Praise for

The Greatness Mindset

"What Lewis has written is a message so many
need to hear right now. In a world overcome with burnout,
stress, and anxiety, *The Greatness Mindset* will help readers
reconnect with their purpose, unlock their inner strength, and
use their gifts to better the communities around them."

— *Arianna Huffington, co-founder of* The Huffington Post
and founder/CEO of Thrive Global

"It's been so incredible seeing Lewis consistently overcome
obstacles to achieve his dreams over the years, and it all starts
with his mindset. I'm thrilled that he took the time to document
his frameworks into this book so others will be able to break
through their own self-doubt and live a fulfilled, rich life."

— *Jay Shetty, #1* New York Times *best-selling author of*
Think Like a Monk *and host of the* On Purpose *podcast*

"Whatever you do in life, adopting the right mindset is
the most important ingredient to fulfilling your dreams.
In this wonderful book, Lewis Howes gives you the
practical tools to achieve true greatness."

— *Dr. Joe Dispenza,* New York Times *best-selling
author of* You Are the Placebo

"Lewis has the ability to share difficult truths in a profoundly empowering way. Inside these pages, you will feel seen and supported to bravely face your own truth to return to your best self. I highly recommend *The Greatness Mindset* to anyone ready to elevate their life."

— *Gabrielle Bernstein*, *#1* New York Times *best-selling author of* The Universe Has Your Back

"Your limiting beliefs have held you back for far too long. Lewis Howes is here to help with *The Greatness Mindset*. Change your beliefs and you change your life."

— *Mel Robbins*, *international best-selling author of* The High 5 Habit *and* The 5 Second Rule

"Lewis's practical, science-backed approach to a potentially overwhelming topic is a breath of fresh air. I highly recommend *The Greatness Mindset* for anyone looking to reconnect with their vision, to revitalize their relationships, or to reinvent themselves."

— *Tara Swart Bieber, M.D., Ph.D.*, *neuroscientist and professor at MIT Sloan School of Management*

The Greatness Mindset

ALSO BY LEWIS HOWES

The School of Greatness

The Mask of Masculinity

The Greatness Mindset

Unlock the Power of Your Mind and Live Your Best Life Today

Lewis Howes

HAY HOUSE, INC.
Carlsbad, California • New York City
London • Sydney • New Delhi

*I dedicate this book to my younger self
for having the courage to carry me through pain,
my current self for facing my shame and learning
how to heal, and to my future self, because the
journey to greatness has only just begun.*

CONTENTS

Chapter 1

CHASING GREATNESS

I was 23 years old, sleeping on my sister's couch in Columbus, Ohio, and freaking broke as a joke. But it wasn't a joke. It was my life. And it was anything but great.

Up to that point, my life had been defined by sports. I had achieved All-American status in the decathlon, but my real passion was football, where I also was an All-American. I held the world record for most receiving yards in a single football game (all divisions at every level). And I had finally realized my dream of playing football professionally in the Arena Football League as I was pursuing my chance to go to the NFL. But then, in the middle of a game, I broke my wrist. The prognosis? Surgery. They cracked open my hip to take a piece of bone and fused it to my wrist—six months in a cast and another year to heal.

I was only in the first month of that cast-wearing stage in September of 2007 when I found myself wondering if I would ever be able to step on the field again. To make it even worse, my dad had been in an accident the previous year while traveling on the other side of the world in New Zealand. He had suffered severe brain trauma. After being in a coma for months, he had finally regained consciousness, but it was clear his healing journey would be a long one. After he returned to the U.S., I was able to go visit him weekly, but he could remember very little of everyone who had meant so much to him prior to the accident and showed no signs of improving.

My nights were haunted by so many fearful questions: *What if my wrist doesn't heal? What if I can't play football again? What if my dream is over? Who will I be then? What if my dad never remembers me? What if I can't figure out what to do next? What if no one will ever love me? What if I try and fail? What will people think? Even worse, what if I can't live up to my own expectations?*

> **I knew this couldn't be how the story of my life went.**

It felt like all I could do during those dark days was flip through TV reruns and infomercials with the remote as I felt my chance at greatness not just slipping away but sprinting as fast as it could go. I didn't know what to think, how to feel, or how to process my own emotions. And on top of that, I hadn't even finished college at the time. I was financially, physically, emotionally, and spiritually broken. . . . I wondered what to do next, and from my perspective, I was now very much alone.

But I knew this couldn't be how the story of my life went. I knew there had to be more to my story—that there had to be greatness inside of me—but I didn't know where or how to get started. Yet deep down, I knew I would eventually figure it all out.

MINDSET MATTERS

Maybe you've had one of those moments when you realized the awful truth: you're just trying to survive, running out the clock, hoping someday something magical will happen that changes everything for you. You may actually have a dream that has remained just that—a dream, something to be done someday, but someday never seems to come.

As I write these words, the COVID pandemic has left a lot of people paralyzed, stressed out, and depressed. But of course, it doesn't take a pandemic to produce stress as who-knows-what comes our way next. There will always be something. Life happens. Maybe something unexpected happened to you in recent years: you lost your job, experienced a divorce or heartbreak, lost a loved one, or had career-ending surgery—and you just feel stunned and dazed, uncertain about what to do next.

Or maybe you got off the couch of life a long time ago. You've been busy getting things done, chasing your dreams, and looking good doing it. Perhaps you've grown a side hustle or a successful dream-chasing business or career, but inside, you feel like it just isn't enough. Even though you may be pretty good at getting results, you feel like there is something missing, and you are meant for more.

> **You feel like there is something missing, and you are meant for more.**

It's good, but not *great*!

One reason many people struggle is that they feel their identity is tied to the results they achieve. Maybe that's you. I've certainly been there, done that. The old adage in golf is that you're only as good as your next shot, but that mindset can leave you feeling pretty unfulfilled, as if you could never quite do or be *enough*.

One of the hardest things to break free from is a "good but not great" life. I hear it so often from people who make what most would consider good money and have what seems to be a good career with kids and family—but they still have an underlying sense of pain or unfulfillment. There's an ache for something *more*.

Does that resonate with you?

Now, don't get me wrong. There's nothing wrong with living a "good" life. No doubt, millions of people in the world would happily trade places with you. But the question is this: Is it the life you want? Is it the story you want your future self to tell?

These are the intentional questions high performers ask, and if that's you, I don't want to leave you out of this conversation. Maybe you're already chasing and achieving your dreams, pursuing greatness at the highest level in business, sports, the arts, politics, charitable work—you name it. You've put a lot of effort into intentionally developing your mindset, but you know no one ever truly arrives. You want that extra edge and are always looking for ways to harness the power of your mind. I get it.

So, whether you feel stuck in neutral or broken down and barely surviving life right now, or you're living what most would call a good life but still feel unfulfilled inside, or you just want to break through to that next level and find any edge you can, you've come to the right place.

The Greatness Mindset will help you unlock the power of your mind by showing you how to find your very own Meaningful Mission, overcoming your fears and self-doubt, and finally accomplishing those goals and dreams that may have felt so elusive for so long.

Is it the life you want?

You *can* rewrite the story of your past to propel you forward into a brighter future rather than becoming a story that replays endlessly in your mind and holds you back. But how do you want to write that future story? Who do you want to be? Where do you want to go? Do you even know? And then, how can you exercise the courage to overcome the fears and self-doubt and develop a game plan to pursue your dreams with greater clarity about who you are and who you want to become?

Whatever dreams you may have, or even forgot that you had, I ask you this simple question:

Would you feel happy or fulfilled if your dream died with you? If not, what are you going to do about it?

MASSIVE, IMPERFECT ACTION

Fortunately, my story didn't end on my sister's couch. And my sister had made it clear I wouldn't be living with her for the rest of my life. In fact, one of the greatest gifts she gave me was eventually telling me I needed to help pay for rent or find another place to go. So after wallowing in self-pity for a month or two, I got up off the couch and stumbled forward.

My first move was to call Stuart Jenkins, a mentor of mine I looked up to who was the headmaster of my old high school, and just ask the obvious question: *What can I do?* He said he had heard people were finding jobs on some start-up digital platform called LinkedIn. It was the first time I had heard of it, but I figured if he thought it was a good idea, I would check it out. So I went *all in*, obsessing about it and learning everything I could.

You *can* rewrite the story of your past to propel you forward into a brighter future.

Then at Christmas, my brother gave me a gift. Our family had a tradition of drawing names to decide who gave a gift to whom, and he had drawn my name. His gift was a book. He didn't even wrap it. He just handed it to me, still in a plastic bag. The book was *The 4-Hour Workweek* by Timothy Ferriss. The subtitle definitely got my attention: *Escape 9–5, Live Anywhere, and Join the New Rich*. I devoured that book in a few days at Christmastime, holding it awkwardly, flipping pages with my one cast-free hand. The book opened me up to a world of possibilities about things like digital business, online marketing, and launching something new. Then I just went deep, reading blogs by all the top leaders at the time, and reaching out to everyone I could think of on LinkedIn to develop relationships over that next year.

Two things really helped me during this time. One was getting serious about learning salsa dancing (a story I'll tell later). The other was choosing to master the skill of public speaking—a fear that held me back my entire life that I felt I needed to overcome. I met a guy who was a professional speaker and told him I wanted to learn how to do what he did, but I couldn't speak in front of anyone to save my life. He treated me to a cup of coffee (no, I still couldn't even afford my own cup of coffee!) and gave me his best advice: "You've got to join Toastmasters and give a speech every week for a year." *Well*, I thought, *this guy clearly knows what he is doing, so I'm in!*

At a Toastmasters event in Columbus, Ohio, this one guy gave an amazing speech. After the event, I cruised to the back of the room. As I was stuffing snacks in my mouth while wrapping more in napkins, I heard a man ask, "What are you doing?"

I froze, then turned to see who had asked the question. It was the speaker who had just delivered the incredible speech! I gulped and tried to swallow, acting like it was the most natural thing in the world to be cramming free food into every empty pocket I had with only one hand.

"Well, I, uh, really don't have, um, a lot of money, so I'm taking some of this home for later." If I could have crawled under the snack table I would have, but I doubted I could have fit my six-foot, four-inch body underneath the tablecloth without him noticing— and besides, I would have crushed the food in my pockets.

"Let me buy you lunch," he replied, and turned toward the door as if he encountered hungry, pocket-stuffing people after every speech.

His name was Frank Agin, and he began to mentor me in public speaking, but he also had a local business networking company. As our relationship grew, I told him about all the work I had been doing learning about LinkedIn, and I helped him upgrade his profile there. He gave me a check for $100 and told me this was going to be a game-changer for his business. I was stunned. *Do you mean people will pay money for me to do this?* With his encouragement, I started helping more people who also paid me. Real money!

But he didn't let me stop there. Before long, he had another challenge for me: "You should write a book about LinkedIn."

What? I had no idea how to write a book. I was only 24 years old. Who would listen to me? Besides, I almost flunked out of English class in high school.

He wasn't deterred. "I'll help you write it." He had written a few books before, so we decided he would write a section about offline networking, and I would write about using LinkedIn to network online. It wasn't a Pulitzer Prize–winning book, but we got it done, and it was offering value to people. Before I knew it, I was an author, making money and moving forward.

Then I went to a Twitter meetup and thought, *Maybe I could do this on LinkedIn.* As far as I knew, no one had ever done a LinkedIn networking event. So I did 20 LinkedIn networking events over the next year, all over the country, using my network, which led to my doing more consulting and ultimately to my first webinar, which launched me into the online and digital business world— and I haven't looked back since.

Fast-forward 14 years, and not only did I return to playing sports, but I also played on the U.S.A. men's national handball team for nine years at the Olympic competitive level. Meanwhile, in the business world, I built a growing business with a seven-figure annual revenue stream. Out of millions of podcasts in the world, my podcast, *The School of Greatness,* is consistently near the top of the list and features some of the most successful people in the world, with more than 1,200 episodes and half a billion downloads. Plus, I have the number one personal development show on YouTube and have written multiple books, including a *New York Times* bestseller. I've been featured on shows such as *Ellen*, the *Today* show, and *Good Morning America* and have been able to build a following of more than eight million on social media.

All of it has made it possible to make an impact in the world by serving on many nonprofit advisory boards and serving causes I care about for the last decade. I've been able to leverage my personal network to bring in many millions in donations to help Pencils of Promise and other causes like Charity: Water and Operation Underground Railroad, freeing children from sex slavery.

I've been able to figure out a lot on this journey and have learned directly from some of the greatest minds in the world, people who have devoted themselves to the pursuit of greatness in their respective fields. But at the end of the day, I knew I needed to write this book about finding meaning, overcoming fears, and creating a game plan for significance and fulfillment in life because of what I feel inside on a daily basis.

THE PATH AHEAD

As we journey together, I'll share more about how I've grown, even in recent years. Greatness is what I've been studying and trying to apply my entire adult life. Across different seasons, I've had to overcome physical, emotional, and mental challenges in the three big areas of life: health, relationships, and in my businesses and finances. And it has not been easy. I've encountered fears and insecurities at all levels, but I have overcome so many of them with help from some of the greatest minds in the world. As an interviewer of—and learner from—these great minds, I've been able to tap into their expertise to see how they've overcome their pain, challenges, and traumas to accomplish the most incredible things.

But you may be asking, what do I mean when I say *greatness*?

From the time I took that initial massive, imperfect action to today, I've developed a working definition of what greatness is:

Greatness is discovering your unique gifts and talents to pursue your Meaningful Mission and make the maximum positive impact on the people around you.

It's not complicated. It's all about figuring out who you are and how you can make an authentic and unique contribution that makes the people around you better and the world a better place. It sounds simple. So what keeps so many of us from living it out?

One key reason people do not pursue greatness is that they quickly encounter the Enemy of Greatness: **the lack of a clear Meaningful Mission.**

When you don't know what you really want to do, it's pretty difficult to do it. So, Step 1 is figuring out your purpose. As Viktor Frankl, Holocaust survivor and author of *Man's Search for Meaning*, said, "The first thing that gives life meaning is a project that demands your attention."[1] Apart from that, you're simply wandering aimlessly. I'll equip you with practical guidance on how to get clear on your mission.

Not having direction or purpose creates a vacuum in your soul, a vacuum that fears, sadness, and mental health challenges rush to fill. That's why Step 2 is critical: I'll show you how to overcome the most common barriers to greatness. I'll walk you through each one of the debilitating fears—fear of failure, fear of success, the fear of what others think about you, and finally the fear of what you think about yourself. The truth is that, left unaddressed, these fears all lead you to the same place: self-doubt and the belief that you are not enough. The only way to overcome and convert those fears is to tackle them head on. In these chapters, I'll show you how and give you a practical Fear Conversion Tool Kit.

Step 3 is where you will actually learn how to develop the Greatness Mindset. At the heart of this mindset is the unwavering belief that "I am enough!" That doesn't mean you have arrived, achieved perfection, or done all the good you could possibly do in the world. It means you are still a work in progress, for sure, but you're still moving forward, trying, failing, learning, and growing while helping other people do the same.

> **It's all about figuring out who you are and how you can make an authentic and unique contribution that makes the people around you better and the world a better place.**

The Greatness Mindset begins to take shape when you begin the journey to heal the pain and trauma in your past. Until you do that, you may often find yourself at the mercy of past pain without ever realizing how or why. We'll explore the psychology and brain science behind how our past shapes our present responses and how to choose to listen to your inner coach rather than your inner critic.

Only when you have begun the journey to heal your past can you engage in an authentic evaluation of the four key elements of the Greatness Mindset in what I call the Mindset-in-Motion Cycle:

1. **Identity.** You are the hero of your own adventure, but heroes are only made by confronting and overcoming challenges.

2. **Thoughts.** Your thoughts shape your reality, especially the chatter inside your own head. We'll take a closer look at how the latest brain science can help us understand what goes on inside our heads.

3. **Emotions.** Your feelings are intimately connected to your thoughts and your body. Once again, the latest brain science and psychology offer critical insights. Paul Conti, author of the excellent book *Trauma: The Invisible Epidemic*, warns us to invest time in healing the pains in our past because "trauma changes our emotions; changed emotions determine our decisions."[2]

4. **Behaviors.** Your actions bring the internal mindset to life as you live it out in the physical universe. We'll examine the role habits and routines play in fueling the Greatness Mindset.

Finally, Step 4—you need a Game Plan for Greatness. These seven actions give you a proven plan drawn from my own experience and the considerable expertise of so many experts from whom I've had the privilege of learning:

1. **Ask courageous questions.** When you dare to ask yourself courageous questions, you begin to make the impossible possible.

2. **Give yourself permission.** Once the door is open, you must give yourself permission to wake up every single day and walk through it.

3. **Accept the challenge.** If you want to become fearless, you need to go *all in* on the fears until they disappear. I'll show you how to use a 30-, 60-, or 90-day challenge to make it happen.

4. **Define your greatness goals.** I'll share my own proven process for goal-setting and achievement that will empower but not overwhelm you.

5. **Enlist support.** You cannot get there by yourself. You'll need internal help via habits and routines as well as external support from peers, coaches, and other voices to help you stay the course.

6. **Get stuff done.** Now it's time for action. I'll share the keys for actually getting stuff done and engaging in meaningful activity to keep moving forward no matter what.

7. **Celebrate!** It all comes down to resting in the reality that you are enough, being your authentic self, no matter the result.

DO YOU REALLY WANT THIS?

In the pages ahead, I'll draw from the many experts who've been my teachers over the last decade and share insights of my own. I don't have all the answers. None of us do. But together we can achieve something more, something greater, hopefully even greatness itself.

I'm not saying I have arrived. Not at all. The journey continues. But . . . I. Am. Enough. I've learned to love and accept myself, and every day I'm learning and growing. I have come to realize there is a path forward to a place where I can live out my Meaningful Mission and feel deep fulfillment and life significance.

Now, chasing greatness may mean you'll stumble and fall a few times along the way. Are you willing to take that risk? You were once, back in the day when you were first learning to walk. You fell. A lot. But you kept getting back up and trying again. And again. And again. Until you did it. Now you don't even think about it. That's the attitude you'll need now. You'll need to become comfortable with trying, failing, and learning, knowing that failure is the only path to success.

It will mean tuning out the critics and the opinions of all the people who choose to sit in the stands instead of taking the field (including tuning out the loudest critic in your head). One thing I've learned on this journey: criticism happens no matter what. It is the price of admission to life. You can't let that decide how your story will be told.

> **Are you ready to discover your unique gifts and talents, and go *all in* on pursuing those gifts and talents?**

It will mean finding and listening to coaches who can help you see past your fears and raise your vision of what's possible in your life. It may mean enlisting the help of trained professionals or therapists who can help you heal your past so you can move forward. I don't claim to know the details of the particular support you will need, but I know leadership expert John C. Maxwell is right: "One is too small a number to achieve greatness."[3]

It will mean giving it your all, taking courageous action, but then letting go of the results. The results may not be what you expect them to be. They may be better. Or they may just be different. And that's okay. If you continue to act on your Meaningful Mission, the things you know you will one day be proud to have done, the results will take care of themselves.

So, my question to you is this—and be gut-level honest with yourself here because no one else's opinion matters: Are you ready to discover your unique gifts and talents, going *all in* on pursuing those gifts and talents, and, in that pursuit, making the maximum impact on the people around you?

If you are, you can master the Greatness Mindset and adjust your life story so that instead of you chasing greatness, greatness will chase you.

Chapter 2

THE GREATNESS ALTERNATIVE

On September 13, 2007, Lieutenant Jason Redman, a U.S. Navy SEAL, was nearing the end of his deployment in the Anbar province in Iraq. Nearly every night he and his brothers-in-arms conducted missions, engaging in life-or-death gunfights in what had been the most intense deployment of his 15-year career. One week more, and he would be headed home to his wife and three young children to enjoy a fun Halloween celebration.

That night, intelligence indicated they might have finally located the top leader of Al-Qaeda for the Anbar province, who surrounded himself with a security team known to choose suicide bombing rather than surrender. That leader was also responsible for the death of a fellow Navy SEAL. As Jason geared up for the mission that night, he set his body armor side plates aside, thinking he would need to move quickly in the coming conflict. He didn't want any extra weight holding him back. Yet something gnawed at him, urging him to just put the plates on. So he did, and without another thought, boarded the helicopter for the flight deep into enemy territory.

But when they landed and entered the house where the leader was thought to be hiding, whoever had been there was gone, although they did find weapons and bomb-making materials. As Jason sat on the porch with his team waiting for the explosives to be destroyed, word came in that five individuals had just been spotted running from a house about 150 yards away and were hiding in thick vegetation. His nine-member team was tasked with tracking them down to find out what they knew.

As they advanced in the darkness, they checked with air surveillance: Any weapons? *No.* What are these guys doing? *Can't see them.* As they made their way through the dense brush, Jason's "Spidey sense" alerted him something was off. He chalked it up to stress and pushed forward, following what they had been trained to do.

And then it happened. The medic on the team found one of the guys they were searching for—by literally stepping right on him. The shadowy figure on the ground rolled and reached for the medic, who promptly shot him while getting shot himself in the process. What none of them knew at the time was that the five men they had been tracking were the last of the Al-Qaeda leader's suicidal security detail of about 15 people and that the enemy had set up an ambush line in that field. To make it worse, the medic had been bringing up the rear of the SEAL team, which meant Jason and the rest of the group were already in the middle of the hornet's nest.

As they dragged the medic to a large John Deere tractor tire lying in the field, other team members got shot. Out in front, Jason found himself less than 45 feet from two belt-fed machine guns firing massive bullets that punched through the air around him with supersonic force, with tracer rounds lighting up the area like explosive fireflies.

Jason was immediately "stitched," riddled with bullets across his body armor. As he fell, he felt like an 800-pound gorilla hit him with a baseball bat as he took two rounds in his right elbow, then a lightning bolt shot up his arm and slammed him in the back of his head. A quick reach with his left hand found nothing.

He presumed his arm had been shot off. Jason kept returning fire and shouting orders to his team, a move that caused the enemy to focus both guns on his position.

Bullets slammed into his helmet, off his gun, and shattered his night vision device off his head. Then a single bullet struck just in front of his right ear, traveled through his face, and exited the right side of his nose. The force shattered his jaw all the way to the chin, broke all the bones around his right eye, blew off his nose, and knocked him out.

When Jason came back to consciousness, he tried to make sense of what had happened. *My arm is gone.* His left hand explored the place where the side of his face used to be. *My face is gone.* Tracer rounds streaked by, just inches above him. *Don't move!*

Unable to reach his tourniquet to stop the bleeding, he called to his team for help. For the first time, they realized he was still alive. Another round slammed into body armor side plate he had almost left at base. As painful as the impact was, it kept the round from hitting his kidney and demolishing his spine.

Somehow, his team leader dragged Jason back to the cover of the tire. They called in a close air strike, and by the time the blur of helicopter transports and medical personnel working frantically to save his life had passed, Jason had lost about 40 percent of his blood.

Shortly after he arrived at Bethesda Naval Hospital in Maryland, doctors performed a CAT scan and created a 3D model of his skull to figure out possible reconstruction options. The image looked as if someone had hit Jason in the face with an ax. His right arm was still attached, but doctors discussed the need to amputate it.

The reality of his situation still hadn't completely kicked in. He had planned to attend his sister's wedding in the Virgin Islands in October of that year, so at one point, he wrote a note to the nurse asking how long it was going to take to put him back together so he could go. She gave him an incredulous look and simply said, "It's going to take years to put you back together."

As he lay there one night with nothing to do but wrestle with his own thoughts, a voice began speaking. Someone had come into his room and, thinking he was asleep, said how overwhelming the hospital experience was. They droned on about how terrible it must be for all these wounded warriors who were broken and never going to be the same. And Jason realized they were talking about him.

WHEN THE ENEMY WINS

If anyone had an excuse to stand down at that moment and settle for a life that was less-than-great, it was Jason Redman. But as you'll see, Jason chose a different, more intentional path.

So many great people live lives absent of greatness because they live by *default* and not by *design*. They let themselves be limited by fears, anxieties, and pain from the past instead of embracing a limitless, abundant mindset. That doesn't mean they never deal with tough stuff. Of course not. It comes to all of us in different ways. But you don't have to run from it when it comes. You can choose to accept the challenges and face the fears—and enjoy the journey!

When people live in the darkness of fear and uncertainty, they don't have what I call a Meaningful Mission, an underlying purpose that gives their lives a greater significance. As a result, they don't feel freedom within or peace on their journey. They unknowingly let fear control their life decisions and shape their perceptions of what their choices might be. As a result, they feel stuck where they are, even trapped, which can cause them to feel lost or resentful and angry at themselves and others.

This internal uncertainty can produce tremendous anxiety. As their body reacts to those emotions, they may even experience physiological responses or panic attacks. We're seeing this anxiety manifest itself more and more. Anxiety is the most common mental disorder in the U.S., affecting 40 million adults.[1] According to the Cleveland Clinic, every year, up to 30 million Americans experience some sort of panic attack.[2] And it is often people who are in what most would consider to be the prime of life who face the greatest struggle. According to the National Institute of Mental Health, over 31 percent of adolescents experience an anxiety disorder, followed by 18- to 44-year-olds at around 22 percent, and 45- to 59-year-olds at a little over 20 percent.[3] In other words, no one is exempt.

This rise in anxiety can be attributed to a number of factors, but the bottom line is a growing sense of uncertainty. And as Dr. Wendy Suzuki told me on my show, uncertainty is the key driver for a lot of our anxieties.[4]

Have you ever felt dissatisfied in your life? With your career or business experience? With your intimate relationships, family, or friends? Or, most of all, with yourself?

A general sense of "blah" can become the rule rather than the exception. Perhaps that is why we have seen a significant decline in happiness in U.S. adults. In a general social survey over more than 40 years (1973–2016), the trends have been toward people saying they are less happy, especially in the past 20 years.[5]

Some turn to coping mechanisms for temporary relief from the stress, like eating more but exercising less. That may explain why, according to the National Institute of Health, nearly 1 in 3 adults are overweight, more than 2 in 5 adults have obesity, and about 1 in 11 adults have severe obesity.[6] All of these behaviors, unfortunately, are self-sabotaging moves that exacerbate the problem instead of leading to solutions. And we are here to get to the root cause and find healthy solutions for your growth, abundance, and greatness.

Some make poor financial decisions in the hopes that spending more in the short term or buying that one magical "thing" will somehow produce a sense of fulfillment. And when that doesn't work, they try again. And again. This pattern can be especially destructive for someone already living paycheck to paycheck. It digs a debt hole that makes everything else in life more challenging and only multiplies the already-overwhelming stress load.

We see this trend in the increased debt levels. For example, the median U.S. household income was $79,900 in 2021, according to the U.S. Department of Housing and Urban Development.[7] That is an increase of almost $35,000 from 2000. However, the typical American household now carries an average debt of $145,000, an increase of over $94,000 during that same time! I'm not saying all debt is bad, but this level of extra debt burden only contributes to the stress load. Instead of helping people feel better, it amplifies the problem.

Some turn to busyness in the hope of feeling better and finding clarity. *If only I could do more,* they think, *then I'll finally feel like I have value and am making a real difference.* Yet it feels like there's never enough time to get done what needs to get done *now,* let alone to do more. As the minutes tick by, the sense of overwhelm kicks in. They feel that familiar tightness in the chest, the weight of the monster sitting on them, making it difficult to breathe or think.

You can't change your life direction if you don't know where you are *right now.*

They just feel drained, like butter spread too thin over toast. Exhausted. Never caught up. On rest. On sleep. On relationships. On working out. On living up to the expectations of friends, family, co-workers, and society. Drowning in responsibilities. And then the physical pain follows. Headaches and migraines. Tightness in the throat. Heart palpitations. Stomach sickness. Back pain. Take your pick. The body sounds the alarm: *something is off.*

And the more intense this downward spiral becomes, the more isolated and alone they can begin to feel. *No one understands how I feel. Can't talk to anyone about this, because everyone else has it all figured out but me.* Then, of course, if that is true, the stage is set for bitterness to sink in. *Why me? Why am I the only one who feels emotionally, financially, relationally, spiritually (and every other kind of -ally) broken? And why is everyone and everything out to get me?* I don't think it is a coincidence that nearly 20 percent of all Americans experienced mental health issues[8] (and that was before the COVID pandemic!).

Can I be really transparent with you? I just described all that pain and anxiety in the third person—*they* feel, *they* experience, *they* fear. But I've felt almost all of those things myself at many points. And maybe you have too. I've already shared some of my own struggles and will share even more about them in the pages to come. So can I just challenge you to reread the description above and change *they* to *you*. *You* feel. *You* experience. *You* fear. Or, if you're really serious about pursuing greatness, change it to *I*. *I* feel drained. *I* experience overwhelm. *I* fear not doing or being enough. *I* feel the painful consequences of it every day.

I'm not trying to create more problems for you, but I do want to challenge you to be honest with yourself. Because you can't change your life direction if you don't know where you are *right now*. You can't have any hope of reaching a new destination unless you get real about your current situation and location. If you want to scale the highest mountain, it helps to know if you are already halfway to the summit, or stuck in the mud in the lowest valley, or a thousand miles from nowhere.

> **The struggle for greatness is part of what makes us human.**

If any of those descriptions sound familiar to you, you are not alone. Anything but! You are normal. That's not to trivialize the intensity of the challenges or the reality that some people face more painful pasts, higher barriers, and deeper biases than others. But as I've interviewed so many experts from around the world, studied the insights of countless others, and engaged people just trying to live better lives, I've learned that the struggle for greatness is part of what makes us human. To struggle is to live.

This doesn't mean, however, that you have to suffer.

It matters how we respond to the struggle, because each of us has the potential for something more—greatness. You will have fears. You will have challenges. The difference is in what you choose to do about it.

Other people see signs of the Enemy of Greatness manifesting itself in unpredictable outbursts of rage. Often these outward manifestations of an internal reality seem to come out of nowhere, triggered by who-knows-what. It can be easy to dismiss them when they are small, but over time, they may increase in frequency and intensity. They usually stem from some unresolved trauma or pain in the past.

Each of us has the potential for something more.

I love the analogy of a juicy orange. Squeeze it, and you find out that what's inside of the orange is juice. When you look at a human being, and you apply pressure to them, what comes out all depends on what's inside. If you have peace and love and patience inside, then that's what will come out when "life happens." If you have anger, resentment, shame, and stress inside of you and haven't learned to process that pain, then that's what will come out of you when everything doesn't go according to plan.

Some people have learned how to keep it all bottled up inside. They've learned not to verbalize their anger or frustrations. But keeping it all inside only causes them to manifest in other ways.

No matter what we do, the pain within will manifest itself somehow.

I used to have a lot of fear and anger within me. When I was poked by life in certain ways, it would come out. It wasn't pretty. But the healing journey I have undertaken has moved me to a very different place, a place of peace and contentment.

THE OPPOSITE OF NOT BAD: NOT GOOD

Several years after I had gotten off my sister's couch and stepped out into the world of LinkedIn, I had managed to build a seven-figure digital business. It was making me a lot of money and helping a lot of people. And for a while, that was enough. But I slowly began to realize that if I had to talk one more time about how to maximize your LinkedIn bio, I would, well . . . I'd probably have one of those outbursts I mentioned earlier.

It wasn't the first time I had been passionate about something for a season. For example, I loved playing baseball from the time I was 5 years old until I just decided it wasn't a fit for me anymore when I was 17 in my senior year of high school. I was good at it—one of the best players on the team—but I wasn't that fond of it and didn't see where it would take me in terms of my life direction and future. So I quit baseball and focused on football, track, and basketball. The move gave me more time to develop the skills to go to the next level in college and become a two-time All-American—in football and as a decathlete.

Like baseball, the business was something I had been really excited about—until I wasn't. I wasn't using my inner genius to the max in the business—even though I wasn't sure what else I could do. It did feel good to have built a successful business, and it felt even better to have money in the bank. But when I told some friends that I was thinking about making a change, they were shocked: *What are you doing? You already have this business that's making all this money and helping a lot of people. Why would you change anything?*

I just knew I wasn't in my sweet spot (something we'll explore more of in the next chapter). Like most people, my mission was evolving. I had the sense that what I had set out to do was no longer my focus. It was time to make a change.

So with a multimillion-dollar business that was growing year after year, I told my business partner I wasn't doing it anymore. It had become apparent to me for a while that he and I had different visions for the company, but I had just put my head down and continued killing myself by working until 3 A.M. to keep the business going. Despite the fact that we had a 50-50 split of the company, I was doing three to four more times the work. I was the sales and marketing guy as well as the content creator, while my partner hand-led backend operations. When I stopped working, everything slowed down. When I said I wanted to step back, he said he would pick up some of the sales load. He ran a webinar that I had been delivering and produced zero sales, nothing at all. Same product. Same content. No sales. And I knew it was time to change direction.

Once again, just being transparent with you, we didn't really have the maturity or the skills to communicate about the situation in a healthy way. I suspect we were both frustrated with each other and, speaking for myself, young and egocentric. There was a lot of blaming on both sides, so we pretty much just didn't speak for several months.

It was only after I began to find my way toward my own Meaningful Mission and take steps to begin healing my own past that I was able to come back to him with a radically different perspective.

When I reached out to my business partner again, I was able to do so with gratitude and peace. He was shocked: *What happened to you?* I simply told him I was grateful for him and all we had built together. I came from a place of appreciation rather than frustration. The program we had built was still producing significant revenue, and I sold my shares to him for seven figures and turned my full focus to getting clear on the next evolution of my Meaningful Mission.

WHAT IF YOU SETTLE?

The more Jason Redman thought about the negative voice he had overheard in the hospital, the angrier he got. He awoke and wrote a note to his wife with his good hand, letting her know nobody would be allowed to come into his room and feel sorry for him. Never again. He asked her to post the following notice with a big sign on his door:

ATTENTION
To all who enter here:

If you are coming into this room with sorrow or to feel sorry for my wounds, go elsewhere. The wounds I received, I got in a job I love, doing it for people I love, supporting the freedom of a country I deeply love. I am incredibly tough and will make a full recovery. What is full? That is the absolute utmost physically my body has the ability to recover. Then I will push that about 20 percent further through sheer mental tenacity. This room you are about to enter is a room of fun, optimism, and intense, rapid regrowth. If you are not prepared for that, go elsewhere.

From: The Management[9]

As Jason chose to embrace a positive mindset, he began the slow, painful healing process. Meanwhile, the manifesto he had posted on the door went viral. Eventually, President George W. Bush invited him to the White House, and First Lady Michelle Obama mentioned the note in two of her own written works. It was also highlighted in a book by Defense Secretary Robert Gates. More importantly, it inspired millions of people facing overwhelming challenges to embrace the same positive

Greatness won't happen by accident.

mindset. The note was signed by President Bush and now hangs in the halls of the Wounded Warrior wing at Bethesda, inspiring more people, as a recovered Redman continues to pursue his own Meaningful Mission.

Here's what he told me: "We need to build more resilient people and help them to get this idea that sometimes nobody's going to come save you but you. It starts with you. You have to be the one that gets up and starts to drive forward. There's a level of resiliency that comes with choosing to drive forward."[10] In other words, greatness won't happen by accident. No one ever accidentally slipped and fell into it. Dr. Jordan Peterson, a Canadian professor of psychology, even cautions parents not to make their children's lives too easy, because doing so can cause them not to be resilient. A lack of challenges in life can actually hurt their development.[11]

And if you choose not to pursue greatness and embrace this positive mindset? What might life look like for you then? It could be a range of outcomes with all of them circling around suffering and sadness or feeling alone or like a victim. On the surface you may look like you're living a great life—family, kids, cars, boats, travel, or however you might define outward success—but a truly meaningful life will pass you by.

> **You can choose to stay stuck . . . but you'll never fully discover your highest, most significant contribution to the world.**

John Glenn, one of the first Americans to go into outer space and orbit Earth, served as a senator for many terms and was awarded the Presidential Medal of Freedom in 2012 by President Barack Obama. He was also the oldest person to go into space at the age of 77. "If there's one thing I've learned in my years on this planet," he said, "it's that the happiest and most fulfilled people I've known are those who devoted themselves to something bigger and more profound than merely their own self-interest."[12]

You may follow a life path that fits what you think you're supposed to do, but it's not what you were meant to do. Or maybe it was the right path for a season, but now your story has evolved, leaving you stuck in a place that feels *off*. You can choose to stay stuck, doing what you think other people want you to do, but you'll never fully discover your highest, most significant contribution to the world.

Even worse, you may get frustrated by it all and become bitter and angry, rather than responding to the challenge like Redman did. The world is full of people who choose to become a villain instead of the hero of their story after encountering challenges. They then begin to hurt other people. None of us sets out to be that person, but it happens nonetheless.

I want something much, much better for you—something great. And if you're still reading, I assume you do too. So, let's invest a little time together figuring out where you are before you get intentional about discovering your own Meaningful Mission.

GREATNESS PERFORMANCE ASSESSMENT

Achieving a life of greatness is possible when you focus on three different areas of your life. I like to call them the Three Players—Business, Relationships, Wellness. It may be tempting to focus on one or two of them, but it's important to develop all three players.

As part of our Greatness Coaching program, we help people assess how well they are living out each aspect of these Three Players. This simple assessment will help you understand your strengths and weaknesses and show you where you need to improve to achieve greatness.

Here is a condensed version of the assessment we use in Greatness Coaching:

Give each statement below a score of 1 to 10.
(1 = "I completely disagree" and 10 = "I strongly agree")
To what extent do the following statements accurately describe you right now?

Business and Career

1. I am doing what I love and want to do professionally.

2. I am earning the revenue or income I want based on my ability.

3. My business or professional efforts make an impact on others in a positive way.

4. I make steady, measurable progress toward achieving my business goals.

5. I have an intentional plan to grow professionally and financially for the next three years.

   (Add your total points for 1–5)
                         Business and Career Total Score: _____

   (Divide the total score by 5)   Business GPA: _____

Relationships

1. My family and/or partner relationships are healthy, fulfilling, and where I want them to be.

2. I regularly engage in social connection (meetups, happy hour events). ☐

3. I invest time and energy in relationships with my family, partner, friends, and colleagues. ☐

4. I practice honest communication, even when the topic is uncomfortable or difficult. ☐

5. I have an intentional plan to grow in my relationships for the next three years. ☐

(Add your total points for 1–5)

Relationships Total Score: _____

(Divide the total score by 5) Relationships GPA: _____

Wellness

1. I am physically healthy and exercise regularly. ☐

2. I make mindful nutrition choices regularly. ☐

3. I am a great sleeper and make it a priority. ☐

4. I frequently practice self-care and strategies to optimize my mental health. ☐

5. I have an intentional plan to better my health for the next three years. ☐

(Add your total points for 1–5)

Wellness Total Score: _____

(Divide the total score by 5) Wellness GPA: _____

Your Results

Your Cumulative GPA: _____

(Add your total Business + Relationships + Wellness GPA and divide the total by 3.)

How did you do?

Use the simple scale below to assess where you are right now:

REBUILDING	ACCELERATING	WINNING	PLAYOFF BOUND	CHAMPIONSHIP LEVEL
2.0–4.4	4.5–5.9	6.0–7.4	7.5–8.9	9.0–10.0

The Enemy of Greatness

Chapter 3

MISSING YOUR MEANINGFUL MISSION

Seven bucks. That's all he had left in his pocket when he hit rock bottom.

For years he had devoted his time, effort, and energy to one dream—pursuing greatness on the gridiron and reaching the NFL. He had the raw materials to make it happen. He worked out with a fervor, and by the time he was offered an athletic scholarship in college, he was six feet, five inches tall and weighed 290 pounds.

But talent and desire are not always enough.

He played all four years with modest success, playing alongside future NFL Hall of Famers. But when he reached his senior season, he injured his shoulder and had a dismal year. When the NFL draft came, he didn't get picked. But his football dream was still alive, so he accepted a $250-a-week contract with a Canadian Football League team. (Coincidentally, this is the exact amount of money I made while playing in the Arena Football League while chasing my dream to make it to the NFL.) He showed up every day with focus, passion, and determination to do his very best, but the team already had a stacked defensive bench.

The coach called him one day asking him to turn in his playbook: "I respect your hard work and determination, but unfortunately this isn't your year. I'm sorry, but we're going to have to cut you." It seemed like his football dreams had died.

He bummed a ride to the airport and anxiously hopped on the long flight back home to South Florida. When he landed in Miami, he did the only thing he knew to do. He called his parents, who lived in Tampa, for a ride and place to stay. On the long ride through the Everglades in his dad's little red pickup truck, he wondered about his next move. Here he was, a 24-year-old with dreams of being a millionaire professional athlete, and he was moving back in with his parents. As he pondered his purpose, he pulled out his wallet to see how much money he had left: a $5 bill, a single, and a handful of change.

What made it especially painful was that his life had not been easy. He had bounced around from place to place as a kid, living in over 13 different states. As a teen, he had lived with his mom in Hawaii while his parents were separated, and they had been evicted, living out of their car. He remembered well the nights when he watched her cry, "What are we going to do now?"

To help his mom out, he started stealing from tourists who came to Hawaii to help pay the bills. As a result, he had landed in jail eight times over the years. He had thought that by going to college and then pursuing his dream of greatness in the NFL that things had finally changed. Now here he was, looking at the measly seven bucks, hearing his mom's question echoing in his head: *What am I going to do now?*

He spent the next couple of weeks on the couch alternating between watching the O. J. Simpson trial on television and "cleaning up every scuff and scratch around the apartment with a bottle of 409 cleaner."[1] Then after about two weeks, he had a revelation:

I realized there was something else for me. The world was going to hear from me. I didn't know how. I didn't know when. But I did know my life was more than just sitting around in this little apartment, cleaning up scuff marks and being depressed.[2]

He knew he had a Meaningful Mission. He just needed to find it. And he wouldn't find it sitting on the couch. He decided to put his size to work as a professional wrestler. So he headed to the gym and started working out like a man on a mission.

His dad had been a famous wrestler, so he asked for training help and applied all of the perseverance and tenacity he had once devoted to football to his new mission of becoming great and making a significant impact in some way. And although success didn't come all at once, it paid off. He started out wrestling under the name Rocky Maivia, a play on his father's and grandfather's names, but was booed soundly by the crowd. He then became the Blue Chipper, with much the same negative reaction. But he was learning both the athletic skills and the show business expertise that eventually led to his developing a new, record-breaking wrestling persona.

Dressed in all black, he became the villain everyone loved to hate—and the crowds loved him. For the next seven years, he dominated the wrestling world, winning the world title every single year. He had finally succeeded in his mission. But he wasn't done.

You may not have followed wrestling during those seven years, but you've probably heard of this determined young man, because as Dwayne "The Rock" Johnson excelled at the show business side of the wrestling world, his mission evolved as he aimed for something bigger—Hollywood.

THE ESSENCE OF THE ENEMY

When Dwayne Johnson wasn't clear on his Meaningful Mission in life, he struggled to make any progress. But once he confronted that Enemy of Greatness, he set events in motion that propelled him to greatness—and he's not done yet.

Why do I call the lack of a Meaningful Mission the Enemy of Greatness? It's simple. If you don't have a clear path forward, you'll never move forward. Why would you? Most people would think it safer to stay put when confronted by the unknown. If you are more adventurous and ambitious, you may try to move, but you feel scattered and confused by chasing after every shiny object that comes your way. You get really busy but feel like, at the end of the day, you're right back where you started. And that can feel even more frustrating. After all that effort, you got nowhere. That's when some people begin to lose hope and turn to coping mechanisms to dull the pain. Ugh. No one wants that.

> **If you don't have a clear path forward, you'll never move forward.**

And yet that's how it can feel every day when you have not confronted this Enemy of Greatness. It lurks in the background of life, shadowy and unseen, unidentified but unbelievably powerful, shaping stories in ways people never fully realize until life has passed them by. "Your purpose needs to be the most important mission of your life. If you're not walking in your purpose, you're just working and living to die," said Nicole Lynn, the first female agent to represent a top NFL agency, when she chatted with me on my podcast. "You've got to figure out what that purpose and calling is."[3]

Sri Sri Ravi Shankar, often referred to as Gurudev, is an Indian yoga guru, humanitarian, spiritual leader, and an ambassador of peace. He is the founder of the Art of Living Foundation, which has helped millions of people over the last 40 years find inner peace and fulfillment in their lives. When I asked him what happens if human beings don't find a Meaningful Mission, he replied:

For one thing, they live a routine life, like boredom, where the intellect goes to sleep. Then you don't need to look for a purpose in life, because you just exist. But it's when you are more mature that you start thinking, *What's the purpose of life*? That's a sign of a mature intellect. And once we have the spirit of inquiry about life itself, then our spiritual journey begins.[4]

Truth be told, not having a clear mission fuels the fears that are core to all of us: What if we're really not good enough to achieve? What if we don't have what it takes to succeed? What if the problem is us? When you don't know where you are going or why, you're naturally going to doubt yourself more. If you do have clarity, however, you can learn how to convert those fears into confidence and overcome that nagging sense of self-doubt.

Having a Meaningful Mission enables you to end the inertia and the temptation to wander aimlessly and label it "success." Believe me, I know what it feels like to drift—I still can't get all those late-night "get rich quick" infomercials out of my head from when I was living on my sister's couch. And I know what it's like to achieve success, but to feel that it's not really what you want to do or it doesn't make you happy.

For me, everything changed when I found the beginnings of my own Meaningful Mission while stuck in L.A. traffic.

BACK TO SCHOOL

On one hot summer day, I was on the 405 highway in traffic. The AC barely worked, and I felt it even more on that sweltering August day. I had moved less than two miles in two hours, so I had plenty of time to play the drums with my fingers on the steering wheel and think. The car itself was a classic that seemed stuck in time: a 1997 Cadillac Eldorado two-door with leather seats, a radio that didn't work, and a CD player. I had bought it for four grand from a mentor of mine. It felt like my grandpa's car, but it got me where I was going.

I had just moved to Los Angeles a few months before and wasn't feeling at home yet. I had sold my previous business to my business partner for seven figures. It hadn't all worked out beautifully, but it was done. I was free to move in a new direction, but what exactly that would be, I had no idea.

I kept moving forward, believing something would materialize, but I was frustrated with so much of my life. I mean, here I was, young and healthy. I had made what most people would think was a good deal of money, but I felt empty. My relationships felt off too. As a result of the lack of purpose, I felt my physical health beginning to slip and my emotional health along with it. I felt like my life was breaking down.

So as I sat in the car that day with the radio going in and out in the background, I asked myself: *Why am I not feeling good inside? Why am I feeling unfulfilled? Why do I not feel satisfied when I've been so driven for the last several years?* I'd been goal-oriented and gotten things done, but I don't feel fulfilled inside. *Why?*

I knew I loved interviewing people, asking questions, and learning, but I had no idea how to make a living doing that. Then it hit me: I'm stuck, and I'm literally surrounded by all these other people who are stuck. They're obviously frustrated based on their honking and yelling—and not just about the traffic. Their frustration is deeper, like mine, with life in general. Then I realized there must be millions, if not billions of people, just like them and just like me. What if I could get in front of them and help them and help myself in the process while making a living doing it?

The wheels started turning, unfortunately not on the highway, but in my mind. At the time, I had heard about podcasts, but they really weren't anywhere near as popular as they are today. You had to explain what a podcast was to most people when it came up in conversations, and it seldom came up. The handful of people I knew who were into podcasting weren't really making money at it yet. But I began to wonder if I could do it. After all, I was already interviewing all kinds of people, but just for my own benefit and learning. What if I could do what I love, record these interviews, and share them with the world to help others? Hmm.

So while still sitting in dead-stopped traffic, I started dialing a few friends who were into podcasting. Both Derek Halpern and Pat Flynn encouraged me to dive in, saying, "It's one of my favorite things," and "It's the best tool for engaging an audience." Since I hadn't moved more than 10 feet, I called my friend James Wedmore to get his input too. He echoed the positive feedback, and we started brainstorming a name for the show.

Out of that place of keen awareness of my own brokenness in life, I told James I wished school had taught me the things I really needed to know. Instead, I had always felt slow and stupid and just *not enough* in school. But I wish there had been a school where I could have felt empowered—a school that taught me how to overcome fear, failure, and insecurities; how to manage my finances; how to enjoy fulfilling relationships; how to maintain my emotional health; or even how to eat nutritiously and be physically healthy.

All those things felt like they were breaking down in my life at that time, and I just wished there was a school about these meaningful things, not just about accomplishing goals and being successful. *I just want to live a great life.*

If only there were a . . . *school . . . that taught about how to do this . . . a . . . School of Greatness.*

Bingo!

The name of the show came to me right then and there. Just as I was stuck, in traffic and in life, the idea began for starting a podcast that could, quite literally, help not only me to get unstuck, but also all the people around me—and millions more—to live a more meaningful and fulfilling life.

MEANING AND MISSION

Someone I have interviewed on the show many times and shared a number of powerful interactions with is Tony Robbins, and he tells me most people struggle to have a big vision for the future because they focus on *how* it can be done instead of *why* they want to do it. Once you are clear on your why, the how takes care of itself.[5]

None of us can see how a mission can be accomplished at the start because our only perspective is what we have at that moment. That perspective is shaped by what we've experienced in the past, not by what we might experience in the future. But when we start moving forward, our perspective begins to change. Opportunities we never imagined were suddenly open to us. Connections we didn't realize were possible open doors we didn't even know existed. Resources we assumed were unavailable suddenly become accessible because we learn secrets we didn't know were once hidden from us. And it all starts by having a Meaningful Mission.

Now, there are two fundamental questions you might already be asking: What makes a mission *meaningful*? And then, even more basic, why are you calling it a *mission*?

> No one else can choose your Meaningful Mission for you.

For a mission to be meaningful, it must first be personal to you. It has to resonate with you individually. It can't be a mission someone else wants you to tackle. It can't be imposed on you against your will or something you fall into by accident. It must be an intentional embracing of a direction that is significant to you. And that is key, because it means no one else can choose your Meaningful Mission for you.

The first step to discovering your Meaningful Mission is to be honest with yourself about yourself. If I hadn't been in a place of honesty with myself about my life situation when I was sitting in traffic that day, I never would have reached out for help. I never would have looked for something more. I might still be stuck in life's traffic, waiting for someone to save me from myself.

Once I saw myself clearly, I began to ask the key question: *What do I really want?* And that leads me to why I call it a *mission*. A mission taps into something more significant than, say, an outing or a trip. It is *not* a vacation. It calls upon the deeper parts of our souls and moves us to attempt something greater than ourselves.

Like a heroic quest, a mission has a singular focus or purpose, as well as a call that compels you to push through resistance to complete it. That's why we don't use the word *mission* to describe a visit to the grocery store, the dentist, or a theme park. A mission by definition is *greater*. It takes time. It requires determination and grit to achieve. It often remakes the people who are part of it into something better. And it always implies that the destination is grander or greater than any you have previously achieved. After all, if it were something you had done before and could easily do again, it wouldn't be much of a mission.

As I began to get honest with myself about where I was and what I wanted out of life, my Meaningful Mission began to take shape. Now my mission is clear:

> **To serve 100 million lives weekly by helping them improve the quality of their lives and overcome the things that hold them back.**

A mission calls upon the deeper parts of our souls and moves us to attempt something greater than ourselves.

Giving my mission a concrete number allows me to quantify the actions and evaluate progress to reach that goal. And once I reach that goal, I'll reevaluate the mission and my next season of life.

And that is key. My mission is *not* to be a podcaster, an author, a TV host, etc. The podcast and these other platforms are the mechanisms to serve the mission.

Having clarity about your Meaningful Mission right now doesn't mean it will always remain the same. In fact, in order for any mission to remain meaningful to you, it must evolve over time as you grow and change. For many seasons, I loved playing baseball. Until I didn't. I found the LinkedIn business to be fulfilling. Until I didn't. And that's okay. The mechanism through which I serve others right now is through *The School of Greatness* show, using multiple platforms to package and distribute the show and similar media efforts. But someday the details of that mission might change as technology shifts or other opportunities arise. I don't know what the future will look like, but I know that my Meaningful Mission will evolve to continually help people improve the quality of their lives and overcome the things that hold them back.

> **For any mission to remain meaningful to you, it must evolve over time as you grow and change.**

Katy Milkman, award-winning behavioral scientist and professor at the Wharton School of the University of Pennsylvania, describes the essence of greatness as being clear on your purpose or mission so that it serves as your North Star. She told me that when someone has that clear North Star and has built their life to support and "lean toward it" in all aspects, she feels like she is in the presence of greatness. That's why when you get clear on your mission, you can start structuring everything else around it and live a more intentional life, no matter the mechanism you choose.[6]

In other words, the mechanism may change. But no matter how the mechanism evolves, your passion and strengths will always drive you to make a significant impact in the world from your sweet spot.

It's important to consider what mechanism resonates with you in the season of life you are in. For example, you may have passion for serving people, but that doesn't necessarily mean you should be an Uber driver. Or maybe that is the thing that really energizes you, which is fantastic if you know that! There are literally a million different mechanisms you could choose that would allow you to do a lot of good for a lot of people. The key is to be intentional about taking incremental steps toward getting clear on your Meaningful Mission and setting yourself up for the mechanism of service that works for you.

Let's be honest about one thing: money can cloud your perspective here. As Zig Ziglar put it, "Money isn't the most important thing in life, but it's reasonably close to oxygen on the 'gotta have it' scale."[7] I've had no money at times, some money at times, and then a lot more money, and, all things being equal, I'd rather have it than not. But it doesn't mean there aren't challenges and pressures to overcome with having more of it.

Your passion and strengths will always drive you to make a significant impact in the world.

Money buys a lot of things and brings you other choices and options and freedoms, but it doesn't buy fulfillment. Try to separate yourself from the money when assessing your Meaningful Mission. Ask yourself: *If money were no longer an issue, what would I do? What would light me up every day?* Be careful that the choices that drive your mission aren't fueled solely by wanting more money, because it won't last.

The bottom line is that your Meaningful Mission is not something you can choose once and be done. It's part of a constant assessment on your journey through life. I started with an audio-only podcast. Now, thanks to my awesome team, we have one of the most popular YouTube channels with video and ever-expanding social media. We're branching into different languages and exploring all sorts of other mechanisms to achieve the mission.

Grasp your mission securely but hold the mechanism loosely. Don't let the *how* stop you from focusing on and pursuing your *why*.

FIND YOUR SWEET SPOT

Is what you are doing right now in life the best use of your time and talents? Knowing your sweet spot helps answer the question. To discover your sweet spot, consider three factors:

Passion

Your Meaningful Mission starts where your heart is. The Rock loved football and used his size to be physically active, and then he grew to love the showbusiness side of wrestling. I loved asking questions, interviewing, and learning.

Ask yourself questions like these, and truly listen to what your heart tells you:

- What lights you up?
- What makes you want to jump out of bed?
- If money were no object, what would you love to do?
- What would you do all day, every day, even if you didn't get paid to do it?
- What causes and experiences excite you?

Power

Passion alone isn't enough. You may really love doing something but lack the strengths to excel at it. When that happens, you've probably discovered a hobby that could have an important place in your life but isn't your sweet spot. For me, I love salsa dancing, and it's more than a passion—it's an expression of my life. I used to travel the world seeking out the best salsa dance clubs in New York City, Miami, Los Angeles, San Francisco, Vancouver, Mexico City, Buenos Aires, London, Paris, Bangkok, Sydney, and beyond. Every wedding I go to I ask them to play salsa, and anytime I hear it at a restaurant, I get up and start dancing. I'm kind of weird about it, but *I love it*! I could do something to make money with it and make it part of my mission, but it doesn't call to me enough inside to make this my life's work (at least not this season). So I keep it a passion for now.

Your unique strengths are components of your natural hard-wiring that give you an advantage in some situations. No one is naturally wired to do everything well. That's why we all need each other. Your strengths give you power in those situations that call for them. You can then develop the skill sets needed to make the most of that power. For example, I love asking people questions and learning from them; that is part of my natural strengths. But I have also become a student of the interview process to develop that skill set in support of my strengths. Together, these strengths and skill sets position me to make a power-driven contribution in my sweet spot.

Problem

Many people spend their lives running from problems. But pursuing a Meaningful Mission from your sweet spot means you actively seek out a problem to solve. Rather than running from the challenge and letting it define you, you courageously run toward it—and redefine the world as you do.

In short, you can become the hero of your own story. Donald Miller, author of *Hero on a Mission*, described it to me in this way: Every good story requires a problem and a hero willing to solve it. Otherwise, there is no story. You find your Meaningful Mission when you find a problem that needs to be solved in the world.[8]

For example, Kelly Simpson, a member of the Greatness Academy community, was a veteran real estate agent who saw a serious problem: an epidemic of violent attacks on real estate agents. Very little was being done to actively equip these agents to be proactive and defend themselves, so she formed the National Safety Council of Real Estate, set out to write a practical guide for agent safety (*Not Today Predator*), and developed training and materials to keep agents safe. She saw a problem that aligned with her passions and strengths and made it part of her own Meaningful Mission.

Whatever the problem is, finding a solution must resonate with you. When I was at an event with Gurudev, a young woman asked him what can be done to end global warming. His response went right to the heart of the issue: "You are clearly passionate about creating change, so I trust you will take action to make it happen. Passion leads to action. If you're not passionate about it, you simply won't be able to sustain your activity."

This focus on solving a problem is consistent with what fuels our sense of fulfillment and happiness. Dr. Laurie Santos, Yale professor and host of the podcast *The Happiness Lab*, told me, "There is a mistaken notion that happiness is all about self-care. But what the science suggests is that happy people are really others-oriented. They're reaching out, making social connections, and worrying about how they can help other people and other people's welfare. That's what seems to lead to a happy life."[9]

In the same way, Gurudev describes three levels of intelligence:[10]

1. Unintelligent people look for instant pleasure for themselves.

2. Mid-level intelligent people shift to doing things out of a sense of duty and focus on following the rules.

3. The highest level of intelligence belongs to those who desire to spread joy by serving others.

Beyond themselves and not merely out of a sense of duty, highly intelligent people, as defined here, care about helping spouses, families, and their communities solve problems. The beauty of this intelligence or awareness is that it is not something anyone is born with. It can be chosen, pursued, and cultivated by everyone.

Former CIA director John Brennan once told me he defines greatness as "accomplishing something that is beneficial to more than yourself and making a contribution to humankind."[11] He added that it doesn't require a large public profile but a willingness to rise to the occasion and meet a need. To be meaningful, he said, it needs to be something that affects more than yourself.

To be clear, we don't always get total clarity on our sweet spot right away. Sometimes we get more clarity as we engage in the process of putting our passions and strengths to work. You might need 5 or 10 years to really figure it out, and even then, you may need a game plan for developing needed skills.

Robert Greene, the *New York Times* best-selling author of books such as *The 48 Laws of Power, The Art of Seduction, The 33 Strategies of War,* and *The 50th Law,* told me he didn't always know his own sweet spot. He tried being a newspaper writer and was good at it, but he always felt friction. He tried screenwriting for television, then for movies. Those were also okay, but they still didn't feel quite like his sweet spot. After a decade of jumping from thing to thing, he decided to pursue his own unique passion for a particular topic with his growing skill sets, and he published a book few people believed would be popular: *The 48 Laws of Power.* At the time of this writing, the book has over 35,000 reviews on Amazon alone, and his impact on the world is still growing.[12]

It's okay if finding your sweet spot and Meaningful Mission takes time. That's normal. Just keep moving forward and never settle until you do.

ENGAGING GREATNESS

Exercise 1: The Perfect Day Itinerary

The Perfect Day Itinerary (PDI) may be one of the most powerful exercises you ever do for yourself, so make sure you have plenty of time dedicated to finishing this exercise. I've coached many unfocused entrepreneurs through this exercise, and most of them have told me it changed their lives. I'm never surprised to hear that because I believe this exercise set me up to create the beautiful life I'm living today.

STEP 1—CRAFT YOUR PERFECT DAY

In this exercise, your job is to map out what your perfect day looks like along the path to achieving your vision. We will start at the macro level by asking ourselves a series of questions.

- How do you want every day to look?

- How do you want to feel every single day? What are you creating daily?

- Who are you with?

- What places are you exposing yourself to? What passions are you fulfilling?

Take out a blank piece of paper or open a new document on your computer and fill the first half of the page with the answers, in broad terms, to these questions. Below are my results from the very first time I did this exercise years ago:

MY PERFECT DAY

On my perfect day, I wake up next to the woman of my dreams. I'm preparing to compete in the 2016 Olympics with U.S.A. Team Handball, so I head to an intense training session with my coach to increase my physical strength and athleticism. Then I'm working on my TV show on a major network and supporting my company team with my projects that inspire entrepreneurs to follow their passions and make a living around what they love.

Of course, not every day you live will be exactly the same. Each day will look a little different depending on what happened the day before. Thank goodness for variety; otherwise, life would get boring and monotonous.

STEP 2—WRITE THE ITINERARY

Next, write out a detailed itinerary for the *next* perfect day on the bottom half of your page. This itinerary should include your obligations and your desires, and the timing for each. Every successful sports season, I had included detailed daily itineraries that, I believe, set us up to win. The schedule listed out every step we needed to take to reach our end goal. Professional sports teams do this as well to help them collectively achieve their vision. That's the point of this exercise—to help you achieve your vision.

Here is a version of my daily itinerary from when I wrote my first book:

TOMORROW'S PERFECT DAY

7:30 A.M. *Wake up, meditate, and enjoy the views from my balcony.*

8:00 A.M. *Healthy breakfast with green juice or a smoothie.*

9:00 A.M. *CrossFit/kickboxing or private skills-training session.*

10:45 A.M. *Check in with my team about projects of the day.*

11:00 A.M. *Complete the top three tasks that were on my list before bed.*

12:00 P.M. *Healthy lunch at home or lunch meeting with someone who inspires me.*

1:30 P.M. *Back to the top three on my to-do list, recording interviews, doing videos, or working with the team.*

3:00 P.M. *Physical therapy to increase flexibility (two days a week).*

5:00 P.M. *Pickup basketball, hiking with friends, swimming in the ocean.*

7:30 P.M. *Healthy dinner at home or out with friends.*

9:00 P.M. *Read, watch a movie, go to events with influencers on the town.*

11:00 P.M. *Make a list of what I'm most grateful for today, create a "completed list" of what I did today. Write the top three things I want to create tomorrow.*

11:30 P.M. *Meditate, sleep, dream, recover the body.*

STEP 3—SET A MICRO GOAL

Choose one or two things on your itinerary that you will do tomorrow. To start working toward your perfect day, you don't need to overhaul your existing routine. Instead, you need to find small, achievable wins that will help you improve your life and feel hopeful.

Pick those one or two micro goals and put them in your calendar or set an alarm for them. Commit to doing them. Tomorrow, you'll be one step closer to your perfect day. If you let it, the PDI can be a powerful exercise that will set up your year (and many years to come) to include the best days of your business and life. It will also help validate your vision and vice versa. If your vision doesn't fit in with your perfect day at either the macro or micro level, consider changing your vision or be more open, honest, and creative about what it will take at a daily level to work toward achieving your Meaningful Mission.

Exercise 2: Write Your Obituary

I recently spent some time with Donald Miller on my show. He had just written *Hero on a Mission* and challenged us to write our own eulogies. He believes that understanding our narratives and objectives helps us to keep growing. I agree. In this exercise, we will write our own eulogies and craft our growth path. As Donald Miller says, a "hero knows what they want."[13] So let's figure out what we want.

STEP 1—CRAFT YOUR NARRATIVE

Get out a sheet of paper and prepare to get honest with yourself. Remember, you're the only one reading this. You can get as aspirational and hopeful as you want. I want you to set aside at least 30 minutes to think about the questions and write your answers.

1. How long do you want to live?

2. What Meaningful Mission did you accomplish before you died?

3. When asked, what do people say is your legacy or your most outstanding achievement?

4. What do your loved ones say at your funeral?

STEP 2—PUT IT TOGETHER

Now it's time to put our goals together to craft a eulogy. If you don't feel like you are a natural writer, this may feel overwhelming, but stick with it. Follow the order of the previous questions for the structure of the eulogy.

Here's a sample to show you what yours might look like:

Lisa Anderson, age 90, was known for the way she supported and advocated for art education in local communities across metro Atlanta. She met with local community leaders, churches, community developers, and schools to help them figure out how to fund and launch art programs for children, teens, and young adults. "Art," she said, "has the power to change a life. By teaching young people skills to express pain, vulnerability, confusion, and beauty, communities could be changed for the better."

Lisa believed that art, whether we were observing it or creating it, had the power to change policy, social discussions, and culture. She spent her life making sure people could embrace the power of art, regardless of their socioeconomic status.

Because of her, young people were changed for the better. It wasn't just art she loved. She loved people too. She was fiercely dedicated to helping anyone she met flourish and thrive.

According to her daughters, Lisa's art, while important, wasn't her greatest accomplishment. "The way she loved people, showed hospitality, and treated you like you were her oldest and dearest friend are the things we will miss the most about her."

Her surviving family and friends are creating the Lisa Anderson Art Coalition. The Coalition will help expand the reach of art scholarships and education in communities of poverty across the United States. In lieu of flowers, the family requests donations to the Coalition.

STEP 3—SAY YES

Okay, now that you've taken the time to craft your own growth path, it's time to start enthusiastically saying yes to everything that will get you there. Understanding where we want to go in life helps us say yes to the things that keep us on the path to greatness and say no to those that do not. Let's start by removing your known barriers.

Chances are, you already know some of the biggest challenges or barriers in the way of your legacy. Is it fear? Anxiety? A job you hate? Lack of training? Refer to the legacy you laid out for yourself. What are the things that are preventing you from achieving those specific goals? Now is the time to take concrete steps to knock those barriers down.

What is the length of time between now and how long you want to live? If you said 90 years old, how many years do you have left? Fifty? Sixty? Twenty? What milestones do you need to achieve within that timeframe in order to fulfill your self-prophesized legacy?

This week, I want you to do **one thing** that will lessen your biggest challenge. If you're going to become a personal trainer but don't even know what certifications you want, set aside 30 minutes for research this week. If you want to teach people how to feed their families for less than $100 per month, find and claim a URL for your future website. As I've said before, every step counts, even baby steps. The important thing is to start saying *yes*.

Exercise 3: Find Your Sweet Spot

If you've spent any amount of time following me on social media, listening to my show, or watching any of my videos, you know that I think you've got what it takes to be great. Yes, *you*. We might not have met, but I *know* you have something you do better than anyone else. *You* have a sweet spot in life. *You* have a talent or skill where your greatness truly shines. I will walk you through a discovery process below to help you identify your sweet spot.

STEP 1—FIND YOUR PASSION

Your sweet spot starts with understanding your passion. Most people naturally know what they are passionate about when they are younger, but it's so easy to lose sight of it as we get older. Our responsibilities and obligations can turn down the volume of our natural passions, but they are still there. Take a few minutes to reflect on your childhood, teen years, or even your young adulthood and rediscover what you loved.

- What did you enjoy doing with your free time?
- What dreams did you have of what you might love to do in life?

Take a moment to write these things down, even if they don't seem viable at the moment. Perhaps you were obsessed with creating cookie recipes when you were younger and putting together cookie baskets for your family when you were younger. Write it down!

Next, list seven things you love to do. They could be anything— as long as you *absolutely love* to do them!

- What lights you up? Inspires you? Energizes you?
- When do you find yourself losing track of time because you are so absorbed in an activity and can't wait to get back to it and do it again?
- What would you love to do even if you didn't get paid to do it?
- Fast-forward to your golden years. What might you wish you had done more of?

Now take a moment to compare your lists.

- What common themes do you see in your answers?
- What words get repeated? What activities keep getting mentioned?

- What threads are woven consistently throughout your story?

Summarize the patterns you see by circling common words or writing a few summary sentences below both lists.

STEP 2—FIND YOUR POWER

Discovering your strengths and skills is next. Like I said earlier, *everyone* is really good at something. Let's figure out what it is with some intentional exploration.

Just because you are passionate about doing something doesn't mean you have the skill set to do it (and that's okay). Your skills can be natural or learned. Here's the difference:

- **Natural strengths** are what you are *naturally good at* based on your personality hardwiring.

- **Learned skills** are what you have *learned to be good at* through life experiences.

I have no doubt that you already know some of your strengths and skills and that you have hidden talents you may not recognize as keys to greatness because they feel so normal to you. I want you to take a moment to think about what you are good at, considering both your natural and learned skills. Write them *all* down.

STEP 3—BECOME A HERO

Now that we've looked at your passions, natural strengths, and learned skills, it's time to look at the problem you want to help other people solve. Do you want to teach people how to grow vegetables to feed their families easier? Do you want to teach people how to get out of debt to have the abundant life they desire? Do you want to teach mindfulness so that children can better overcome the effects of trauma?

Perhaps an easier way to look at this is philosophically. What is just *wrong* in your world, community, or circle of influence? I'm willing to bet that your passions, strengths, learned skills, and mission intersect at many points or one central point. Can you find the overlap?

Take a moment to write down some declarative sentences about your problem-solving mission. Utilize some of the eulogy-writing skills we learned in our earlier exercise.

Here's what it might look like:

I am passionate about cooking and gardening. For some reason, I've always known how to create delicious concoctions in the kitchen, with or without a recipe. In the last several years, I have taught myself how to get better at cooking through YouTube videos, cooking classes, and two cooking vacations to Tuscany. Now I want to take these skills and teach them to single moms, college kids, and low-income families. I believe everyone deserves delicious food and the know-how to create it from affordable ingredients and their own gardens.

REDEFINE YOUR WORLD

The overlap between your passion and your power is your sweet spot. When we pursue our purpose and Meaningful Mission from our sweet spot, we become mission-oriented in our problem-solving. We courageously run toward problems and redefine our world. When we pursue greatness, it's not just ourselves that change. The world changes too.

The Barriers to Greatness

Chapter 4

FEAR #1: FAILURE

Sara Blakely was a frustrated consumer with a problem—she wanted underwear that didn't show lines, was flattering to women's figures, and was not heavy or uncomfortable. "It actually started with my own butt, because I couldn't figure out what to wear under white pants."[1]

So, with a sharp pair of scissors, she cut the legs out of a pair of control-top pantyhose as a prototype—and the revolutionary idea for SPANX was born. At the time she came up with the idea for SPANX, Blakely was in her late twenties and a former Disney cast member turned door-to-door fax machine salesperson, a career she had pursued for *seven years*. She didn't have a business background. She didn't have a lot of capital to invest. She didn't have connections to hosiery manufacturers.

She was even told by some business*men* to get ready, because "business is war."

She didn't want to go to war. She wanted to help women.

It was a perfect recipe for failure, but Blakely had a bit of a secret weapon that no one knew about. When she was a kid sitting around the dinner table at night, her dad would ask her and her brother a seemingly odd question: "What did you fail at today?" Then her dad would encourage them to write down the "hidden gifts"—the lessons that came from their failures.

Not exactly typical dinner table talk in most parenting books, but it helped her get in the habit of destigmatizing failure and building her risk-taking muscles. In fact, she says that if she *didn't* have a failure to share, her dad would be disappointed. So she learned to define failure differently and embrace it as an important part of life. "Failure for me became *not trying* versus achieving the outcome. Once you redefine that for yourself and realize that failure is just not trying, then life opens up to you in many ways."[2]

What is your definition of greatness?

For two years, Blakely heard "no" from dozens of hosiery manufacturers who wouldn't give her a shot. She was priced out by patent lawyers, so she drafted her own patent agreement using a book she found at Barnes & Noble, only turning to an attorney for the things she couldn't do. Department stores refused to sell the product, saying it was too risqué. She came up with the name SPANX because by changing the *-ks* in *spanks* to an *x*, it was easier to trademark and market.

But still, she persisted. She *knew* she had a good product, so she ignored the chatter, trusted her intuition, and pushed forward. After all, to her way of thinking, failure wasn't *not launching* SPANX. Failure was *not trying*.

Fast-forward 20-plus years, and in October 2021, this pioneer form-fitting shapewear company was valued at $1.2 billion.[3] Now the market is littered with competitors.

The fear of failure didn't derail her, because the fear of *not trying* was stronger. In an Instagram post, she summed up her philosophy:

Two things are required to pursue your dreams: hustle and willingness to put yourself out there! The two things people are most afraid of are fear of failure and fear of being embarrassed. I'm constantly working on both of these fears so I can live the life I want free from the burden of caring what other people think of me.

What I've found is that it actually becomes fun and funny. The worst thing that happens? You end up with a great story. So what are you waiting for?[4]

At the end of our conversation on my show, I asked Sara the same question I do of all my guests: "What is your definition of greatness?"

"My definition of greatness would be going for it no matter what, despite fear, and making the absolute most of the life that you were given, because it's not a dress rehearsal."[5]

THE FUNNY THING ABOUT FAILURE

Failure is a funny thing.

Not in the sense that every failure should be followed by a full-on chuckle or a belly laugh of epic proportions. Maybe that's true in some cases, but most of the time failure is painful, embarrassing, and not a lot of fun. We certainly don't seek it out.

Failure is funny, because for something that we each do so well and so often, most of the time we don't want to think about our failures, remember our failures, or in some cases even *admit* that we have failed.

And yet, without failure, we can't move forward.

Without failure, we'd never try anything new. Without failure, we'd never discover a better way.

Failure is a critical part of the fabric of life.

Without failure, we'd never get any better, stronger, or tougher.

Failure isn't something to be shunned, overlooked, or wasted. Failure is a critical part of the fabric of life.

Robert Greene, an American author, has found that depending on how we choose to avoid failure, insecurities can operate one of two ways. First, we can choose to let our insecurities hold us back and avoid the pain of failure by never trying anything. From this perspective, you might try your hardest and find others who are still better than you, but if you don't try, you can always be the best slacker.[6]

Second, we can choose to let our insecurities motivate us and avoid failure by working our hardest. As Sara's story shows, the fear of failure, when channeled properly, can actually cause us to develop persistence, build resourcefulness, and fuel innovation.

THE DOUBT DIAGRAM

In her book *Good Anxiety*, Dr. Wendy Suzuki identifies an array of common anxieties, including the fear of public speaking, financial insecurity, social anxiety, and general anxiety.[7] These anxieties can lead to obsessive compulsions until all you can think about are your fears. Add to that things like pandemics and all the uncertainties of life, and none of us have a shortage of candidates for fear.

> **Self-doubt is simply the killer of dreams.**

I've wrestled with debilitating self-doubt at times myself, the belief deep down at my core that somehow I was not enough. I wasn't good enough. I wasn't smart enough. I was too young. I didn't have enough connections. My talents weren't enough. I even had other people tell me that I wouldn't be able to realize my Meaningful Mission. And my fears contributed to all of it.

Self-doubt is simply the killer of dreams. When you doubt yourself, it's really hard to have the confidence to chase what you want and take action to pursue your Meaningful Mission. That sense that you are just "not enough" can usually be traced back to one of three core fears. It might help to think of them in what I call the Doubt Diagram:

1. *Fear of failure*
2. *Fear of success*
3. *Fear of judgment*

The Doubt Diagram

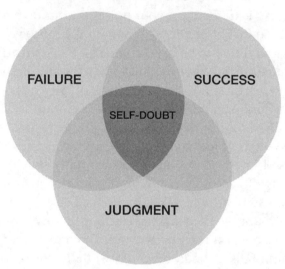

In her book *Woman Evolve*, Sarah Jakes Roberts says we are in relationships with our fears.[8] Like an overbearing partner, they constantly influence us and often dictate our actions. They go where we go. They pretend to keep us safe, when in reality they just consume and manipulate us. That is why Sarah says we need to break up with our fears.

And the first fear you may need to break up with is the fear of failure.

OUR DEFAULT POSITION

Dan Millman, an American author and lecturer in the personal development field, often says, "Raise your hand if you've ever been afraid of failure." He told me that at least 80 percent of the people in the room always raise a hand. I've seen that same trend when I make the same request. Clearly the fear of failure is common to us all. But that fear holds so many people back from pursuing their Meaningful Mission. As Millman told me, our self-doubt inhibits a purposeful life. Dan has learned that the best way to get out of your own way is to focus on your purpose, your own Meaningful Mission, not on what might go wrong on the journey.[9]

I have found that to be true for me as well. As an athlete, I was taught that failure is a part of the journey toward success. You fail your way to learning how to catch the ball. You miss a shot, and then you adjust. You make a mistake, learn from it, and make a change. Failure for me was just part of practice, part of my daily learning to improve and move me toward my goals.

Because I knew emotionally and mentally that failure was a necessary step to accomplishing success for my goals, I was never afraid to fail as an athlete. Like I mentioned earlier, all of us know this from a young age. When we're learning to walk, no one expects a child to succeed on the first attempt. Of course not. Every child stumbles and falls a thousand times while learning to walk. But no one tells the child walking isn't for them. We encourage them to pick themselves up and try again, knowing the only thing that can stop them from succeeding is not trying. But then, as we get older, we let that fear of failure feel abnormal, even though experiencing failure and fear are part of what it means to be human.

"You're always afraid," says Dr. Jordan Peterson, a Canadian professor of psychology, "except when you learn not to be." Fear is our default position as humans. So, if you are afraid of failure, that means you are normal. But running from your fears isn't the answer. Letting them define who you are doesn't work. According to Peterson, "When we are exposed to what we are afraid of, we get less afraid of everything."[10]

Believe it or not, one of my top fears used to be public speaking. After I joined Toastmasters and started speaking every single week to a small audience, I began to feel more comfortable and eventually was regularly getting paid good money to speak to audiences of up to 20,000 people. But I still wasn't always comfortable with it. Not at all.

Every single time I had a speaking engagement, I was afraid of how I would look onstage. I was afraid of saying the wrong thing and being embarrassed while people laughed at me. I thought I would start stuttering and fall all over my words, if I didn't fall on the stairs on the way to the stage.

A few hours before one of my big events, I told one of my coaches, Chris Lee, about my fears. He challenged me to flip the script running in my head by pointing out that my fears were all about me. How *I* might look. How *I* might feel. How *I* might make a mistake. What if I made it all about serving other people? Why was I speaking? For me or for my audience? That shift in thinking about service began the wheels turning. He followed it by asking me questions in what I call the "Then What?" exercise:

What if I forget what I'm going to say next?
Okay, then what?
Well, I'd be embarrassed.
Okay, then what?
I might run off the stage.
Okay, then what?
Everyone would laugh?
Okay, then what?
I'd probably not leave home for a week.
Okay, then what?

I'd probably eventually pick myself back up and keep moving forward.

I realized what Chris was getting at. Even in the worst-case scenario, I'd eventually be okay, and, like SPANX founder Sara Blakely mentioned, I'd have a funny story to tell. So why not just skip all the anxiety in the middle and start with "Everything will be okay" in the first place?

After that awakening, everything changed for me. I realized the power of what Sukhinder Singh Cassidy, president of StubHub, calls "the choice after the choice."[11] And I knew that if my focus was on serving other people, then all my fears about what might happen to me became irrelevant.

WHAT CAN FAILURE TEACH YOU?

There are two general types of fear. The first type is a healthy fear of something dangerous. There are some things we should fear, things that will, in fact, harm us. That is when our fight-or-flight instinct comes in handy to protect us from harm. But the second type consists of wounded fears that hold us back emotionally, spiritually, mentally, and physically from making decisions that will make our future greater. These fears keep us living in the past. They are psychological fears as opposed to being driven by real-life danger.

> **If my focus was on serving other people, then all my fears about what might happen to me became irrelevant.**

Our fear of failure usually falls into this psychological fear category rather than the threat of real-life danger. Even though it sometimes feels like it, the world probably won't end if you fail at most things in life. (Some notable exceptions might include skydiving, atomic fusion, landing on Mars—but I digress.)

Remember, there is something worse than failing: the regret of *not trying*.

On the other hand, failure can help us learn and grow. You might fail and may even receive criticism, but if you take that failure as an opportunity to learn what didn't work, you'll create something better, maybe even great, the next time. For example, after his wildly popular book *The 48 Laws of Power*, Robert Greene worked on another book he just knew would be a breakthrough success. He labored over the manuscript for a year. But when he submitted the manuscript to the publisher, they dropped the project.

Robert was stunned. The feedback he received was that his audience wanted to hear more of his thoughts, but he had collaborated with rapper 50 Cent and made the book more about his collaborator than his own perspectives. Instead of quitting, Robert chose to learn from his spectacular failure. He took the feedback to heart, rewrote the book in eight months, and found another publisher. *The 50th Law* by 50 Cent and Robert Greene became another huge success.

> **There is something worse than failing: the regret of not trying.**

As he told me, Robert has learned to see failure as a chance to reorient or better yourself. And he knows all about a disrupted life. When he suffered a stroke in 2018, nearly half of his body stopped functioning the way it did before. Yet he calls it a "blessing" because it taught him that any day could be his last. "Defeat and failure are the greatest things that could ever happen to you," says Robert. "Failure teaches you your limits and makes you realize what you did wrong. It shows you what you could do differently."[12] With this mentality, he has pressed forward, working on yet another transformative book.

Successes rarely spark much reflection. Failure is how we grow.

Sarah Jakes Roberts's theory is that people quit after failing because they are looking to add to their own value. But as Sarah says, "Success is in the process, not the outcome."[13] When you don't depend on a specific outcome to define your worth, you are free to become great by failing, learning, and moving forward.

Dan Millman is another terrific example of someone who embraces the failure-is-learning mentality. When he was 60 years old, he decided he wanted to learn to ride a unicycle. He borrowed one from a friend, who gave him sage advice: practice on a tennis court. Dan donned a helmet and mounted the unicycle, gripping the chain-link fence with white knuckles. On his first attempt to peddle, the unicycle shot out from under him, leaving him dangling from the fence. Again and again, he failed. It took a week of humbling practice every day to reach the point where he could pedal six times before falling. After two weeks, he could do about 12 pedals. By week three, he was doing figure eights.

From this experience, he learned two things. First, whether it's changing habits or learning to ride a unicycle, everything is difficult at first. Second, there were intermittent days when everything fell apart. He would be doing well one day and then the next would be worse. This trend confused and discouraged him—until he observed a pattern. He discovered that his "breakthrough days" came right after his "bad days." It was on those alleged bad days that the learning happened.

Failure is how we grow.

The struggle to climb out after our failures explode can give us perspective and make us stronger and wiser. Dan told me he believes this same pattern is true with other life skills: "Sometimes we feel like we're getting worse, vegetating, or even going backward, but we may be backing up to get a running start."[14] Even when we can't see the progress, learning can take place if we keep moving forward.

SOMETIMES YOU'RE GOING TO SUCK

Back in 2009, Ryan Serhant was a fledgling real estate agent in New York City. One of his first clients was a woman who was hunting for an apartment in the West Village. He was excited about the possibilities because the commission would have set him up for a while. However, Ryan was not on his home turf and without a GPS. The morning that he drove her to check out apartments, he got himself and his quickly disappointed client lost not once but twice. He was, she told him at the end of that day, *the worst agent and should never be allowed to practice real estate again.* Ouch.

Although the experience shook him, Ryan learned an important lesson from that failure. It doesn't matter how long you've been in any business; new challenges can still catch you off guard. But that doesn't mean you give up. Ryan took an honest look at his performance and admitted that he could have prepared better. He should have researched the area in advance. He should have woken up early and learned the streets.

At that moment, he made a choice. Even though he was not from New York, didn't have the connections, and didn't look the part, he was determined he would be the best real estate agent ever.

Not long after his resolution, an international client approached Ryan. Ryan pushed aside his self-doubt, learned from his failure, and performed the role of the successful broker. He sold the client a $2.1 million apartment, making over $24,000 in commission.

More importantly, the experience confirmed for Ryan Serhant that he could accomplish his real estate dreams if he was willing to learn from his failures.

Now, let me be clear: breaking up with the fear of failure, as Sarah Jakes Roberts puts it, isn't easy. And breaking up with the fear doesn't mean you won't experience that fear going forward. As she says, "Faith makes a demand on courage."[15] It can be difficult to make that kind of leap from total doubt to courageous faith. It is understandable that we may feel indecisive when choosing between two such extremes. It can be tempting to procrastinate making that leap, but if we want to become a master, we have to do what Sarah says:

> We have to come to a place where we realize that not everything you do is going to win. It's like, you're gonna suck sometimes. . . . When your goal is mastery, you recognize that failure is going to be a part of the process. But

because you want to be a master, you dissect that failure, extract the wisdom from it, and apply it to the next try. Because at the end of the day, I'm going for mastery.[16]

I believe that when we allow ourselves to stay in a relationship with that fear of failure, or any fear, for that matter, what we are really afraid of is that we might discover we are not enough. Sarah describes it as the fear "that this will become the evidence that my insecurities need to keep me from being who I'm supposed to be."[17]

The problem with thinking this way is that it becomes a self-fulfilling prophecy. Our fear of falling short causes us to remain frozen and ensures we never fulfill our Meaningful Mission.

YOUR RISK-TAKING EQUATION

Failure is so dependable that the only way to avoid it is to never try anything at all. The people we see as the best, the greatest athletes, the most successful entrepreneurs, or the people making the most impact in the world, are all continuously failing.

Priyanka Chopra Jonas, an Indian actress, model, singer, and winner of the Miss World 2000 pageant, is someone who realizes it is futile to try to avoid failure. "When you want to create a legacy," she told me, "it's what you do *after* failure that matters."[18] As she describes it, when you first attempt something new, failures are inevitable, but if you never try anything new, you'll never evolve, and that is a much greater risk. When you make a habit of trying new things, you diversify, increasing your chances of success. If you only stick with what you know, you put your fate in only a few skills and opportunities. And I love this powerful point she makes: Every successful person has failed along the way to their success, so why should you be any different?

Sometimes the only way to find success is to admit your current state of failure. Actor Ethan Suplee has an inspirational story of weight loss, a journey that saw him lose more than 250 pounds! But before he could begin that journey, he had to first come to the realization that he needed to change. After entering a romantic relationship with a woman who enjoyed physical activities, Ethan realized he would have to get healthy if he wanted to sustain the relationship. His first step to a healthy lifestyle was to voice his intentions to his girlfriend. According to Ethan, that conversation was scary because it felt like, in doing so, he was revealing that his life was a failure.[19]

By voicing his intentions to his girlfriend and feeling the risk of embarrassment if he failed to follow through with his intentions, Ethan leveraged his fear of failure to motivate him to better health and an amazing physical transformation. Instead of letting that fear paralyze him, he looked ahead and realized the price of inactivity (a lost romantic relationship) was greater than the price of standing still.

To overcome paralysis from fear, Sukhinder Singh Cassidy recommends a similar technique called the risk-taking equation. She recommends playing out in your mind the decisions you are afraid to make. By running these scenarios, says Sukhinder, you find there are very few decisions you cannot recover from if they fail. She says we need to let go of the myth of the single choice and stop believing our choices are either/or.

Taking a big risk does not necessarily mean the only two possible outcomes are either a big reward or a major loss. This kind of thinking puts too much pressure on the first choice. There are many possible journeys, and with every choice we discover opportunities to orient ourselves toward success. As she told me, the people she knows who are successful are "measured by small and big acts of possibility." They are "master(s) at the process of risk-taking and constantly choosing."[20]

PAIN POINTS THE WAY

Ray Dalio is another person who embraced failure and learned that pain, not pleasure, is what makes us wise. Ray is the founder, co-chairman, and co-chief investment officer of Bridgewater

Associates, the fifth most important private company in the U.S. according to *Fortune* magazine. He is the 69th richest person in the world at the time of this writing and worth over $20 billion. He has been called the "Steve Jobs of investing" by *Wired* magazine and named one of the top 100 most influential people by *Time* magazine. In other words, if anyone should know something about success, it would be Ray. And yet he told me he learned more from his failures than from his successes.

One of Ray's greatest losses occurred early in his investing career. In 1981, he had predicted that America would experience an economic crisis as a result of the loans American banks had made to countries Ray didn't think were capable of repaying. As it turned out, Mexico defaulted in 1982, proving Ray's prediction true and gaining him a lot of attention.

So he made a second prediction of a depression on the horizon. Instead of a debt crisis, though, the stock market turned around. The point Ray predicted to be the beginning of a downward spiral for the market turned out to be only the dip before the rise. Because of his miscalculation, Ray lost not only his money but also that of his clients. He had to borrow $4,000 from his father just to pay the bills.

Surprisingly, Ray calls this failure the best thing to happen to him. He says it taught him to balance boldness with caution. As he reflected on his failure, he evolved. He began seeking intelligent people with different opinions from his own. As a result, he learned to test his theories more thoroughly before risking everything on a prediction.

Since he made these changes, he has seen great success. This success was only possible because he learned he could not know everything and that he needed to lean on a team of diverse thinkers. According to Ray, reality doesn't care if you accept it in the face of failure. The world will keep turning regardless of your actions. All we can do is try to understand reality and learn how to approach it when failure happens.[21]

EMERGENCY RESERVES

So if failure is inevitable, why should we fear it? What if, instead, we gave ourselves permission to fail on the journey to greatness? Marissa Sharif, a professor at the Wharton School of the University of Pennsylvania, was inspired when she observed that many people, herself included, failed to meet goals in their lives because of what she called "what-the-hell moments."

These moments come when someone has a small backslide from a healthy direction, which can tempt them to totally abandon their greater goal. For example, someone might set a goal to consume a total of 1,500 calories a day. They might meet that goal Monday, Tuesday, and Wednesday, but then Thursday morning—donuts at the office. Then the small failure of one donut cascades into pizza and potato chips for dinner the rest of the week, because "what the hell, I've already failed."[22]

To attempt to solve this issue, Marissa set the goal to work out every day of the week but allowed herself two emergency reserves, days when life might get in the way and make working out impossible. This structure lets her relax in those moments of tension. Instead of giving up on her bigger goal and not working out the rest of the week, she can tap into her reserves and know she is still acting with integrity toward her goal.

Just having the knowledge that emergency reserves exist tends to motivate people and keep them on track to reaching the bigger goal. Katy Milkman told me she sees this sort of failure recovery technique as a way of forgiving ourselves. She says to avoid permanent failure, we have to arrange a backup plan—and a backup plan to that backup plan.[23]

The fear of failure does not have to derail your journey to greatness. But perhaps it is not the fear of failure but just the opposite that holds you back.

ENGAGING GREATNESS

I'll provide you with a comprehensive Fear Conversion Tool Kit at the end of this section to help you take action to overcome the barriers of greatness. For now, ask yourself some simple questions:

- To what extent do you struggle to overcome the fear of failure?

- How has this fear held you back from wholeheartedly pursuing your Meaningful Mission?

List any failure fears you have here while they are fresh in your mind.

_____

_____

_____

_____

_____

_____

You can use the exercises in the Fear Conversion Tool Kit (page 109) at the end of this section to further identify and find help to overcome them.

Chapter 5

FEAR #2: SUCCESS

Even as a little girl, Jamie Kern Lima loved the beauty industry.

She would pore over magazines and admire the models who, with their even complexions and slender forms, represented the American ideal. Jamie got the message. She would have to look like that too if the world was to love her.

But it wasn't long before Jamie's love for stories called her into the public eye and in front of cameras. She thought she had arrived when she landed a job as a news anchor. Then, just when she thought she had finally achieved that ideal image, her skin developed unusual red, rashlike bumps.

The horror of her new reality struck her during a live report when the producer told her about some kind of substance on her face. "Wipe your face," her earpiece repeated. "Wipe it off." But no matter how hard she rubbed, it would not wipe it off.

To her dismay, Jamie learned she had developed a skin condition called rosacea. She searched the spectrum from the cheapest to the most expensive cosmetics available, but nothing masked the red, bumpy patches on her face. She wondered how long it would be before her viewers left her—and she lost her job.

As she reflected on that trying season, Jamie shared with me her perspective now. Although she had no idea at the time, her setback was a setup. As she grappled with every brand of cosmetics letting her down, her mindset began to change. She wondered, *Why aren't there any products for me? Why don't any of these models look like me?*

What came next was one of the bravest moves a person could make.

Jamie left her dream job in pursuit of a new vision. She developed a business plan to meet the need for rosacea-friendly cosmetics. As she acted on her plan, she developed a new company called IT Cosmetics and a product specially made for sufferers of rosacea. Despite its proven effectiveness, all the beauty retailers she admired—Sephora, Ulta, QVC—rejected her product.

At one point, she had less than a thousand dollars in her personal and company bank accounts combined. But she was undeterred.

At what felt like a particularly great pitch to a private equity firm, Jamie presented her business plan, product, budget, and entire vision. At the end, as she stood before the panel, she felt certain she was about to finally receive the financial backing she needed to properly market her product.

"We want to congratulate you on your product," the head investor began. She saw her dream manifesting as she heard, "We think that it's awesome." And then came the unexpected, "We want to wish you the best, but we're going to pass on investing in IT Cosmetics."

She could hardly believe it. If she wasn't going to walk away with funding, then she at least wanted some feedback. She held her composure, took a deep breath, and asked the burning question: "Can you tell me why?"

He looked her over, just three feet away from where she stood. "Do you really want me to be honest with you?" With trepidation, Jamie nodded her head. "I just don't think women will buy makeup from someone who looks like you, with your body and your weight."

Jamie walked away from that interaction numb and shocked. While crying in her car, she remembered the motivation behind her efforts and realized this man—the one who saw her appearance as a hindrance—was exactly why her business had to work. *He is just as much impacted by the definition of beauty as everyone else out there.*

Finally, all her past experiences and countless hours comparing herself to unrealistic standards, her fears about her skin condition, and her self-doubt all culminated into one undeniable need. Her Meaningful Mission became clear. She needed to create a beauty brand "for the people." Her ads would show people of all ages, skin types, and gender expressions. She set out to change the culture of beauty "for every little girl out there who's about to start doubting herself, and every grown person who still does."[1]

More motivated than ever, Jamie poured her heart and soul into IT Cosmetics. And she achieved incredible success. But with the success came even more challenges, the kind of challenges many people fear so much that they don't even try to succeed. She spent nearly 10 years working 100-hour weeks, rarely seeing friends or family.[2] She had finally found success, but success had become unhealthy and unsustainable. Jamie attempted to work at an unrealistic pace because no matter how much success she had, each one could be her last and she had to strike while the iron was hot.

It was at this point that the cosmetics giant L'Oreal recognized the revolutionary brand that Jamie had built. They offered her $1.2 billion for IT Cosmetics! Suddenly she was faced with a choice: accept L'Oreal's offer or go public. By accepting the offer, she'd make more money than she could have imagined during all those years struggling to get her idea off the ground. And by going public and maintaining control over the company, she'd probably continue working herself to exhaustion.

But just like when she left her job as a news anchor, Jamie again felt that she needed to leave her comfort zone to pursue something new. She chose to stop chasing success and being constantly afraid of losing it. Jamie sold IT Cosmetics and stepped down as CEO.

Since then, she has maintained a happier 20-hour work week pursuing other greatness opportunities. For example, in 2021, she published *Believe IT: How to Go from Underestimated to Unstoppable*, now a *New York Times* bestseller.

FROM SETBACK TO SETUP

It seems logical that people would fear failure because no one wants to fail. Failure seems to be the antithesis to greatness. But there's a second fear in the Doubt Diagram that is less intuitive.

The fear of success.

This one may seem illogical at first. After all, isn't success what we all want?

When success is the finish line, it can be easy to run the race. But what will happen after you cross the finish line? How will you lead a growing organization? What if you have to deal with the press or the public spotlight? What if people take advantage of you and you lose money and look stupid doing it? That's where doubt can creep in and hold you back from even attempting to succeed. *How will I keep up the pace? Will I be able to withstand the pressure or the spotlight? What if I achieve it and still don't feel fulfilled? What if I'm not good enough to succeed again?*

Let's be honest: there is some validity to these questions, but you can't let them stifle you. If they do, the world will miss out on your greatness and never see the unique value only *you* can provide.

I've asked a handful of people who recently have had a rise of success—massive growth of followers online, more fame, and more money and opportunities coming their way than they had before—to rate themselves on the self-love scale from 1 to 10. Ten meant they fully love and accept themselves and are fulfilled and peaceful inside, and 1 means they hate themselves and don't accept anything about who they are. They all gave me a number of where they were. Then I asked them to go back to the day before all the success and fame started and give me a number.

The answers blew my mind.

Even though from the outside looking in, their success looks amazing, they all scored themselves higher *before* the success! No wonder so many people are afraid. That's why the second fear you must break up with is the fear of success.

KNOW WHEN TO WALK AWAY

When Jamie saw her business taking off, her imposter syndrome told her she couldn't handle it, that it was only a matter of time before her success spiraled out of her control. She told me the only thing that kept her going in those times of self-doubt was her enduring belief in the mission, that her Meaningful Mission was bigger than herself.

The point of success, though, isn't the end of self-doubt. It is normal to be tempted to fear you won't be able to keep up with the demands

> **The point of success isn't the end of self-doubt.**

of your newfound success. This fear can cause you to self-sabotage, running yourself ragged to prove you're enough. That all-too-common imposter syndrome can convince you your success is a fluke, making you short-sighted. You might feel, like Jamie did, that you have to make the most of your success while it lasts.

But that scarcity mindset is not a Greatness Mindset. You have to plan for long-term success in pursuit of your Meaningful Mission, and part of that plan needs to include pacing yourself. Sometimes success can mean closing a comfortable chapter and beginning a new uncomfortable one. In other words, you may need to shift gears.

Dr. Phil, a mental health professional and popular TV show host, shared his insights with me: "The worst thing you could ever do is pursue the wrong dream, or if your dream changes and you don't change with it."[3] Dr. Phil knows a little about shifting gears.

Before he was a television star, he ran two successful psychology practices. However, he told himself from the beginning that if he ever got to the point where the impact he was having on people's lives no longer fulfilled him, he had to stop. That's exactly what happened when he returned to his practice after Christmas break one year. He saw his appointment book filled for the entire next year and thought, *I don't want to do this anymore.* In what he calls his "gut-check moment," he was at risk of staying in a place of comfortable success that was not satisfying. Instead, he referred all his patients to others and shut down his practice.

> **Greatness is being willing to change your definition of success as you pursue your Meaningful Mission.**

Why? His view of success had changed.

Phil has made shifting gears a habit on his path to greatness. He also started a company in trial sciences called CSI. The company helped with trial strategy, jury selection, mock trials, and shadow juries and trials (upon which the CBS television drama *Bull* is based). Again, Phil was successful in this business. He even represented Oprah Winfrey in the mad cow case in Amarillo.

Yet after about 15 years of success, he felt stuck again:

I had done everything you could do. I represented every major airline in the world. I represented all the nine major film studios out here. I represented half of the fortune 100. I was involved in tobacco litigation, breast implant litigation, and everything you could imagine. I'd done virtually everything you can do in that profession.[4]

That's when he realized it was time to do something different. What he created was the now famous *Dr. Phil* television show. But he was only able to create that show because he didn't let a fear of what success might bring limit him. Instead, he took control of his own destiny.

A mark of greatness is the understanding that success itself isn't the endgame. Greatness is being willing to change your definition of success as you pursue your Meaningful Mission.

ONE STEP AT A TIME

Here's the thing about greatness: Greatness is not about being complete at the start. But it is about being *enough*, even while you are still growing, developing, and changing. And that's where the tension comes in: you already are *enough* where you are in this moment *and* you are always becoming *more*. If you aren't willing to become more, then ultimately you aren't willing to grow into the evolution of your own greatness either.

Greatness is a process that is best pursued one step at a time.

As the CEO of ATTACK Athletics, Tim Grover, a businessman and personal trainer, is known around the world for his work with elite athletes across all sports, including the NBA, NFL, MLB, and even Olympic athletes. He was Michael Jordan's trainer when Jordan won multiple NBA World Championships, and Kobe Bryant's trainer too. He told me that everyone is always looking for a specific number of steps that lead to success, but the truth is there are an infinite number of steps because there are an infinite number of definitions of success:

> **Greatness is not about being complete at the start. But it is about being *enough*.**

It doesn't matter how long you've been doing it. Those steps are constantly shifting. Those steps never, never end. And you just can't climb steps. Sometimes you've got to crawl. And when you finally get to the top, everything shifts and you're at the bottom again.

Wait . . . *what*?! The top is the bottom again?

You may get to the top and think you've made it. You look back at where you've come from and feel great. Then you immediately look forward to whatever is next and realize you're back on step one. What you thought was the top is the beginning. And that's when most people just quit.[5]

The journey never ends. When we realize that truth, we can guard against giving in to the fear of success. When the questions start again and greatness seems to fade into the distance, we can remember that the goal is not passing specific success checkpoints but pursuing greatness.

> **The goal is not passing specific success checkpoints but pursuing greatness.**

I know what Tim meant. I spent so many years (my entire lifetime, really) preparing to host *The School of Greatness* podcast. Yet after 10 years at the time of this book launching, I feel like I'm just getting started! Too many people think that constant pursuit of greatness sounds exhausting, so they quit before they begin. In reality, I find it comforting because it means I don't have to have all the skills to get started. With the reassurance that I don't have to have it all figured out, every step I make becomes a sort of self-contained success. I don't need to have answers for what comes after I achieve success; I just need to push past my fears right now and move forward one step at a time.

Here's the truth: You can and will become who and what you need to be on the journey to greatness. In fact, that's the only way to do it.

That is why Amy Cuddy rejects the idea of "fake it till you make it." She has her own version of the saying: "Fake it till you become it." "Fake it till you make it" means you're never authentic, never actually good enough. "Fake it till you become it" means you anticipate growing and becoming the version of yourself you're practicing. Amy calls this "tricking yourself into believing in yourself."[6] I call it a cool tool for use in cultivating the Greatness Mindset. We must be willing to face the things we fear by going all in on them, until those fears disappear and we come out the other side with a new set of skills and inner beliefs.

> **Only when you pursue growth, push past the fear, and become authentic can you begin to position yourself to enjoy success on the journey.**

This reframing practice comes back to defeating that imposter syndrome. Even if you aren't everything you need to be for success right now, you are enough to start right now.

Only when you pursue growth, push past the fear, and become authentic can you begin to position yourself to enjoy success on the journey.

THINK DIFFERENT

It is those long stretches of smooth sailing that are actually most dangerous because too much success can cause you to let your guard down, and that's when failure can hit you the hardest. To avoid that, you have to *think differently*.

From 1997 to 2002, Apple ran an ad campaign called Think Different. In it, they shared powerful black-and-white photographs of creative visionaries ranging from Albert Einstein to Bob Dylan, Amelia Earhart to Jane Goodall, Martin Luther King Jr. to Muhammad Ali, Jim Henson with Kermit the Frog to John

Lennon and Yoko Ono, and Frank Lloyd Wright to Pablo Picasso. All of these people choose to "think different."[7]

To overcome the fear of success, you may need to do the same thing. Think differently.

Let's return to Jamie's story. As her success snowballed, it became a threat to her quality of life because of self-doubt. The more she succeeded, the more she feared losing it all and began to reject the constant struggle to keep up the pace. That is when she had to think differently. Once she believed in her own success and saw it was not a temporary thing, she realized she couldn't keep working 100-hour weeks. She began to learn to have faith in the process, trusting that some things could wait for the next day. As she told me, "I did not need to work hundred-hour weeks to build a billion-dollar company."[8]

According to Tim Grover, we should *embrace the change* that success can bring as a way out of our routines and see the wins in that opportunity. As Tim and I talked, he suggested we move forward on the journey and experience things that might cause us to fear and convert them to opportunities by choosing to see them through that lens. "Count them as wins," he suggested, not as losses or negatives.[9]

Know you are enough *and* you are becoming more.

It's a simple but critical mindset shift. You can't let the fear of actually getting what you want inhibit you. Keep your perspective. Yes, sometimes winning can feel like losing. We can grow to hate the very situation we once longed for. When you find yourself afraid of success or maybe resenting the success you've recently achieved, remember that change is uncomfortable but inevitable. You can't choose whether change happens, but you can choose how you change.

Remember, your role models have insecurities too. Whoever they are, I guarantee they have had to face the same fears and struggles. When you're tempted to believe you aren't good enough or aren't prepared enough to take on the responsibility of greatness, just take the next easy step and know you are enough *and* you are becoming more.

ENGAGING GREATNESS

As I mentioned, I'll provide you with a comprehensive Fear Conversion Tool Kit at the end of this section (page 109) to help you take action to overcome the barriers of greatness. For now, ask yourself some simple questions:

- To what extent do you struggle to overcome the fear of success?

- How has this fear held you back from wholeheartedly pursuing your Meaningful Mission?

List any success fears you have here while they are fresh in your mind:

_____

_____

_____

_____

_____

_____

Chapter 6

FEAR #3: JUDGMENT

Can I be really honest with you? There is one fear I have struggled with more than others. It isn't the fear of failure, although I've had my issues with that, just like all of us. And it isn't the fear of success, although there have been growth challenges I've encountered on the journey. I'm not minimizing those fears at all, but they weren't the things that held me back from creating and going after what I wanted in my life. The one I have wrestled with the most, especially in my early years, has been the fear of judgment by others.

See, I really like making people happy. I want to please them, not create more tension in their lives. That can be a good thing in many ways, but when out of control, it can also lead to detrimental fears that do a lot of damage, both to myself and others.

For many years in my most intimate relationships, my fear of judgment and disappointing the other person led to my abandoning myself, going against my core values, and crossing boundaries I didn't want to cross in order to please them. At least, that's what I told myself as I did whatever it took to make it work.

Let's face it, the idea of love can cloud our own judgment because we're such chemically connected beings. But when we are not aligned with someone emotionally, spiritually, and mentally, trying to make it work is not the best path. My mistake was to try to "fix it" rather than realize that I simply was not in alignment with the other person. That is not intended to be a judgment of the other person but a candid assessment of how I let this fear keep me in certain relationships long after it was time to walk away.

As I have worked with my therapist to understand the relational dynamics, and most importantly, to see my own shortcomings, I realized I felt pressured to stay silent or to compromise boundaries. I was afraid of the relationship not working out and then being judged for it not working out. I didn't want people to think I was a jerk or to see me as the guy who breaks hearts, so I stayed in the relationships, even though I knew deep down that something was off. Plus, I didn't want people I care about being angry with me or disappointed in me, so I just gave in constantly in relationships.

You have to set boundaries that align with your values and vision.

My therapist says I was always trying to buy peace. I would get flowers or a special gift or do something to try to buy peace in the relationship. But you can't buy peace. You have to *be* peace. To do that, you have to set boundaries that align with your values and vision. And that is true in any relationship, whether it be with your business relationships, family, friends, or loved ones.

At the core, my fear of judgment prevented me from doing the right things and being 100 percent authentic in who I was. As a result, I felt like I was out of integrity with myself. Here I was, not being authentic in these most intimate relationships, when my entire mission was to encourage people around the world to be authentic in the pursuit of greatness.

The lack of integrity began to diminish my self-confidence, which made me feel like I was living life at level 6 as opposed to 10. The self-doubt began to creep back in around the edges of my being, which only made it all worse because I knew I was allowing it to happen.

This is all to say, I get it. It's really hard when you're in the moment of stress, breakup, or being fired from your job because it feels like such a big deal. It's messy. It's painful. When you're in it, it's hard to think outside of that moment. You think people are judging you, and they may very well be.

You see, at these pivotal moments, the ego tells you you're not enough because someone hurt you. You'll never amount to anything. You're not worthy. You're afraid of failure. You're afraid of success. You're afraid of other people's opinions. But the ego is what can block you from the flow of abundance.

What I learned to do in those moments is to keep telling myself, *Soon I'm going to have hindsight*. A year from now, I will have learned a lesson from this experience. I will be stronger. I will have more humility. And in six months, a year, or two years, I will be on to something else. People will either move on with me or move out of my life.

My friend Robin Sharma says a bad day for the ego is a great day for the soul, because the ego needs to die at different times in our life so we can purge what is holding us back. Certain parts of the ego can be powerful and positive, but sometimes we need to purge the part that holds us back and limits us to break the invisible chains forged by the judgment of others.[1]

> **Ego is what can block you from the flow of abundance.**

OUR INVISIBLE CHAINS

So many people are hindered by the fear of judgment by other people, their opinions, the embarrassment, what people will think about them, what they'll say about them. Why is that? Why do so many people wait decades to start a creative endeavor they've been dreaming about for so long because they are insecure about someone else's opinion?

When I asked Dan Millman, he observed that many people feel their identity is on the line with the opinions of others, or even their actual self-worth. We both agreed letting our identity be defined by the opinions of others was a mistake. But he made the point that if we focus more on how we can serve others, rather than what they think of us (*It's all about me. How do I look? Do they like me? How do I sound?*), we can move past the anxiety about their opinions.

In fact, Dan calls this the God of Opinion, and I think he is right. We might as well create a little idol called Other People's Opinions and worship it at an altar every day, because that is how so many people live their lives—all because they need the approval of others to define their identity.[2]

Dan Gilbert, professor of psychology at Harvard, makes the distinction between *bumblers* and *pointers*. Bumblers are the ones in the ring, on the field, doing their best to keep moving forward even though they fail often. They keep getting back up, learning, and trying.[3]

Meanwhile, the pointers sit in the stands and ridicule the ones on the field. They don't actually achieve anything, but they do their best to look good. They've got all the fan bling and the most comfortable seats from which they make fun of all the people who are truly trying. They're not bumbling, like the folks on the field because they aren't doing anything of significance at all.

As President Teddy Roosevelt put it:

It is not the critic who counts; not the man who points out how the strong man stumbles, or where the doer of deeds could have done them better. The credit belongs to the man who is actually in the arena, whose face is marred by dust and sweat and blood; who strives valiantly; who errs, who comes short again and again, because there is no effort without error and shortcoming; but who does actually strive to do the deeds; who knows great enthusiasms, the great devotions; who spends himself in a worthy cause; who at the best knows in the end the triumph of high achievement, and who at the worst, if he fails, at least fails while daring greatly, so that his place shall never be with those cold and timid souls who neither know victory nor defeat.[4]

The reality is that each of us can be a combination of critic and bumbler at times. But criticism is not deadly, even though it can feel like it at times. I'm not minimizing the emotional impact, but getting criticized on the Internet or having someone laugh at you doesn't have to determine your life direction. Those people only have power over us when we let them.

So don't let them; take your power back!

For too many years, my fear of judgment drove me to want to succeed in order to prove the critics wrong. But that type of fuel and energy is not sustainable because the accomplishment of my goals then came from a place of insecurity as opposed to doing it because I loved it or because I wanted to inspire and lift others up. Instead of feeling proud after 5 or 10 years of trying to accomplish something and then finally doing it, I would still be depressed 30 minutes later.

We run from our fears, which is why we often distract ourselves or make creative excuses without taking action. For example, one person I was coaching told me they just keep taking courses and going back to school to learn more—but never actually took action because they felt they weren't ready to pursue their goals. But no matter how much schooling and degrees or certifications they received, they would never be ready. They were distracting themselves, feeling like they needed more . . . something. But the reality was they were afraid of failing and being judged for it.

In my conversation with Dr. Ellen Vora, author of *The Anatomy of Anxiety*, we discussed what it feels like when we worry about pleasing others and aren't true to ourselves. She called it "giving a false yes." Here's an example she used: Imagine running into someone you haven't seen for 15 years in a store. You chitchat for a minute, and they suggest getting together next week for coffee. Inside, you immediately run through all you have to do next week and think, *I don't have time to do that.* It's nothing against that person, but it's a low priority for you.

But instead of politely declining, you worry about that fear of judgment and hear yourself say, "Sure, let's do it!" while your brain is screaming, *Say no! Say no!* According to Dr. Vora, that's a false yes.

When next week rolls around, you either flake out and don't go, or you go out of guilt and are thinking about all the other things you *could* be doing. You end up low-key resenting the person because you gave a false yes instead of an authentic no.

As Dr. Vora said succinctly, "It's a little betrayal of the self."[5]

That was my pattern for years. But breaking that pattern has freed me to enjoy better relationships and live with confidence knowing I am pursuing a life of significance and service that is true to my values.

THE TRUTH ABOUT CRITICS

Here is the truth: people will judge you no matter what you do. If you sit on the couch and do nothing, people will criticize you. If you chase your dreams, people will judge you. Either way you are being judged, so you might as well go for your dreams and do the thing you love the most.

When you look in the mirror, you should at least be proud that you gave your all on the field no matter what the critics may say. Be true to you.

One question retired Navy SEAL Commander Rich Diviney posed to me was: *How do you really know what people are thinking?* Usually, you don't. You only *think* you do. The reality is, you usually don't have a clue. Rich suggests we tend to obsess over negative things people *might* be thinking because of the way the brain works:

We consciously lodge a question into our forebrain. Our brain immediately begins to come up with answers. I do this experiment with people in classes I teach. I say, "Just take a moment. I'll give you thirty seconds to answer this question. How could I double my income in the next thirty days? Anything that pops into your head, write down on a piece of paper." They generate a little list.

Then I say, "I don't care what the answers are. I only care how ridiculous the answers are. How many answers did you come up with?" I usually get three, four, five, and sometimes even seven or eight answers. Why? Because they launched a question to their forebrain.

Whatever question we lodge in our forebrain, our brains will begin to answer. But often we do this the wrong way. We ask, *Why am I so bad at this? Why does this stuff always happen to me? Why are these people out to get me?* When that happens, our brains begin to answer those questions and some of those answers are as ridiculous as the answers that someone raised about doubling their income![6]

In other words, our default answers often come from a place of weakness and fear. Our brains easily turn to survival mode, which is a fight-or-flight response that assumes the worst. The answers our brains generate about others may be ridiculous, but they can feel pretty real in the moment.

A lot of our fears of the perceptions of others are imaginary. But some are real. People do judge you and often do so in hurtful ways. And that's okay too.

I asked Joel Osteen, pastor of the largest congregation in America, televangelist, and author, based in Houston, Texas, how he overcomes the tendency to feel insecure about

Either way you are being judged, so you might as well go for your dreams and do the thing you love the most.

93

what others think. When he started, everyone was supportive of him. But as his ministry grew, so did the critics. As he says:

> You can't reach your destiny without people being against you. Some people are not going to understand you. They don't want to understand you. Sometimes we spend time and energy trying to convince somebody to like us, and they're never going to like us. And that's okay. Stay focused on your race. And so what I've been good at, and I encourage other people to do, is to tune out the negativity and run *your* race.
>
> I believe we only have so much emotional energy each day. It's not unlimited. How much am I spending for negativity, for unforgiveness, for what that guy said, for the guy that cut me off in traffic, or for a co-worker who played politics? That's energy that I don't have for my dreams and my goals.
>
> Life is just too short to waste any of our emotional energy on things that don't matter.[7]

Make no mistake—you will have critics. Everyone who is pursuing greatness does. It's what you do after you realize you have critics that counts. It's in those moments that you have to make a decision to shrink back or to stand up, get out on the field, and give it all you've got.

PRACTICAL INSIGHTS

Everyone has an opinion, but not all of them are worth addressing. I like what Priyanka Chopra Jonas told me about cultivating happiness for yourself: "This is your journey and yours only." That means it's up to you to decide how that journey unfolds. If you rely on the opinions of others or their validation, it's going to be a long and bumpy ride. As she continued, "If we're expecting someone else to contribute to your trajectory, it's going to be skewed."[8]

She added that if you're *receiving validation* from others instead of having it within yourself or creating your own validation through the things that matter most to you, then you are always going to be subject to the judgment of others. She chooses to focus on the love, affection, and support from her family and friends and ignore the trolls. "Taking pride in who we are," she noted, "and what we bring to the table is the greatest joy of them all."[9]

> **It's what you do after you realize you have critics that counts.**

This was eye-opening for me!

Rich Diviney suggests another way to push past fear and change our trajectory: "The quality of our lives are directly proportional to the quality of our questions. We ask ourselves questions on a consistent basis; if they are negative, our life is going to suffer."[10] Conversely, if we ask ourselves better questions, our life improves. And the first thing he asks himself is, *What's a better question here?*

It sounds counterintuitive or even sarcastic, but asking a better question halts the negative thought process and creates a new trajectory. And whether it's comparing yourself to others (*Why are they so much more or better than me?*), complaining about circumstances (*Why does this bad thing keep happening to me?*), or wondering about the future (*When is this ever going to change?*), the answer is to ask a better question.

To counteract negativity and stop worrying about what people think of her, Dr. Wendy Suzuki, a professor of neuroscience and psychology at the New York University Center for Neural Science, has a process she calls "joy conditioning." Based on her 25 years of studying how memory works and applying all of her knowledge to addressing anxiety, the process is a direct antidote to fear conditioning, which she says we all experience by default. Joy conditioning takes no training at all, simply a willingness to look back on your life. As she described it, "Joy conditioning is mining your own memory banks for those joyous, funny, or any of your favorite positive emotional events in your life—and consciously bring them up and relive them."[11]

In essence, it is all about mining your life for positive emotions and flooding your mind with them.

Dr. Suzuki says the secret to doing this is to think of a memory with a scent component, a smell that sticks in your mind. She gave me the example of a particular time she attended a yoga class. It was an invigorating experience, but the best part came when the instructor put lavender lotion on her hands, waved them in front of Wendy's face, and gave her a short but relaxing neck massage. It stuck with her so much that Wendy now carries a small bottle of lavender essence and uses it for a pick-me-up.

> ## Don't let the negativity of others derail you.

It's a simple way to condition herself to joy and push past the negativity.[12]

You can do this for yourself. Think about a joyful memory (bonus points if there are good smells involved!) and use that to combat the negative thoughts.

Whether it's drowning out the negative opinions of others with positive opinions from those you trust, asking better questions that pull you out of the negative spin cycle, or joy conditioning so you stop living fearfully, you can and must make the decision to step past the fear of judgment.

You only get one shot on your quest to greatness. Don't let the negativity of others derail you.

ENGAGING GREATNESS

Before you engage with the activities in the Fear Conversion Tool Kit at the end of this section (page 109), ask yourself some simple questions:

- To what extent do you struggle to overcome the fear of the judgment of others?

- How has this fear held you back from wholeheartedly pursuing your Meaningful Mission?

List any fears of what others think while they are fresh in your mind:

_____

_____

_____

_____

_____

_____

_____

_____

Chapter 7

THE DREAM KILLER: SELF-DOUBT

When I was growing up, my father never acknowledged my birthday. No parties, no gifts, no cake. One day I asked him, "Dad, how come you don't celebrate my birthday? Do you not love me?"

"I love you very much," he replied. "I celebrate you every day, but in my work and life experience, I see so many people limited by their age because they have a limiting mindset about time." Sure, I would have loved to have had some presents and cake now and then, but his message was a powerful, shaping influence in my life from an early age.

"I never want you to feel like you're too old to start something," he told me. "I never want you to feel like you're too young or too inexperienced to chase your dreams. I never want you to feel like you're not capable of developing the resources, the intelligence, the wisdom, the skills, the experience to attract abundance in your life." In short, Dad was telling me, *Lewis, I never want you to feel like you are not enough.*

Do you know what kills more dreams than anything else on the entire planet? Self-doubt. So many people fail before they begin simply because they do not believe they can succeed. All the fears of failure, success, and judgment contribute to this one potent poison.

I saw this dream killer at work as far back as in the eighth grade. I looked up to a senior basketball player who was the most talented athlete I'd ever seen at that time. It was freakish how explosive he was. He was totally jacked with a 40-plus-inch vertical leap and could do 360-degree dunks. You name it—the guy had incredible athletic ability. Here I was, a skinny little 13-year-old who could barely jump and touch the basketball rim. I had every reason to doubt my own ability and every reason to think he would go on to be a professional athlete.

> **So many people fail before they begin simply because they do not believe they can succeed.**

But despite his talent, he did not believe in himself. Time and again, he buckled under pressure. Watching him fall short of his potential taught me that incredible talent doesn't matter if you don't know how to believe in yourself. More importantly, if you have the mentality of a winner and are willing to work hard to overcome adversity, you don't have to be the most talented athlete to win.

When I shared this story with pro-athlete trainer Tim Grover, he agreed. In fact, he said he would rather work with less talented athletes if those athletes worked hard to bring their A game. Those athletes were always his best. They were winners. They became great.[1]

NOT ENOUGH?

Maybe at this point in the journey to greatness, you have some sense of what your Meaningful Mission might be. You've identified fears that hold you back. You want to step up and step into greatness, but you're feeling too young or too old. Maybe you feel you have too many responsibilities now in this season of life or think it's too late for you to pursue your mission. Maybe you just don't feel qualified yet. The bottom line is that when you doubt your capability, you intimidate yourself, making it impossible to take action.

You *are* enough. Unfortunately, positivity doesn't come naturally for most of us, including how we view ourselves. And often a person's environment can contribute to a self-deprecating mindset. Joel Osteen is one of the most abundantly positive people I have ever met. He attributes his positivity and confidence to his parents, who surrounded him with encouragement and optimism. They frequently affirmed his abilities and worth.

After ministering for many years, Joel discovered many people have a "natural recording" in their minds telling them they aren't good enough. Their own negativity picks away at their self-confidence, holding them back from greatness.

Incredible talent doesn't matter if you don't know how to believe in yourself.

With that in mind, Joel shared with me a piece of wisdom he received from his dad: "You'll never rise any higher than the way you see yourself."

The only way to silence the negative recording, says Joel, is to pay attention to your thoughts about yourself and align them with the vision you want for your future. Want to get out of debt? Drop 20 pounds? Grow a thriving business? Whatever success looks like for you, you have to be able to envision yourself achieving that dream or you'll never make the moves to achieve it.[2]

Now, you may be thinking you don't doubt your ability; therefore, you don't struggle with self-doubt. However, there is a second form of self-doubt, and that is doubt about your self-worth. Far too many people secretly struggle with thinking they do not *deserve* greatness, or even goodness, for that matter.

That's why I was so grateful when my friend Dan Millman introduced me to the "Yes, thank you" practice. It's simple but effective. When opportunities for success come your way, choose to believe you deserve them, and simply say, "Yes, thank you" to the world. By practicing this response, you acknowledge your own worth and deservedness as a human being.

You aren't more deserving than anyone else, but you aren't any less deserving either. Too often we self-sabotage because we don't believe we deserve success. *I am not enough. I am not worthy.* Because we don't think we are worthy, we conclude that any initial success must be temporary. As a result, we subconsciously make things harder on ourselves simply because we don't believe we deserve the rewards. Your fear of failure becomes a self-fulfilling prophecy all because you don't believe yourself worthy. Your fear of success limits your possibilities all because you don't believe you are worthy. Your fear of the judgment from others causes you to compromise, all because you don't believe you are worthy.

> **When opportunities for success come your way, choose to believe you deserve them.**

Practice showing yourself kindness, or as Dan says, ask yourself daily, "How good can I stand it today?" Every day. Work up your tolerance to goodness until you can say, "I am worthy of greatness."[3]

A WORK IN PROGRESS

Kindness to ourselves is one of the biggest keys to conquering the dream killer of self-doubt. While we might show tremendous gratitude toward others, most of us struggle to show gratitude toward ourselves. For example, I can show myself gratitude for being consistent with what I said I was going to do. Maybe I showed up on time to events, followed through on my 30-day challenge, drank my target amount of water each day, or even got the sleep I needed to deliver my best. In all of those instances, no matter how small, I can be thankful to myself that I was enough. I'm not talking about stroking our egos like an egomaniac narcissist but simply acknowledging our successes and being grateful for our own contribution to them.

I am worthy of greatness.

I saw an example of this when I saw a video of Snoop Dogg after he was awarded a star on the Hollywood Walk of Fame. He rattled off a long list of all the things he was grateful for and thanked a lot of people. Lastly, he said:

> I want to thank me. I want to thank me for believing in me. I want to thank me for doing all this hard work. I want to thank me for having no days off. I want to thank me for never quitting. I want to thank me for always being a giver and trying to give more than I receive. I want to thank me for trying to do more rights than wrongs. I want to thank me for just being me at all times.[4]

It's true. We don't thank ourselves enough. We're not grateful to ourselves when we show up and do the work. When we do something challenging. When we have that hard conversation. When we call to reconcile someone with whom we had a falling-out. When we do the emotional healing work required to move past the trauma in our lives. When we face the fears and insecurities and push past them.

I've found a powerful practice to affirm that we are, in fact, enough. Show appreciation to yourself twice a day, once in the morning and then again at night. By doing this every day, you release a waterfall of abundance that will flow over you and draw other positive opportunities toward you.

Going back to Dan Millman, he believes the way to build confidence in your worth is to appreciate your individual story and growth journey. Dan's book *Everyday Enlightenment* describes "twelve gateways to personal growth." The first of these gateways is realizing your innate worth as a human being. Dan has a beautiful perspective on human value. He believes each person has a story that is completely unique and continually unfolding. As such, we need to appreciate our stories, particularly the painful parts, because those obstacles give us our strength.

We each have a unique past and a unique way forward. Your way forward might not look like the next person's. That is why Dan warns that comparing ourselves to others is a "profound disrespect for our own process." The reality is that your process might not be at the same pace as someone else's. As a gymnastics coach, Dan saw children learn to do somersaults at different paces. Ironically, those who took longer often learned the technique better than those who learned quickly. He sums it up as there is no one right path, only the right path for you at this moment. When you discover the value of your journey, past and future, you no longer need to measure yourself against others and can recognize your worth.[5]

Joel Osteen also believes the way to overcome self-doubt is to focus on you, to locate and celebrate your individuality. In a conversation I had with him about imposter syndrome, he shared how he managed to overcome his self-doubt when he took over Lakewood Church after his father's passing. At that time, his father had led the church for 40 years and grown quite a devoted following. Coming into such a well-established church, Joel felt obligated to pose like his father, to try to change himself to fill the empty space his father had left. *Every person that came had come from my dad*, he thought. *They didn't come to hear me.*

Despite their close relationship, Joel was not his father. His preaching style was laid-back, nothing like his father's loud and passionate sermons. Nevertheless, for the first three or four months, Joel did his best to preach his father's messages from the notes his dad left behind. Although Joel thought he was doing what was best for the church, he was actually impersonating his father. Then in month five, he stumbled across a passage of scripture that said David fulfilled his purpose for his generation (Acts 13:36). In that verse, Joel heard these words: *Joel, your dad fulfilled his purpose for his generation. Now go fulfill your purpose for this generation.* Joel recognized his God-given gift was different from his father's but no less powerful.

When he finally gave himself permission to be himself, the church began to grow exponentially. People responded positively to his style of ministering. While sharing this story with me, Joel offered these powerful words of wisdom: "You're empowered to be you, and nobody can beat you at being you." This is how we combat imposter syndrome. If you aren't trying to be anybody but yourself, it is impossible to be an imposter. On the other hand, when we strive to be like someone else, we might even do a pretty good job of it, but according to Joel, as long as we are trying to imitate someone else, we are "lessening our power." As he puts it, "If you don't realize you're a masterpiece, that you have something to offer that nobody else has, you limit yourself."[6]

> **Being yourself frees you to truly celebrate others.**

By the way, yet another byproduct of being yourself is that it frees you to truly celebrate others. It doesn't minimize your talents to see someone else succeed because although that person might be better than you at one thing, you are great at this other thing in this other way.

If you've been going through life with low self-esteem and low self-worth, the idea of celebrating yourself might seem cocky. Expecting greatness might even seem entitled. Humility and sacrifice are often seen as virtues—and they certainly can be, but to reach your potential and help others at your full capacity, you have to first appreciate your worth and invest in yourself. You've got to fill yourself up first. You've got to take care of your health, your mindset, your energies. Remember, the Greatness Mindset is a growth mindset, not a fixed mindset, and part of the growth mindset means prioritizing your own journey, which is still in progress.

WHICH COACH WILL YOU BE?

What are the practical actions you can take to go from being a self-sabotager to self-maker? Let me begin, not surprisingly, with a sports analogy. As a football player, I've had nasty coaches who criticized and embarrassed me. I could be giving it my all, but they would still hound me and degrade me. I also had coaches who showed me tough love, but in a positive, loving way. They might call me out and make an example of me, but at the end of the day, they showed me they cared and wanted to see me grow.

There's a powerful difference between those two types of coaching. In the same way, we can be either the greatest coach to ourselves or we can be the worst critic of ourselves. The inner love-based coach will tell you, *I am enough. I love myself the way I am, and at the same time I am working to improve.* The inner fear-based critic will tell you, *I'm not enough.* The inner critic's voice calls for improvement too, but from a negative place, whereas the inner love-based coach always comes from a caring place.

> **We can be either the greatest coach to ourselves or we can be the worst critic of ourselves.**

To heal your self-doubt, you have to shift your mindset to the love-based coach and stop comparing yourself to others. Instead, compare yourself to the version of you from the past. When you compare your present self to who you were the previous month or the previous year, you will see all you've accomplished. Then you can acknowledge those improvements and set new goals. The key is not to improve because you aren't enough. You improve because you live in a growth mindset.

The second practical way you can improve your confidence is by surrounding yourself with a supportive learning community. I asked inspirational speaker and author Simon Sinek how people instill belief in themselves if they have self-doubt. He told me a story about a friend who was going through a rough time in her life and doubting herself. After trying to reaffirm her through encouragement to no avail, he switched tactics. He asked her to help him learn a skill he was weak in and that he knew she was talented in. When she was the one giving advice instead of receiving it, her confidence suddenly rocketed.

So if you're afraid you aren't enough in one area, find ways of serving your community with the skills you are confident in. Then give the same opportunity to the other members of your community and let them teach you the skills you would like to strengthen. This way you'll address the areas you lack confidence in and also grow appreciation for the expertise you do have.

Finally, sometimes the solution to self-doubt is simply to do the work. Seth Godin, author and former dot-com business executive, distills it to the essence of what must be done sometimes to push past self-doubt. He told me that we simply have to remove the debate:

> I've written 7,500 blog posts in a row. Tomorrow morning, which will be a Friday, there will be another post. But it won't be there because it's the best post ever, nor will it be there because I decided to post it tomorrow. It will be there because it's Friday. And I haven't reconsidered that decision in 20 years.
>
> So, I don't have to have a meeting with myself about whether or not it's time to write a blog post. There *will* be a blog post. You chop the wood and carry the water by getting rid of the debate.
>
> Think about how many things you do that were once thought impossible. Driving across town used to be death-defying, but we got used to it. We build a pattern into it. What I've tried to do is make it so that writing a blog post for a million people doesn't make me nervous because I do it every day. I've trained myself so that it's not that risky.[7]

Maybe you can adopt Seth's same approach to an area of life where you wrestle with self-doubt and have allowed it to be your dream killer. Make the decision to show up and do the work. Give yourself a system that empowers you to push past the fears and be your own most powerful coach by putting in the reps.

> **Make the decision to show up and do the work.**

To be great, you can't let your insecurities and fears hold you back, even though we all have real flaws. Flaws are not a reason not to try; they're just something you have to overcome. Step one of overcoming them is to accept yourself as a work in progress. Remember, you are *enough* and you are becoming *more.* In fact, you are becoming *great.*

ENGAGING GREATNESS

The next step is to engage with the activities in the Fear Conversion Tool Kit (page 109). But before you do, ask yourself some simple questions:

- To what extent do you struggle with the dream killer of self-doubt?

- To what extent do you struggle to believe you deserve goodness?

- How has this self-doubt held you back from wholeheartedly pursuing your Meaningful Mission?

- Are you ready to do something about it?

Chapter 8

YOUR FEAR CONVERSION TOOL KIT

This Fear Conversion Tool Kit contains some of my best exercises for converting your fears into fuel for your greatness journey. You can work through each one back to back or choose the ones that feel like the best fit for you right now.

Are you ready to overcome those barriers to greatness? Let's get started!

Exercise 1: The Fear Converter

It's time to identify your fears and confront them head on—then flip the script on each of them to embrace an abundance attitude rather than a fearful perspective.

STEP 1—CREATE A FEAR LIST

We are going to clear our minds by dumping all the fears swirling around in our heads onto a piece of paper. I call this the Fear

List, and it is one of the most informative and productive exercises you can do for yourself. This exercise will not only reveal what you are feeling, but it will take them from scary and intimidating thoughts to simple words on a piece of paper. Anytime we can get things out of the recesses of our minds and onto something concrete (like a piece of paper), we can move forward consciously.

> **What would it mean for me to truly embrace greatness?**

There are no rules for listing your fears. The key is to just get them out on paper. Are you scared of failing? Are you scared of looking ridiculous? Are you scared of people judging you? Are you fearful you'll lose money? Are you scared you're going to let your family down? Or maybe you're just scared of taking the first step toward your Meaningful Mission. When listing your fears, be sure to write down every fear that comes to mind.

Some of my fears early on included public speaking, putting myself out there and meeting strangers, learning to salsa dance, learning to speak Spanish, and singing in public. They were all tied to the fear of judgment. What would people think of me? Would they laugh at me? Would they accept me if I didn't look perfect?

If you're having trouble getting started, ask yourself, *What would it mean for me to truly embrace greatness?* Or, *What would it look like to live in abundance instead of scarcity?*

STEP 2—FORMULATE THE FEARS

You may have heard the term *limiting belief* before. It's a familiar phrase psychologists and coaches use to help their clients identify restricting beliefs about themselves that are fundamentally untrue. These beliefs keep us small instead of allowing us to live our fullest and most confident life.

Take a look at the list of fears you've written and identify the top three to five that you feel are the biggest recurring restrictors when it comes to living out your passions. For example, let's say you wrote down "fear of public speaking." Let's go more in depth with it using "if . . . then" statements to truly define what it is that scares you.

> *I'm scared that if I speak in public, then I will stutter and sweat. I will forget what I came to say, and I will look foolish and underprepared. If I don't learn how to embrace public speaking, then I won't be able to do a pitch in front of investors. If I can't find investors, then I'll never launch my new business. I'll be stuck at this job that I hate forever.*

In this example, it's not actually public speaking that is scary; it's the fear of looking foolish and underprepared. These things can be conquered with hard work, a little sweat, and a healthy dose of preparation. The key is to use "if . . . then" statements to climb down the ladder of abstraction and discover what is causing your fear.

When our fears are just swirling around in our brains, we can't get good information out of them. But when we are "formulating the fear," we are figuring out the drivers and finding ways to combat the *true* sources of our restricting beliefs.

STEP 3—FLIP TO ABUNDANCE

Using the top three to five fears you formulated, it's now time to flip the script by moving out of your restricting beliefs and into abundance thinking. The old thought patterns will die, and new thought patterns will take root.

Instead of saying, *I'm scared of public speaking*, say, *I know I have a message that will help a lot of people. I know that, within me, I have everything I need to be a good public speaker. With enough preparation and practice, I can speak publicly and confidently.*

The Greatness Mindset is ultimately about embracing the potential of your life and moving forward in your Meaningful Mission.

Do this with your fears. Pay attention to your body as you go through the exercise. Do you feel a little relief every time you make an abundance statement? Do you feel a little excitement tingling at the bottom of your spine? That's good. You're going to need both of those things in your pursuit of a new mission.

Just as we train our muscles at the gym, we have to train our mind to stop overthinking and get comfortable with action. Formulating our fears and choosing abundance over scarcity is one way we can halt overthinking and embrace action.

We have to move from *I can't* to *I will*, from *I don't know how* to *I did it anyway*. The Greatness Mindset is ultimately about embracing the potential of your life and moving forward in your Meaningful Mission. Gaining traction starts with facing your fears head on so you can convert them to greatness fuel.

Exercise 2: The Magic Minimization Formula

My guess is you've had a worry or fear pop up when you've tried to pursue something new or prepare to make a significant change. You might feel like there is nothing to do except ride the wave of emotions that comes with a big change or new undertaking, *but that's where you're wrong*. Dale Carnegie, probably one of the most influential self-help gurus of all time, had a strategy he called a "Magic Formula for Solving Worry Situations."[1] It's a calm, detached process to conquer worry and find peace.

With some advanced planning, we can learn to *control* the wave of emotions and move forward peacefully and wholly grounded. In this next exercise, we will learn to handle our worries to support our mission.

STEP 1—ANALYZE THE PROBLEM

Carnegie's magic formula starts by looking at our problem with a little more detachment than may feel comfortable. The first step is to analyze our problem *fearlessly and honestly*. Start by writing down what worries you, even if it feels personal or private. Whatever it is, write it down.

Continue writing down everything that is clouding your mind at the moment. The key here is not only to clear your mind of each worry but to write out the worst possible outcome. As you write down each worry, ask and answer, "What is the worst that could possibly happen?"

I am worried that if I pursue my true passion, then I will lose my job because they won't support me doing this outside working hours.

STEP 2—ACCEPT THE WORST POSSIBLE OUTCOME

After we've written down each worry and each worst possible outcome, the next thing we do is *accept* that the worst may happen. We must accept the worst-case scenario so that we can *relax*. When our minds are distracted by fear, we can't focus. We can't make decisions confidently. We can't understand the true nature of the battle before us. But the good news is that *as soon as we stop resisting the scenarios that scare us*, we start to relax. Our problem-solving skills will activate, and we will be able to move forward in our Meaningful Missions more quickly.

In my example above, the worst-case scenario is job loss. Here's how one might accept that.

I am worried that I will lose my job. If I lose my job, then I know other positions are available at a different company. I can use my LinkedIn account to connect with other people in my field. If that doesn't work, then I can reach out to alumni from my college to see if I can get connected with job opportunities I might like. Whatever happens, I can start to pursue a new job . . . maybe even something I want more.

Take a few moments to take each problem in the first step of this exercise and write down how you will accept it. I think you'll be surprised at how easily and quickly you will feel relief in your body as you do this.

STEP 3—MINIMIZE THE PROBLEM

In the final part of this exercise, we need to take time to figure out how we can improve upon our worst outcome. This may seem unnecessary, as we've already accepted the worst that may happen, but this is where some of the real magic happens. This step is where we will "minimize the problem," as Carnegie says.[2] We will concentrate on the future, toss out all the what-ifs, blame, and shame. For this next step, we need only to ask ourselves, *How can I minimize these consequences?*

Let's continue with the job loss example from above.

If I lose my job, then I won't be able to pay my bills. However, I would feel a lot less stress if I had six months' worth of house and car payments in an emergency fund. I will start putting aside money every month until I have all of the necessary funds to cover myself for six months if I lose my job. Then I will meet with a financial advisor to find out how to make sure this emergency fund grows the most interest.

Take as much time as you need to go through each problem and worst-case scenario that you've accepted, and write down how you can improve each situation and minimize the consequences.

FINAL THOUGHTS

This exercise is one way not only to write down facts, like real worries and possible consequences of risk; it's also a way to be objective and detached about our fears. Herbert E. Hawkes, former dean of Columbia College, once said to Carnegie, "If a man will devote his time to securing facts in an impartial, objective way, his worries will usually evaporate in light of knowledge."[3] With a little bit of planning, fears will dissipate, and action and a real sense of peace will take their place.

Exercise 3: The Self-Coaching Solution

How many times have you fallen victim to a critical or hopeless voice in your head? As I mentioned in Chapter 1, your thoughts shape your reality, especially the chatter inside your head. There is a way to coach yourself to deal with your inner critic and get out of the quicksand of negativity. In this exercise, we will change how we talk to ourselves by using third-person pronouns and our own names to refer to ourselves. Studies by Dr. Ethan Kross, experimental psychologist, neuroscientist, and author of *Chatter: The Voice in Our Head, Why It Matters, and How to Harness It,* have shown that talking to ourselves in the third person not only diffuses stress but can

> **Your thoughts shape your reality.**

also actually change our mindset from *I can't* to *I can.* When we talk to ourselves the same way we would talk to people we love, we can learn to control and engage with negative thoughts instead of letting them run the show.[4]

STEP 1—ACKNOWLEDGE THE LOOP

Chances are, you have a script that plays in your head during times of personal stress. *I'm not going to make it. I don't have what it takes. Everyone is going to laugh at me. I'm stupid. I suck!* These are likely leftovers from significant emotional events we experienced in adolescence or even inherited from our parents.

I'm willing to bet that there is at least one thought on loop over and over in your head. It might not even be anything you've ever said aloud. It's time to acknowledge these thoughts. Carl Jung once said, "Until you make the unconscious conscious, it will direct your life."[5] Take a few minutes to make these negative thought loops more conscious by writing them down. If you have more than one piece of chatter that interferes with your confidence frequently, take a moment to write it all down.

STEP 2—RUN THE MATH

Negative chatter is almost always hyperbole. If one of the loops that plays in your head is, *People are always looking and laughing at me,* take a moment to acknowledge the voice. Then dissect it.

In this example, we would start with the word *always. Always* means every moment of every day. Do you believe, on a conscious and rational level, that every moment of every day, the thing that frightens you or brings you stress is "always" happening? Chances are you do not. This is important to acknowledge, because as soon as we realize the voice is most likely a liar, we have much more control over what happens next. We move from the quicksand of chatter into a place where we can move forward freely and quickly.

With each of the loops you wrote down in the last exercise, take a moment to find the hyperbole or dramatic statements. Chances are that your loops are on auto-play and kick in during stressful situations. How many times has your inner critic been proven correct? My guess is that the numbers are surprisingly low. Your success rate is likely much higher than your failure rate.

Next, ask yourself these critical questions:

- When was the last time you experienced that particular stress?

- Did you survive it?

- Did you learn something from it?

- Could it have been worse?

- What positive things emerged from that stress?

Then—and I know this may make you feel self-conscious, but I want you to do it anyway—I want you to stand in front of the mirror and pair each negative loop with a new statement of confidence. Use your own name and say these statements out loud.

Here's how it might work.

Statement from Step 1: *Every single time I give a presentation at work, I mess up and look foolish. I stumble over* *my words, I sweat, my mouth gets dry, and I know everyone is judging me for not being better at public speaking.*

Confidence Statement: *Lewis, the last presentation you gave at work was easier than every single one before it. Your boss mentioned he enjoyed it. Your co-workers even laughed at the joke you said at the end. Sure, you got a little sweaty, but that's body language for "I'm nervous right now." No one mentioned that, but they did say that it was an excellent presentation. In our next presentation, let's accept that you might get a little sweaty, so wear lighter clothes or layers so others don't see the sweat marks. Let's assume your mouth will be dry, so be sure to have a bottle of water handy. No one has ever laughed at you up there unless you told a joke. Your chances for success are higher than failure, as long as you prepare well. Lewis, you are equipped with everything you need to nail the next public speaking event at work.*

Speaking to ourselves the way we would talk to someone we love is an effective way to distance ourselves from stress, fear, or pain. On the surface, it may seem to be just a bunch of "soft" affirmation stuff. But I promise if you use this strategy while you also go all in and embrace your fear until it goes away, magic will happen. Continue writing and speaking new confidence statements for each newly conscious auto-play loop until you've acknowledged them all.

STEP 3—COACH YOURSELF IN THE MOMENT

To bring this exercise into an in-the-moment application, I want you to find a picture of yourself as a younger person. If you can't find one of those, find a photo of yourself that you love. If it's more effective, print it out and keep it somewhere you can easily access it. You might consider keeping it in your purse or wallet or on your phone.

The next time your inner critic takes center stage with one of the negative chatter loops, move to a private room and talk to your picture as if you were talking to a friend.

Lewis, I just heard you think that you don't have what it takes to start your own business, and I want you to know that opinion is wrong. First, you've worked hard to be ready for this. Second, you deserve the good things that will come from launching your own business. Third, there is great joy on the other side of this fear. So let's do this together. Whatever happens, we will survive it. I know you can do this.

Talking to your picture may make you feel silly, but it is something that will help you acknowledge the negative chatter, soften its influence, and remind yourself that you can do amazing things. The goal here isn't to silence the negative chatter but to take power away from it. Claiming confidence aloud is a powerful tool that can help us emerge from negativity. And you can do this *anytime* the negativity threatens to keep you from taking action.

STEP 4—ENGAGE YOUR INNER CRITIC

It is vital to engage with our inner critic along our path to greatness. Stress will occur during certain events or situations that are out of our control. Instead of re-experiencing this stress repeatedly by reliving the memories on auto-play or by listening to the chatter inside our head, we need to take back control and diffuse the toxicity.

> **Remind yourself that you can do amazing things.**

Are you living a safe life? Are you living a comfortable life? Is it too comfortable, or are you doing things daily to help you get beyond your insecurities, your fears, your doubts, and the things that hold you back from greater joy in your life? Every great thing comes when you overcome insecurity. Lean into your insecurities and go all in on making your unconscious chatter conscious because

I'm telling you—there is magic and beauty on the other side. You are loved, you are worthy, and you matter. It's time to go out there and do something great.

Exercise 4: The Fear Sit-Down

Fear isn't a boogeyman. It is human nature to avoid actions and emotions that scare us. I don't know anyone who gets excited about walking into pain intentionally. The problem is, when we avoid our fears, we cannot be truly happy, because we will know that something is holding us back from our greatest self.

Although we may try to ignore it, it *will* strike. Let's start by learning to sit with it.

STEP 1—VISUALIZE TRIUMPH

In Exercise 1, you listed all your fears and acknowledged their role in keeping you from abundance. Go back to this list and identify the ones that have been the most crippling over time. For three to five minutes at a time, allow yourself to sit with these crippling fears.

The key in this exercise is to allow yourself to think about situations that bring on your most significant, most burdensome fears. Give yourself space to feel your body's responses, acknowledge your inner hyperbolic chatter, and sit with any overwhelm that happens.

Every great thing comes when you overcome insecurity.

As you do this, breathe in and out while picturing the waves of an ocean. Think of your fear as that wave. Fear comes aggressively at first, but then it lessens. When we acknowledge our fears and practice sitting with them, our fears will slowly ebb away.

Here's what I mean by "sitting in the fear."

1. Set your timer for five minutes.

2. Imagine yourself doing something that scares you.

3. Visualize every piece of the scenario.

4. Take deep, slow breaths in and out.

5. Mentally note any changes in your body.

Let's say social anxiety is keeping you from going to the gym, which you used to really love. Imagine yourself getting dressed for the gym. Visualize driving to the gym. Imagine yourself walking into the gym. See yourself greeting people. Watch yourself putting your things into a locker. Visualize yourself finding the right playlist and putting in your ear-buds. Imagine grabbing your workout journal and heading to the weights or cardio area. Imagine the feeling after your workout. You're sweaty but accomplished. Imagine the smile on your face as you drive home.

When you visualize yourself overcoming your fear, you will probably feel a response within your body like sweating, shortness of breath, etc. That's okay. Your job is to get to the other side of this fear in your mind's eye. Do your best to keep your breathing slow and methodical—in for four counts, hold four counts, exhale eight counts.

When your timer ends at five minutes, take a moment to appreciate the courage you displayed while sitting in your fear.

STEP 2—REWARD YOURSELF

Next, immerse yourself in an activity you love for 30 minutes. Do you love to paint? Dance? Do you have a friend you love to FaceTime with? Do you have a favorite meal you love to eat? Do you love going to your basement and punching a boxing bag? It doesn't matter what it is. Give yourself a moment to enjoy something amazing for the next 30 minutes. Doing things we love is a confidence builder and helps us feel more capable.

STEP 3—TAKE A SMALL STEP FORWARD

After challenging yourself with your fear and rewarding yourself, it's time to take a small step forward. You will be well prepared for that at this point. Using the gym example:

> Consider calling a few gyms in the area and asking: What are the peak times? Are there any classes that can be translated into 1:1 training sessions? Do you have low-sensory hours?

We don't have to be instantly ready to take giant leaps forward. We just need to take a small step forward. Small steps add up over time, and every action we take is meaningful, no matter how small it may seem at the time. Take some time to figure out a few small steps you can take, then do at least one of them to move forward.

After you've completed that small but monumental step, take another moment to appreciate your courage. Feel free to borrow from the previous Self-Coaching Solution exercise (page 115) and talk to yourself in the third person: "Good job, Lewis. That took courage, and I'm proud of you."

Moving past our fears requires both thinking and action. We can't go all in on our dreams and find the courage to bet on ourselves if we don't do both. I believe this is an exercise that will help set you on that path.

When we avoid our fears, we cannot be truly happy, because we will know that something is holding us back from our greatest self.

Exercise 5: Your Alter Ego Locator

Adopting the mantle of an alter ego is a practice adopted by musicians, professional speakers, creative people, athletes, and business people alike. Alter egos can be very powerful because they separate us from our core selves. You may have heard stories of Beyoncé's alter ego, Sasha Fierce, who helped her overcome fright and inhibitions while on stage. Adopting an alter ego when I was out on the football field before a big game or when competing in the national championships in the decathlon helped me to better separate from any failures and better prepare for my successes. In this exercise, we are going to use the same concepts I used when building my alter ego.

STEP 1—FIND INSPIRATION

As an athlete, I was hungry to find a hero, someone who could inspire me and convince me that I could do what I wanted to do. When it was football, I found inspirational players and watched their highlight tapes. I found out who *their* heroes were and watched those tapes as well.

In this step, I want you to do just that. Chances are, you already have influencers in your life that are in the field you're in or in the field you want to be in. If you're ambitious or competitive, you may have already sized up who's out there. But let's formalize it. Find people doing what you want to do. Watch them. Study them. Find out who inspires them. Find *their* mentors.

Then study them. Follow them on social media, listen to their podcasts, and read their books. If they're not a public figure, reach out to them and ask for an interview. This is your chance to do some research and find out what makes them tick and decide which qualities you want to embody. Try to identify a few key people in this phase.

After a few weeks of studying your heroes, write down the characteristics and qualities they have that you want to learn. Do they seem fearless? Do they never quit? Are they able to laugh at themselves? Do they reframe failure into a stepping-stone to greatness? Use what you discover to help identify exactly what it is that you want for your own path to greatness.

Inspirational Heroes	Characteristics to Embrace
1.	
2.	
3.	
4.	
5.	

STEP 2—VISUALIZE

When training for the decathlon, I knew the pole vault would be my hardest event. I was scared that I would get stuck upside down, fall on the pavement, and crack my head open. So every night, after watching videos of pole vaulters at the top of their game, right before I fell asleep, I would visualize myself going over the bar. I would do this over and over. Not surprisingly, it helped practice go better the next day. When it was time to go over the bar, I would remember myself going over that bar in my visualizations. I would manifest my alter ego as one of the great athletes I'd watched in the highlight films, and I would believe I could do it. I did this every night for six months, until I felt like I could fly.

And that's exactly what I want you to do as well. Every night, I want you to visualize what it is that you want to do. You can even practice the acceptance of your greatness with language, which we know from previous exercises is very powerful.

I am so happy I did open mic night at the club. It was so exciting to be up there and do well.

Rumination and self-talk help us in big and small ways. In the same way that we can make ourselves feel bad about things that have never happened during these practices, so can we make ourselves feel powerful and confident.

Take a moment to write down some concrete things to visualize.

STEP 3—FIND A TOTEM

After studying the greats and visualizing yourself becoming great, you're well on your way to overcoming fears that threaten to derail you. The next thing I encourage you to do is to find a totem to help bring your alter ego to life. Winston Churchill used to put on different hats to help him evoke different personalities. Martin Luther King Jr., who had perfect eyesight, wore eyeglasses because he felt he commanded more respect when he looked "distinguished."[6]

Your courage will give way to growth, which will give way to mastery.

What can you use to make yourself feel more confident? Is your artifact a pair of glasses or a hat? Maybe it's a shade of lipstick or even something as simple as a pair of socks. My guess is you might already have something like this in your home that you've already used to feel more confident. Make it more official. And now, you're well on your way to becoming your own version of Sasha Fierce.

STEP 4—BE A SUPERHERO

To pursue greatness is really an audacious goal. When James Lawrence set out to do 50 Ironman Triathlons in 50 states in 50 days, he started out as a mere mortal. But by day 30, he had created the Iron Cowboy, his superhero alter ego. Every time he put on his glasses, he wasn't James Lawrence. He was the Iron Cowboy. On day 30, the Iron Cowboy was James's self-assured version of himself who was ready to run the next 20 days. Without the Iron Cowboy, James may have succumbed to his own fears or anxieties.

When you can't outthink your fear, move forward as your alter ego. You'll not only engage your playfulness; you'll also give yourself courage. Your courage will give way to growth, which will give way to mastery.

Exercise 6: The Joy Conditioner

Understanding our fears can strengthen our resilience, improve our creativity, and even enhance our emotional intelligence. I had a conversation with Dr. Wendy Suzuki where she shared her theory of joy conditioning. I think it's an exciting way to start overcoming some of the natural anxieties some of us face, either in our everyday lives or in the pursuit of our Meaningful Mission.

In this exercise, we will learn how to reframe our anxiety triggers and counteract them. Many of these concepts are adapted from Dr. Suzuki's book *Good Anxiety: Harnessing the Power of the Most Misunderstood Emotion.*[7]

STEP 1—UNDERSTAND YOUR TRIGGERS

When you understand precisely what makes you anxious, you can channel the energy in a more positive direction. The understanding can take us from feelings of lack into the feelings of abundance.

To begin, write down three to five of your known triggers for anxiety. Do you get nervous when your boss calls an unexpected meeting? Do you feel fear when plans are changed at the last minute? Whatever it is, write it down.

Next, write down a recent thought or memory that brought on anxious feelings. Get descriptive. Don't just write, *Dinner last Wednesday*. Write a paragraph or two about these thoughts and memories.

Now write down how you *feel* right now as you are reliving these memories. Do you feel ungrounded? Sad? Mad? Whatever it is, write it down. Take some time here to sit with these emotions. Remember these emotions and feel them all the way through. This kind of leaning in reminds us that we can *survive* these feelings of discomfort, fear, or anxiety. Here, we are conditioning our muscles of resiliency.

STEP 2—REMEMBER YOUR JOY

Next, write down five joyous, funny, exciting, or cheerful memories and, just as before, be descriptive. Write down as many details as you can remember: what you wore, who you were with, and what your body felt like.

Then next to each of these memories, write down any smells associated with them. Scent memories are so powerful and can help us bring back the positive feelings associated with these memories. If one of your memories was the triumph you felt after a 12-mile hike up to a scenic overlook, what smells are associated with that? Sunscreen? Nature? Campfires? The rubber grip on your walking stick? If you have an incredible memory of going to Disney World as a youngster, what do you remember smelling in the air? Main Street Bakery? Roasted nuts? Whatever you can remember, write it down next to your joy memory.

Finally, write down how you felt during each of these moments. You'll probably start to feel positive just by doing this exercise. You might even find yourself with a big smile on your face as you write. Let these positive emotions sweep over you. If you felt triumphant or sated, giddy, or completely relaxed, let yourself feel it all over again.

STEP 3—COUNTERACT THE TRIGGERS

Now that you have allowed yourself to deep dive into both the joyous and the anxious, it's time to create an action plan to counteract your anxiety triggers. First, go back to the list of memories you recorded in the first Fear Conversion exercise. For each memory, take a moment to see how you can condition yourself to feel positivity amid anxiety.

For example:

The next time an unexpected meeting makes me feel overwhelmed and angry, I will not resist feeling overwhelmed and angry; I will acknowledge the feelings and allow myself to feel them. Next, I will cut open a lime and inhale the fragrance. I will remember how happy, relaxed, and peaceful I felt when my spouse and I ate the most delicious key lime pie after a long walk during our honeymoon.

While experiencing anxiety, this action plan may not dissipate your anxious feelings entirely but it will likely help you relax long enough to move forward feeling better than before. Instead of focusing on the negative (scarcity), you will be focusing on the positive (abundance).

After you've written an action plan for each of your five triggers, take some time to find ways to access the scents associated with your positive memories easily. Is there an oil, candle, or room spray that can keep on hand? Find these items and pick a place to keep them, whether that's in your car, home, or office (or even all three!).

Anxiety is informative. It is a feeling that alerts us to the need to find solutions, a different path, or even to set new boundaries. If we don't allow ourselves to feel it, we deny ourselves the opportunity to become more empowered and resilient. And when we lean in to discomfort and pair it with joy, we become a powerhouse that can move forward, *even in the midst of overwhelm or anxiety*. What could be better for our Meaningful Missions?

WORTHY OF MORE

I was reminded of this Ramakrishna quote recently: "An ocean of bliss may rain down from the heavens, but if you hold up only a thimble, that is all you receive."[8] So many of us have been holding thimbles up to the heavens because we think that is all we are worth. We've been letting fear drive the bus because we think that our fears and doubts deserve center stage. They don't. *You do.*

> **Your breakthrough is coming.**

Don't let your fears keep you from your purpose. There will be easy days and difficult days, and they will be interspersed with one another. Everything is difficult until it is not. The important thing is to keep coming back to your purpose. Keep setting goals and taking action. Even on your bad days, something is happening.

You are worthy of more than a thimbleful of bliss. You are deserving. You *matter.* You have been created for something greater than what you've currently accepted as the status quo. There is a reason you are here. You are worthy of love, abundance, and more opportunities.

Persist through difficulty. Keep moving. Your breakthrough is coming.

For additional resources to help you live out the Greatness Mindset, visit TheGreatnessMindset.com/resources.

The Mindset of Greatness

Chapter 9

HEALING YOUR PAST

During one recent Uber ride in Atlanta, I struck up a conversation with the woman who was driving. As a child, her father had abandoned both her and her mother, who suffered from a drug addiction, and she was left alone to care for her mother. As an adult, she continued this practice of caring for needy people in her romantic relationships. She found herself drawn to men with drug addictions and tried to heal them. As a result, she endured a string of physically and emotionally abusive relationships. As she shared more details, it became clear that the trajectory of her life stemmed from her childhood trauma. She accepted toxic relationships because her inner child was trying to heal itself by fixing others.

Sitting in the Uber that day, however, I didn't hear defeat. Yes, the physical evidence of her past still remained, but the energy she radiated was full of positivity and kindness. Then she said something that stuck with me, "It doesn't hurt me anymore. I've learned how to heal it and turn the pain into wisdom."

Wow! So that was it. This incredible woman was in the process of becoming something new, something not determined by her past trauma. In fact, she was healing her past so she could move forward in a healthy way. She told me how she was now married to a wonderful man. The two of them had a blended family, whom they supported together as a team. She had taken intentional action to bring the cycle of trauma to an end.

Whatever your trauma—and we all have past trauma of some sort—if left unhealed, it will direct your future too. Trauma perpetuates trauma. To stop the cycle, you have to let your *adult* self make the decisions instead of the younger, wounded self.

My own healing journey has revealed a lot about my inner child and his needs. In the midst of some of my own relationship struggles, I was fortunate to interview Dr. Ramani Durvasula, a leading expert on narcissism. She explained that narcissists often go undiagnosed because they refuse therapy. Therapy forces a person to face their decisions and consequences. Narcissists would much rather project their problems onto someone else and play the victim.[1]

When Ramani said this, something clicked for me. In three different relationships, I had asked each girlfriend to attend couples therapy with me, and each of them refused. I was so confused by that. I thought most women would love a guy willing to talk about his feelings and work on their relationship in therapy. Yet even in the instances when the relationship was in total disrepair, and I finally convinced them to go talk with someone, they would not listen to the therapist.

Now, I'm not saying I was perfect in any of my past relationships. Far from it! Part of the problem was, of course, me. I could not set appropriate boundaries in my relationships because I was willing to sacrifice parts of myself just to keep peace and make others happy. Another person who helped me realize this tendency was Nedra Glover Tawwab, who wrote *Set Boundaries, Find Peace: A Guide to Reclaiming Yourself.* I realized I was choosing partners who were living in a state of emotional chaos. They had an insecurity or criticism for themselves, so I entered their world wanting to fix them and convince them of their worth.

Looking back now, I should have realized I could not force someone to grow when they were not ready. I should have seen that I can accept people where they are but not necessarily be in a relationship with them. They each had their own trauma involving past abandonment, and their trauma collided with my own like a personalized poison.

You see, my father was affectionate with me, but for the first 13 years of my life, I feared his temper. When he came home, the rise in tension was palpable. On the other hand, my mom was passive. She did anything to keep the peace, even giving up pieces of herself. As an adult, I played the part I had seen my mom play, surrendering boundaries for the sake of keeping peace. I remained in toxic relationships for far too long, thinking I could fix them. I naturally practiced what I had witnessed as a child.

Until I did the healing work my inner child needed, I ended up feeling shamed and wronged in every romantic relationship. Everything would start fine, then my triggers would activate. I could see the relationship was not working, but both my fear of being alone and my commitment to succeed drove me to try anything to make it work, even abandoning myself. Yet all along I felt I was not being true to myself and resented myself for losing my voice.

Only when I started to heal my inner child and the trauma from my past did I finally start to feel like I was acting authentically as my true self. I learned to tell my inner child what he needed to hear. Once

I was not being true to myself and resented myself for losing my voice.

I acknowledged that child part of myself, I felt capable of becoming a new person. Now when I am faced with a trigger, I can say those unhealthy behaviors are not who I am anymore. I do not have to react emotionally or continue the unhealthy patterns of my previous self. Don't get me wrong. It is an ongoing healing journey. I have to continually remind myself that I am a new person and no longer need to react to the fears I held as a child.

I had other wounds to heal with my inner child too. As I wrote about in *The Mask of Masculinity*, I suffered sexual abuse as a child. I was teased for being in special needs classes in school. My brother went to prison when I was eight. I essentially lost my father after a car accident resulted in severe brain trauma that changed him forever. All this trauma caused a constant fear within me that I was not enough.

Dr. Gabor Maté is an addiction expert who also specializes in childhood trauma. He has educated the public on how childhood trauma can lead to self-soothing addictions. These addictions go beyond alcohol or drug addiction. "If you get the message that you're not good enough, that you're not worthy enough," says Dr. Gabor, "then you might spend the rest of your life trying to prove that you are."[2] Such children can grow up to be extreme people pleasers, like myself, who sacrifice parts of themselves in an attempt to feel enough.

My solution was to become the biggest, strongest athlete I could so no one could make me feel small again. And in some ways, it worked! It got me external results. But it also left me even more insecure and ashamed about my past. It wasn't until I started healing the past that I could experience any inner peace.

> **It wasn't until I started healing the past that I could experience any inner peace.**

The truth is, most people have a traumatized inner child with unmet needs. Often, like in my own case, this child's coping mechanisms are not healthy. The only way to move on from these unhealthy habits is to reconnect with the inner child and give the child what was needed in the first place. Maybe you need to tell the child they are loved, that they are enough. Or maybe assure them that they are protected, that you have their back. In short, you need to speak positively to your inner child to make it possible for you to fully embrace the Greatness Mindset.

UNADDRESSED TRAUMA

Living with unhealed trauma made me physically ill. Often I felt suffocated, like my throat was closing up and a massive weight sat on my chest. I was exhausted all the time and felt like I was living a 6 out of 10. I felt I had sacrificed integrity because I wasn't being authentic to my values or vision, all just to unsuccessfully make one person happy. Or so I thought. As it turns out, the one person I was really trying to satisfy was my own inner child.

> **No one needs to live a future defined by blame of another person.**

Unhealed trauma can hold us back in so many ways. One way is through victim consciousness. Dr. Shefali Tsabary, the author of *Radical Awakening: Turn Pain into Power, Embrace Your Truth, Live Free*, defines victimhood as a real state in which some people find themselves. If people are raped or physically abused, they are victims. People should feel justified to call their suffering by its true name and unapologetically say, "I have been a victim." But victim consciousness happens when people tie themselves to that perpetration. People with victim consciousness begin to live by and define themselves by that event, unintentionally leaving the power with the perpetrators. "True empowerment," says Dr. Tsabary, "is to take all power back, including blame."[3]

This does not mean the perpetrator is free of blame or that you necessarily have to forgive what happened. The perpetrators are always to blame for their injustices, but no one needs to live a future defined by blame of another person. Instead, people can choose to live a future worth taking credit for. And the first step toward that is to do the healing work.

Even if you are free of victim consciousness, your unhealed past can hold you back in other ways. Often, we develop coping mechanisms to help us survive immediate trauma. This natural ability for self-preservation is a biological gift. However, these temporary solutions can become an unhealthy pattern. What worked as a defense mechanism in an emergency when younger can become an unhealthy coping habit when older.

Dr. Nicole LePera, author of *How to Do the Work: Recognize Your Patterns, Heal from Your Past, and Create Your Self*, shared an example of someone who did not feel accepted when they displayed sadness. This person might learn to avoid similar trauma by bottling their emotions in the future. The appeal of these coping mechanisms is the relief they give in the moment. With enough repetition, unhealthy coping can become second nature.

For Dr. LePera, stress loops became her familiar coping mechanism. At one time, she did not have the tools to combat the stress in her life, so she found solace in the excitement of the stress. Stress gave her an adrenaline rush, a hit of cortisol, and that was the best she could do at the time. She told me she now sometimes finds herself seeking negative reviews for the agitation they create. Why? Because it is a familiar state. Our subconscious, says Nicole, operates from the familiarity principle. Our subconscious convinces us that the familiar is always better than something unpredictable, even if—and this is important—taking a new approach might turn out better.[4]

> **The key to *being* peace is to set relationship boundaries in alignment with your Meaningful Mission with people who share and support that mission.**

My own familiar state often held me in toxic relationships. I was afraid of hurting the other person and couldn't bear the thought of hurting someone I cared about. Plus, I was afraid of others' judgment since she might talk badly about me afterward.

Over the course of a year, I engaged in therapy to intentionally find peace. At the beginning of the year, my therapist asked me an empowering question: "What is your intention for therapy?" I said, "I want clarity, peace, and freedom." In every session, she asked me the same question: "What do you want?" I gave the same response, "Clarity, peace, and freedom." At the end of the year, she asked. "Have you found this?" And here is what I realized. I didn't *find* these things. I had *become* them. I AM peace. I AM clear. I AM free. I tell you this because before you chase anything in the world, you have to be your own peace and joy.

The key to *being* peace is to set relationship boundaries in alignment with your Meaningful Mission with people who share and support that mission. This applies not only to romantic partners, but work relationships, family, friends, or anyone close to you.

When you take back the power, heal your past, and start aligning with your vision, you will feel unlimited. Your confidence will grow because you will be showing up in a positive loop instead of a negative loop.

COACH OR CRITIC

Let's return to the idea I mentioned earlier, that everyone has an internal coach and critic. I experienced firsthand the difference between a demanding yet encouraging coach versus a purely negative critic. A loving coach will challenge you to become your greatest without degrading you.

Life works the same way except *you* are your own most effective coach or critic. You get to intentionally choose to be the inspiring coach who accepts yourself as the work in progress that you are. You

> **Compare yourself to a past version of yourself rather than to others.**

can accept yourself while you improve yourself. Compare yourself to a past version of yourself rather than to others and celebrate how far you have come.

Through his research on Alzheimer's, Dr. David Perlmutter, a board-certified neurologist, has established himself as an expert on the brain. According to him, the brain has two parts: the fear-based part and the compassionate part. The fear-based part is reactive. It urges us to seek immediate gratification and creates the fight-or-flight sensation. The compassionate part is future thinking. This part of the brain is responsible for bringing the adult into the room when you feel triggered. The adult makes conscious, clear-minded decisions as investments in the future. According to Dr. Perlmutter's research, it is impossible to make conscious decisions when the fear-based part of your brain is activated because you cannot calm down enough to make a conscious decision. That is not what that part of the brain is for. It is for making quick survival decisions.

What Dr. Perlmutter calls the fear-based state, I call a negative state. Often, the negative state involves heightened emotions, which in turn can cause you to react in a way that does not align with your authentic self. The opposite, the positive state, allows you to say, "I don't like this situation, but I'm going to make a conscious decision not to be triggered by irrational fears." This kind of control requires monitoring your emotions.[5]

Being limitless is about discovering how to live in a beautiful state of being.

When I went to India a few years ago, I studied meditation at One World Academy. For two weeks, we did nothing but meditate. The Academy uses another set of terms for these positive and negative states of mind: the beautiful state and the suffering state. A beautiful state is all about living in love, joy, abundance, and appreciation. A suffering state is living in anxiety, stress, jealousy, and doubt. What I learned there is that being limitless is about discovering how to live in a beautiful state of being. This means fostering enduring relationships, conquering challenges consciously, finding fulfillment, and becoming a more compassionate leader.

So we've got the beautiful state and a suffering state, the positive mind and the negative mind, the fear-based mind and the compassionate-future-based mind, the coach and the critic. At the core of all these concepts is the need to learn to love yourself and heal a thought, a memory, a traumatic experience.

What if we could always lean in to love and positive coaching, the beautiful state? For that to happen, you must practice disassociating yourself from the past in order to heal it. As you do so, your journey will still be challenging, but those challenges won't hold you back. Instead, they will give you more power to lean forward because you won't be living in fear of failure, success, or judgment.

A greater future is going to happen because of intentional actions based on a clear vision.

The fear-based critic will tell you, *I'm not enough.* The love-based coach will reinforce you are enough: *I love you for where you're at, and let's also improve and grow.* Growth and healing will be an ongoing process. A hero says, *This adversity is not going to define the rest of my life. It is a roadblock. It is not the end of the road. And this hurdle is going to make me so much more powerful when I learn to get over it.*

If you want to create a greater future, it's not going to happen by accident. It's going to happen because of intentional actions based on a clear vision, and you simply will not have a clear vision as long as you live in a chaotic state of mind.

Psychiatrist Paul Conti, M.D., author of *Trauma: The Invisible Epidemic,* studies mental illness from a treatment standpoint, specifically societal prevention of trauma. He advises us to imagine a disease that has only subtle outward symptoms but can hijack your entire body without notice, one that transfers easily between parent and child and that can last a lifetime if untreated.

According to Dr. Conti, this is exactly how society should view trauma, as an out-of-control epidemic with a potentially fatal prognosis.[6] The bottom line is that it is treatable. We can make changes as individuals and as a society to ease trauma's effects and prevent further traumatization if we embrace one critical realization: trauma is both treatable and preventable.

ENGAGING GREATNESS

To help you discover the trauma in your own story and begin to heal your past, here are some activities that you might find helpful.

Exercise 1: Your Coping Mechanisms

Everyone has ways to numb pain, cope with disappointment, or process triggered trauma. These can be everything from the extreme (drug addiction) to more "acceptable" ones (workaholism). Whatever they are, we've all got them. In this exercise, we will take a deeper look at our coping mechanisms and what we gain (or don't gain) from them.

STEP 1—IDENTIFY YOUR NUMBING DEVICES

It's time to get even more personal. Get out your trusty journal or the notes app on your phone and take an inventory of your coping mechanisms. You can use the following questions to help get you started. These questions are not meant to incite self-judgment; they are intended to help you identify the powerful things in your life that help you numb your pain.

- Do you drink alcohol?
- Do you binge eat?
- Do you smoke?
- Do you smoke weed?

- Do you watch porn?

- Are you a workaholic?

- Are you an extreme people pleaser?

- Do you binge television at night?

You can see the types of questions I want you to ask yourself. When I was younger, I was willing to negotiate *anything*—even my own boundaries and desires—to manufacture peace and clarity. Because I wasn't at peace within myself, I was an extreme people pleaser who would do whatever it took to find peace. When we experience pain or trauma, we often find comfort in our coping mechanisms (like I did). It is part of how we soothe ourselves.

Spend some time in reflection to identify your own. If you find yourself at an impasse and unable to identify your own, ask a trusted friend or partner to share with you how they've noticed you cope in difficult circumstances.

STEP 2—WHAT DO I GET FROM THESE ADDICTIONS?

Next, I want you to investigate what you receive from these coping mechanisms. You may note that I've called them "addictions" because that is what they can become. When we have tried and true methods to numb our pain and avoid feeling our feelings, we have given something else control of our well-being.

Take a moment to review your list of coping strategies. How are they providing value to you? When you work too much, are you able to stop intrusive thoughts? When you drink alcohol, are you able to feel like you can laugh easier? When you smoke weed, is that the only way you've been able to find enough calm to go to sleep? Are you dependent on any of these activities?

There are no wrong answers here. I want you to take an honest look at your coping strategies and identify their appeal. If they weren't serving you in some fashion, you wouldn't keep turning to them.

Write down everything that comes to mind.

STEP 3—IS MY HIGHEST SELF SERVED BY THESE ADDICTIONS?

At this point, you've discovered your sweet spot, you've done some work around your purpose, and you've identified your path of growth. To get to where you want to go, you will need to become the highest version of yourself. I want you to take a moment to visualize your highest self (we'll do some more work around this shortly) by imagining yourself on your Meaningful Mission, living out your legacy.

Does this version of yourself numb the pain? Or do you do whatever you can to face your pain?

Coping mechanisms serve us well until we are ready to move from numbness into the fighting zone. To become the highest versions of ourselves, we have to take conscious steps into the ring of life. We've got to lace up our metaphorical gloves and fight through to healing.

What do you need to do to get yourself ready for a fight? If you were to stop cold turkey with any one of your dependencies, what would you need to help you do it? A therapist? An accountability partner? A doctor? A coach? Spend some time thinking about the emotional, spiritual, and physical equipment you need to move away from your dependencies and into the realm of healing.

When you're ready, write them down.

YOU ARE AMAZING

This exercise might have been challenging for you. It took me years to identify my own dependencies and gain the ultimate courage I needed to leave them behind to embrace healing. I want to remind you that you are good enough. You are worthy enough. You are *enough*. You have what it takes to live a life of purpose and meaningfulness. Everything you need to succeed is already inside of you. Part of the path of greatness is finding the tools you need to excavate your integrated self.

Exercise 2: Mind and Body Check-In

Up until a few years ago, my nervous system was the master of my thoughts, relationships, and body. I was constantly reacting with my body and thought patterns to situations or conversations that I found stressful. I would get sweaty, feel panicky, or raise my voice in situations that didn't seem to call for that kind of response. It seemed I was always in and out of fight-or-flight mode, but I wasn't quite sure why.

It wasn't until I was able to create awareness around these reactions and trace them back to their origin that I could start the process of healing. When it comes to painful or traumatic memories, being conscious of our bodily reaction and *why* it's happening is the first step to a more whole self. In this exercise, we will do a little work around our triggers and check in with our bodies' reactions.

STEP 1—REACTIONS INVENTORY

The first step to becoming conscious of our bodily reaction to being triggered is to take a step back and assess things when we are no longer feeling those reactions. Don't do the first part of this exercise if your emotions are heightened. You'll want to do this exercise when you feel grounded so you can take a fair assessment of your own reactions.

Get out your journal or a sheet of paper and spend some time reflecting on and answering these questions:

- When do you get angry?
- What annoys you about people?
- When do you feel the loneliest?
- What happens right before negative self-talk happens?
- When do you feel the saddest?
- When do you feel reactive?

- What are the situations in which you feel out of control?

- What situations bring on anxiety or panic attacks?

The key here is to get you thinking about your physical and emotional reactions from a *conscious* place. We want to get to a place where we can be in a positive, energetic state, *even when we are triggered*. When we are in this empowered state, we can better create abundance and opportunities and set out on our Meaningful Missions.

STEP 2—IDENTIFY YOUR BODILY RESPONSES

Next, let's take an inventory of our bodily responses to triggers. Write down what you know you feel in your body when you are in the situations you've detailed in the previous step. For instance, when you get angry, do you clench your fists? Or clench your jaw? When you feel sad, are you also very tired?

Here's another set of questions to help you discover some of your physical reactions to emotional triggers.

- What makes you sweat (outside of physical activity)?

- What makes you want to roll your eyes?

- What causes your fists to clench?

- When do you raise your voice?

- Outside of sleeplessness, what makes you feel tired?

As you go through your triggers and assess your bodily responses, write down every reaction you can think of. You want to bring as much as possible out of the unconscious and into the conscious.

STEP 3—COMMIT TO A NEW PATTERN

Now that you've identified your triggering situations and your bodily responses to them, it's time to commit to a new way of handling your responses. Learning to do this is a long journey, and you will need to practice your responses over and over until they start to feel more natural.

Committing to a new pattern may look something like this:

- When I start to sweat or feel panicky, I will excuse myself and take a break for a moment.

- When I feel triggered, I will take deep breaths and relax my jaw, fists, and shoulders.

- When I raise my voice or yell, I will immediately apologize for my tone and speak at a calmer level. If I can't, I will excuse myself and continue the conversation later.

- When I lose my temper or can't get ahold of my emotions at a particular moment, I will commit to journaling about the experience. I will identify what made me feel so angry and write about how I can do better in the future.

As you think about your responses, take your Meaningful Mission into account:

- As a person with a Meaningful Mission, how do you *want* to respond in triggered situations?

- Is there a way you can respond that gets you closer to your mission?

- How can you be consciously responsible in your responses?

We all have bodily responses to triggers because we live in some pain from our past. Bringing our reactions out of the unconscious and into the conscious is one way we nurture and love ourselves better. Life is long and sometimes brutal. Regardless of healing and changes in behavior, we will still react physically to stressful or scary situations. It's one of the gifts of our bodies! Of course, we will still "get triggered," *but we will be aware.*

Take time to journal new patterns you will try to establish. Take your list from Step 1 and write out sentences that start with the reaction.

HEALING IS A JOURNEY

The goal of healing our triggers isn't to never be upset or triggered. Our goal is to understand the things that hold power over us. Our goal is to acknowledge the things that cause our bodies, minds, and spirits to react—either by fighting, freezing, or fleeing.

What kind of person do you want to be? Do you want to be a reactive person or a person who understands yourself so well that you can pull yourself out of a reactionary phase, either before it happens or very quickly after it happens? When you create awareness around your triggers, you will start healing, allowing yourself to feel safe and better care for yourself.

Have patience with yourself. Healing doesn't happen overnight. It's a *journey.*

Exercise 3: Your Trigger Origin Stories

Depending on the source of your trauma, you may want to consider doing the next few exercises with your therapist or counselor. If this exercise starts to feel overwhelming to you in ways that feel unsafe, stop and come back to it with your therapist or counselor when you're ready.

One of the most significant steps we can take to heal past trauma is to find the origin of our pain. I've had to do this several times in my life to move forward with my business, take chances in relationships, and learn how to communicate better with the people I care about.

STEP 1—WRITE DOWN YOUR MEMORIES

Do you have a list of regrets or a list of memories that cause pain every time you remember them? For instance, do you remember being bullied in school or have a memory of feeling humiliated in a group of people?

In this exercise, I want you to take as much time as you need to dump out every memory, event, or problematic person from the past that you know still has a hold over you in the present. You've already cataloged your bodily responses and your coping mechanisms. Now it's time to find what drives them.

Get out a sheet of paper or your journal and write down every past event that has caused bodily reactions and triggers in your present. It may help to go back to your list of physical reactions and use that as a guide to trace them back to your original trauma.

Here are some guiding questions for this exercise:

1. What are the memories or events that have caused triggers?

2. Who are the people who have caused triggers?

3. Where, who, or what are the sources of your pain?

4. What painful memories can you write down that connect you to this feeling?

This exercise may take a few attempts over a few days. Feel free to stop if you seem overwhelmed or triggered just by recalling the memories. Healing is not a straight path. It is a journey, and this stop on the line might take a few days.

STEP 2—WRITE YOUR YOUNGER SELF A LETTER

In the second part of this exercise, I want you to write your younger self a letter for each memory or event you wrote down. If you don't want to do it for every single one, make sure you do it for the ones you feel are the most powerful in your life. The point of this exercise is to give yourself agency in your painful moments and thank your younger self for their strength and resiliency.

Here's an example of what I mean:

Dear Becky,

It wasn't easy when Katie started the "I Hate Becky Club" in sixth grade because she was mad at you. It was mean and wrong. No young kid should have to go through that!

It took a lot of strength to endure that. I know it was a lot of pain to handle at 11 years old. I'm so proud of you for still going to school every day and doing everything you could to have fun with your friends, even though it was so hard every day to deal with your bullies. You were so strong! I'm so proud of you for never being mean back and still helping others whenever they needed it. You didn't deserve to be treated like that, and I'm impressed that you could still be kind.

I wonder if there is anything you need now to let go of that pain. We are older now, and we have more skills and more power than we did at 11 years old. How can I help you let go of this pain?

After you're done with your letter, take a moment to see what your younger self inside of you needs to move away from the pain. Like we've done before, check in with your body as you write the letter. Are you starting to feel sweaty? Or are you relieved? Sad or angry? None of these feelings are wrong, and it's good to take an inventory of how you feel as you write each letter.

Remember to give yourself agency in these letters by asking your younger self what they need. This kind of exercise can be potent as it can help integrate parts of us into a more whole person.

STEP 3—DECIDE TO STOP RUNNING

One of the biggest reasons our trauma continues to cause us pain is because we keep trying to run away from it and not feel the feelings as they rise to the surface. When I decided to confront the pain of my past, I was able to move forward in leaps and bounds. It can be scary to face past trauma, so we need to make an agreement with ourselves to face it, accept it, and write a new future.

The pain that has happened to us may be unfair, wrong, or even illegal. *But it happened.* The sooner we can say, *I accept that this happened to me. It wasn't right, I didn't deserve it, and I accept it,* the sooner we can embrace Meaningful Missions and walk a new path of growth.

This doesn't mean you need to be friends with the people that hurt you or keep them in your life, but holding on to the pain of the past will only cause you more pain in the future.

Today, as you sit with your list of painful events, take a moment to accept what you have experienced. Commit to yourself that you will face your trauma and heal from it, whatever it takes.

Donald Miller said to me, "I would not be so grateful for my life if I had not had my heart broken. I just wouldn't. Pain serves us tremendously."[7] Like me, I'm sure you've endured much pain and disappointment. When we face our trauma, we are walking a new path. We are walking the way of a hero on the path to greatness.

Chapter 10

FINDING YOUR IDENTITY

For many years, I felt like something was missing inside. No matter what level of success I obtained or how many goals I accomplished, I would feel let down afterward. I expected to feel fulfilled, but instead, I felt empty. Don't get me wrong. It felt good to check something off the list, but deeper fulfillment eluded me. After years, even decades, pursuing a goal, I felt like, *Now what?*

As I shared in my book *The Mask of Masculinity*, in the early years of building my business, I was succeeding on the outside, making money and growing my brand. But I didn't feel fulfilled because I hadn't healed a lot of different things in my life. I actually felt frustrated because I was out of alignment with my integrity, values, and vision. I was more focused on how to make more money, get more influence, and prove people wrong than on serving others and fulfilling my Meaningful Mission.

What I have come to realize is that for most of my life, I was accomplishing things just to prove people wrong—whether the bullies from my childhood or the people who picked me last to be on their teams. I was focused on trying to heal scars from the past and prove I was something other than what they thought I was. Or something other than what I thought they thought I was. My fuel to succeed came from my wounded inner child, but it wasn't meaningful or sustaining fuel. It led to me pursuing goals for self-centered reasons and not from a place of pure love.

In short, I let other people define my identity. It tried to be someone I was not. Through getting clear about my identity through my journey with *The School of Greatness*, I transitioned into becoming someone who focused on serving others. My fuel became, *How can I collect wisdom from experts to improve my life and deliver it to others so they can become better versions of themselves?*

The process of healing your past is essential to you being able to ask one of the most important questions you will ever answer: *Who are you?*

And only you can answer that question.

CULTIVATED OR PRUNED

As a child Payal Kadakia, ClassPass founder, artist, and author of *LifePass*, lived two lives. Around her American friends, she was all-American. Around her Indian friends, she was a proud Indian. In addition, she is an MIT business graduate who also studied dance.

No matter which community she found herself in, she felt pressure to feel ashamed of the seemingly opposing other part of herself. In truth, she was authentically a part of both. Now older and equipped with more insight, Payal says when you live to please others, "you don't know what success looks like anymore."[1] She calls it plan B success. It's not the success path you chose for yourself, but one you sort of fell into accidentally. And no wonder it doesn't feel fulfilling to you. It's not yours!

I think we could all benefit from Payal's reminder that "we are allowed to grab from different types of our identity."[2] As she looks back now, she told me she can see how it is the combination of her identities that gives her the ability to solve the problems she was meant to solve. And she is grateful she got to experience both the business and the creative worlds so she could explore different thoughts and processes.

Who or what has shaped your identity? Did you cultivate it yourself, or did someone else choose to prune you to grow in a particular direction? Often, this pruning happens unintentionally and is the product of the environment in which we live.

You have to nurture your own growth in the direction of your own Meaningful Mission, or it will flow wherever other people take it. This nurturing process is both a self-directed and openminded journey. You should intentionally choose your path but be prepared to explore new directions. Organizational psychologist Adam Grant shared with me an interesting psychological term called *identity foreclosure*, which is what happens when people commit to a single identity—even one they're excited about—before exploring other options. Adam has seen this story play out with college students who commit themselves to one career before really testing out any other options. Such students often reach a point when they think they chose incorrectly but feel trapped because their identity is then firmly tied to their work.[3]

Maybe you can relate to that close connection between identity and work. Or maybe you define who you are more by the community you associate with. In that case, you need to be careful not to place your membership in this community ahead of your own values. Social psychologist Dr. Amy Cuddy spoke with me about this temptation. She reminded me that our values make us who we are, so compromising those values for a group means giving up agency over our lives.[4] It can be tempting to conform to peer pressure and

> **You have to nurture your own growth in the direction of your own Meaningful Mission, or it will flow wherever other people take it.**

adopt the same beliefs as the people closest to you, but hold true to what is right for you and your mission.

SEE YOURSELF CLEARLY

To live out your own greatness and not someone else's idea of it, you have to be intentional about crafting your identity. Part of this intentionality might mean rejecting some old parts of yourself and visualizing the new you that you want to become.

While speaking with me about the need for change, Leon Howard, South Carolina state representative, shared a story he read about two men who decided to quit smoking. One of the men, when offered a smoke, responded, "No, I'm trying to quit." He still visualized himself as a smoker, one who was trying to quit, but a smoker nonetheless. The other replied, "No, I don't smoke." He was fully invested in a new identity by taking off his old self and claiming a new identity.

It goes back to the reality that you *are* enough *and* are becoming more. Not either/or but both/and. As Leon shared with me, "I appreciate where I'm at now, but more importantly, I appreciate where I'm going."[5] The reality is that your identity will continually evolve and include diverse elements, so you must be careful not to limit yourself.

You are a combination of all your experiences, communities, and beliefs, and that one-of-a-kind combination is what makes you the best person to pursue your unique Meaningful Mission. If you hold a clear image of your ideal self as your North Star, you will make incremental life changes that will bring you closer to the meaningful success that *you* find fulfilling.

Research shows that the most successful people are ones who try on multiple identities. Herminia Ibarra, a professor at the London Business School, has been studying how people build careers. She discovered successful people try on and switch out many identities and do not simply accept identities to please others. They take the initiative to explore different roles to find the combination that feels right for them.[6]

Sometimes, as was the case for Adam Grant, your experimentation may involve taking off identities that you have worn for a while. Adam wanted to share his ideas on public stages, but he had long worn the identity of an introvert who feared public speaking. To help him adapt his identity, he listened to other introverts who delivered powerful speeches, people like Brian Little, Susan Cain, and Malcolm Gladwell. He decided to let go of his past identity as a self-conscious speaker and tried on a fresh identity that served his mission. Now you can find his inspirational speeches all over, from YouTube to TED Talks.

Dr. Benjamin Hardy, an organizational psychologist, also acknowledges the importance of having a flexible identity. He shared with me that having a flexible identity does not mean it is out of your control. You should always be the one directing the changes to your identity, but

> **To pursue greatness, you have to first know yourself.**

your identity will inevitably change. Your past self had different approaches for meeting a different set of goals, which is why Ben warns us to always work with goals and beliefs that serve the *present* you, not a previous version of you. He encourages you to ask what you should be focusing on right now, without holding yourself to old standards. This current focus mindset, he says, will help you selectively put your attention on the things that will help you achieve the next great thing in your life.[7]

When life coach, inspirational speaker, and entrepreneur Tim Storey joined me on my show, he shared this wisdom: "When you find out where you came from, who you are, and what your purpose is, you cannot be stopped."[8]

To pursue greatness, you have to first know yourself. No one else can do that for you. There are problems you are meant to solve. Don't miss out on knowing yourself and feeling completely fulfilled by the success meant for you.

HERO OR VILLAIN

Donald Miller gives us a good way of looking at how our identities get shaped. He told me that identity is everything because we will operate out of how we see ourselves living our identities in stories. As Don describes it, there are essentially four primary characters in every story: the victim, the villain, the hero, and the guide:

> The victim believes they are doomed and have no way out. They are looking for a rescuer. The villain is the one who makes others small. They demean others in order to feel powerful. The hero is the one who really doesn't have what it takes, but accepts the challenge and transforms until they can get the job done. The guide is the one who has played the hero for so long that they have the expertise to turn around and help somebody else.[9]

The key point Don makes is that these four characters simultaneously exist in every story because they simultaneously exist in you and me. At any moment, you and I are playing the role of one of those characters. And that role can and will change many times throughout the typical day. We may not be able to choose what happens to us, but for the most part, we can choose the role we play in the story.

"The more you identify as the victim, the worse your story will go," Don told me. "Victims do not transform. They are only bit parts to make the hero look good and the villain look bad. When we play the victims, our stories go nowhere. We never get what we want. We don't build a legacy. We're not remembered."[10] To put this in the perspective of the previous chapter, victims don't work to heal the trauma in their past. They let it define who they are.

But there is another subtle yet more important distinction to be made about what we choose to do with the pain of the past. Don puts it this way:

> Villains and heroes actually have the exact same backstory. Both the villain and the hero backstory are painful.

At the beginning of the movie, the hero has pain of some sort. Likewise, the villain has a painful backstory. So, the difference between the villain and the hero is one thing: how they respond to pain. The villain says, *The world hurt me. I'm gonna hurt it back.* And the hero says, *The world hurt me. I'm not gonna let this happen to anybody else.*[11]

> **Healing is a journey, one you must take to discover who you are.**

How you decide to react to the pain that has come your way in life causes you to be the victim, villain, or hero of your identity story (and you may well serve as a guide to others along the way). As Don pointed out to me, often the learning takes place as the hero takes action—going to therapy, engaging in a relationship, learning from past mistakes, or helping someone else. Healing is a journey, one you must take to discover who you are.

ENGAGING GREATNESS

If you are ready to uncover your identity so you can see yourself clearly, I encourage you to engage in the following exercise to help identify who you are and want to become.

Exercise 1: Your Current Identity

If you don't love yourself for who you are, it's hard to pursue a Meaningful Mission and carve out the life you are meant to have. I truly believe that you are a gift to the world, and you deserve an abundance identity. Even if these things don't feel true, I know they are true for you. The best place to start building a stronger, nonlimiting abundance identity is to figure out who you are now and chart a path to who you want to be. This exercise will get you started.

STEP 1—TAKE INVENTORY OF YOUR CURRENT SELF

Self-awareness is key to cultivating a new identity. You can't get to the finish line if you don't know where to start. Rate yourself on a scale of 1 to 10 on the following statements below. Be sure to record your answers here or in a place where you can review them in a few months. You'll want to be able to track your progress.

I am happy with the identity I have.

Strongly Disagree				Agree			Strongly Agree		
1	2	3	4	5	6	7	8	9	10

I want to attract opportunities, abundance, and meaningful relationships.

Strongly Disagree				Agree			Strongly Agree		
1	2	3	4	5	6	7	8	9	10

I want to feel much better about myself than I currently do.

Strongly Disagree				Agree			Strongly Agree		
1	2	3	4	5	6	7	8	9	10

I have bad habits that need reshaping.

Strongly Disagree				Agree			Strongly Agree		
1	2	3	4	5	6	7	8	9	10

I know the new behaviors I need to create for myself.

Strongly Disagree			Agree				Strongly Agree		
1	2	3	4	5	6	7	8	9	10

I know what I need to do to become who I want to be.

Strongly Disagree			Agree				Strongly Agree		
1	2	3	4	5	6	7	8	9	10

I understand what my identity needs to be to support my Meaningful Mission.

Strongly Disagree			Agree				Strongly Agree		
1	2	3	4	5	6	7	8	9	10

I know what my Meaningful Mission is.

Strongly Disagree			Agree				Strongly Agree		
1	2	3	4	5	6	7	8	9	10

I may not have clarity on my Meaningful Mission, but I want to take steps to discover it and build an identity to support it.

Strongly Disagree			Agree				Strongly Agree		
1	2	3	4	5	6	7	8	9	10

These statements are only meant to gauge your starting point. They are not a reflection of how powerful and abundant your new identity can be. Remember, this is *only the beginning* of an incredible journey. Don't get discouraged if any of your ratings were lower than what you want them to be. Instead, take a minute to reflect on any answers above that you want to explore further and write down your thoughts.

STEP 2—WRITE A MEANINGFUL MISSION MANIFESTO (MMM)

Humans, at one point or another, all experience feeling like we are not enough. It's part of the human experience for our confidence to ebb and flow. When our identities are limited and built on negative experiences, the feeling of not being enough can be crushing. People can work 60 hours a week, get every promotion they want, and still feel like they are terrible at their job if their identity is not built on a solid foundation or if their actions are not aligned with their truest selves.

> **You must understand who you ultimately want to become and chart a path to that person, that purpose, and that identity.**

If you feel like nothing you do is good enough and that you are consistently stuck, it might be because the actions you take are out of alignment with your true purpose or because you haven't healed a wound that is driving you to feel this way. No matter what you do, what you achieve, or how many allegedly good actions you take, it will feel empty if you are not on the right path.

To free yourself from a prison of negativity, you must understand who you ultimately want to become and chart a path to that person, that purpose, and that identity. In this step, I want you to take a few minutes to review your answers from the previous step, reflect on a few of them, and get concrete with the outcomes you want.

These are the behaviors I know I want to change: _____

_____

My highest self no longer spends time _____

_____

My highest self wants to spend time doing these things instead:

_____

My highest self wants to help others by _____

_____

When I picture my highest self, these are the characteristics that I have:

_____

Now that you've written these things down, take a minute to put them all together in a Meaningful Mission Manifesto (MMM).

I, _____, am committed to ending the behaviors that are inconsistent with who I want to be. I will stop_____. I will no longer spend time _____. Instead, I will spend time _____ because I want to help others _____. I will spend time becoming the kind of person who _____.
When I move through the world aligned with my truest and highest self, I can achieve my Meaningful Mission, help others, attract abundance, and create positive opportunities for myself.

EXAMPLE

I, Anthony Cooper, am committed to ending the behaviors that are inconsistent with who I want to become. I will stop procrastinating when it's time to meet a deadline. I will be kind and loving to myself when I fail. I will stop getting angry over minor infractions and learn to be more forgiving. I will no longer spend hours bingeing TV or playing video games. Instead, I will limit my time on those activities, spend time with friends, find a business coach, and learn how to journal. I want to help others by teaching them how to write for corporate success. When I move through the world aligned with my truest and highest self, I can achieve my Meaningful Mission, help others, attract abundance, and create positive opportunities for myself.

This manifesto will help guide you as you build a new, more positive identity. If you are out of integrity with who you want to be, the way you think about yourself, and the actions you take, you are not going to feel whole. You're going to feel a profound sense of lack. This is harmful to your identity.

Your Meaningful Mission Manifesto is a commitment to yourself to take the actions that confirm an abundance identity, support your growth, and ultimately assist you in your Meaningful Mission. There will be days, weeks, and months where you won't feel like taking the actions that support your desired identity, but you must press on. The last statement of your Manifesto tells you why.

STEP 3—HONE NEW SKILLS

With your MMM written, it's likely some new skills will need to be learned and developed to support your new path. Reshaping your habits, new skills, and new growth are all things that will help you build a new identity. In addition, the new behaviors and skills will help you feel better about yourself, attract meaningful relationships, and become aware of good opportunities.

Based on your answers from the first step, take a minute to list any new skills you may need to develop below. Next to them, write down how you can achieve them (with a coach, course, book, etc.). I've provided a few examples so you can see what I mean. Complete your own list on a separate sheet of paper or in your journal.

Skill I Want to Build	How I Can Build It
Frugality	Find an online course or book I can work through
Resiliency	Find a self-talk therapist
Not procrastinating	Look for people online who share skill-building in this area; find a person to help with accountability in this area

GET READY FOR GREATNESS

Appreciate the strength it took you to get from where you were to where you are now. If you had feelings of inadequacy or dissatisfaction during this exercise, I want to remind you that you are building a *new you*. You are creating an identity that isn't based on trauma, criticism, or lies about what you can accomplish. Take this moment to breathe deeply. Your innate strength will help you get to where you want to go. Greatness awaits!

Greatness awaits!

Exercise 2: Identity Celebration

When I set out on my own path to greatness, I was reactive, fearful, and anxious. I had built my identity from a past that was mired with trauma and challenging experiences. I had to intentionally pursue healing from my traumas, work through my fears, and create a new identity for myself. One big step in my healing path was *acceptance*. I had to decide to love myself for who I was, who I would become, and every step in between. I had to stop beating myself up for not being perfect and take specific steps to protect myself from harmful inner thoughts.

> **Our inner thoughts shape our identity.**

Our inner thoughts shape our identity. We have to view ourselves in a loving, positive light so that we can build the identity we want. Take some time today to clean your inner house of negativity and celebrate who you are *right now*.

STEP 1—REPLACE YOUR NEGATIVE THOUGHTS

Negative thoughts are energy vampires and can affect your Meaningful Mission, work performance, and, most important, relationships. One of the best ways to stop negative thoughts is to identify them, bring them to the surface, and acknowledge them. It's counterintuitive *not* to suppress negative thoughts, but they're the villains of our identity, and they get stronger and bigger every time we stuff them down or put them on a shelf for "later." In this step, I want you to spend some time identifying the thoughts and feelings that cause you to shut down, react, get defensive, or isolate yourself.

Get out your trusty journal or a new sheet of paper.

1. Identify your chronic negative thoughts and feelings.

2. Ask yourself: *Does this thought or feeling support an abundance identity?*

3. Reframe your intrusive thought with an abundance mindset.

Sketch out a table like the one that follows and fill in the blanks. I've filled in some examples so you can see what I want you to do.

INVASIVE THOUGHT/EMOTION	REFRAME YOUR THOUGHT
I am so messed up. There is no way I can help others.	I am well prepared to provide empathy and help someone who has had negative experiences.
I am too old to start something new. I've lost my chance.	Because of my age, I am equipped to help younger people avoid the pitfalls I experienced.
I will never measure up to my peers. They are all so much farther ahead than I am.	The only experience that concerns me is my own. I am walking a new path of growth that will take me to where I want to be.

So many times, the thoughts and emotions we experience don't belong to our true selves. They were created through our trauma or imagined through our fear. When a painter sits down to paint, if they were to imagine what someone might say on an Instagram photo of their artwork, they would never paint a thing. If a runner sets out to run the Boston Marathon, they would never complete it if they kept hearing their college coach calling them a loser.

Our most authentic identity is not self-critical or disappointed with who we are. Our truest essence is loving, kind, and encouraging to ourselves. When we bring our not-worthy and not-good-enough thoughts into the light, they cannot survive.

STEP 2—CELEBRATE YOU

You are *worthy*.

You *deserve* to live a big life.

You *matter*.

You are a gift.

Take some time to celebrate the wonder that is you. It's time to make a list of the things we love about ourselves. List *anything* you love about yourself. Anything! You don't need to use a lot of words, but be specific. Instead of "I am great at deadlifts," go deeper into why you love this about yourself. "I'm great at deadlifts because I am never intimidated by the weight on the bar." Then take a moment to reflect on how these celebrations can help you on your journey to heal and pursue a Meaningful Mission.

Here is what that might look like:

I CELEBRATE THIS ABOUT MYSELF	HOW THIS CAN APPLY TO MY MEANINGFUL MISSION AND ABUNDANCE IDENTITY
I'm great at deadlifts because I am never intimidated by the weight on the bar.	If I look at obstacles as just another plate on the bar, I can summon the part of me that is never intimidated and move forward with confidence.
I am a good friend because I am very encouraging, and I always show up when I am needed.	I can look at myself as a friend, encourage myself, and work to give myself what I need when I am in crisis.
I love that I am kind to everyone I meet, even when I feel cranky.	When I am feeling angry with myself for imperfections, I know I have the strength to be kind to myself. If I can find strength for strangers, I can find strength for myself.

When you are done, post this list somewhere you can refer to it often. Take a picture with your phone so you can carry it in your pocket. Put it in the pages of your journal or hang it on the fridge. Put it anywhere you can see it. When you feel chronic negativity creeping in, this list will remind you of your worth and help you re-center your thinking.

STEP 3—WRITE A LETTER FROM YOUR FUTURE SELF

Next, take all of the positive feelings you have from Step 2 and channel them into a letter from your future self to your current self. Imagine yourself, just a few years into the future, writing a letter to the present you, right in the middle of the work of healing and growth. You can say anything you want in this letter, and in case it's helpful, here are a few ideas to get started:

- Thank yourself for doing the daily actions that helped build a stronger identity.

- Mention how proud you are of your younger self for doing the hard work of healing.

- Talk about why you're proud of your present self.

- Thank yourself for showing up.

- Mention the obstacles that you had to overcome and celebrate overcoming them.

- Mention the addictions or destructive behaviors you conquered.

- Say thank you for the routines you established.

- Encourage yourself to stay the course.

- Mentor yourself by revealing the consistent behaviors you need to embrace to build a new identity.

- Celebrate the fact that your younger self supported your Meaningful Mission.

Follow your intuition as you write the letter. You are celebrating yourself, in the now, for getting to where you want to go. *You are amazing.*

YOU ARE THE ONE

You've probably heard me say this before: if you want to find the one person who can change your life, look in the mirror. You are the *only person who can give yourself what you want*, and you must be willing to do the work every day. That's why it's so important to accept yourself, celebrate your work, and reprogram your negative thoughts. You're on the path to greatness now. Develop your skills. Own your insecurities and celebrate your abilities. Do the work every day. Build yourself into a force. You have everything you need, right now, to triumph.

Exercise 3: Your Inspiration Finder

Inspiration is a word we throw around, and it's easy for it to get cheapened. But authentic inspiration is *vital* on your journey to build a new identity. Inspiration can give you wings to rise above the fold, help you learn more, and live a better life. When we have people in our lives who inspire us, both personal and virtual (e.g., online coaches), I genuinely believe we have more joy and can make a more significant impact. This exercise will help you find what inspires you, identify what you want from it, and make a plan to achieve it.

> **You are the only person who can give yourself what you want.**

STEP 1—WRITE AN INSPIRATION LIST

In this step, identify the people who you admire, and from whom you get inspiration. It can be anyone—parent, sibling, friend, teacher, online coach, author, celebrity, or well-known figure. Feel free to list anyone who comes to mind, even if you think it might seem odd. If they inspire you, write them down.

- Write a list of people who inspire you.
- Write one to two sentences next to each name about why they inspire you.

Understanding who you admire and *why* can help you identify what you yourself want to embody.

STEP 2—VISUALIZE

Next, get more concrete by listing actual characteristics you want to develop for yourself. It might help to look at the list from Step 1 and dissect which admirable qualities these particular people possess.

- Visualize who you want to become.
  - What qualities or characteristics do you have?
  - How do these qualities or characteristics help you in your Meaningful Mission?

- As you visualize your future self, take an assessment:
  - Are you doubtful or confident?
  - What do you think about yourself?
  - Are you fearful or fearless?
  - What other emotions are you feeling?

- Do the same with the people you listed in Step 1.
  - How do you imagine they feel about themselves?
  - Do they pursue their goals even when they don't feel confident?
  - How do they tackle problems or obstacles?
  - How do they motivate themselves?

When you're ready, get out a piece of paper, journal, notes app (you know the drill by now), and record the characteristics you want to have.

STEP 3—MEDITATE WITH THESE PROMPTS

Now that you've identified the qualities and characteristics you want to build, take some time to meditate on them. It is in the quiet moments of meditation that we can center our thoughts and begin healthy thought patterns around new goals. Meditation can also help us discover the concrete steps we want to take to achieve our goals. A lot of magic can happen in the quiet.

To get ready for meditation, find a comfortable position. Many people report that meditation is most effective when their feet are flat on the ground, but find whatever position is most comfortable for you.

1. Start your meditation with several deep breaths. You may want to bring focus to your breathing by counting the beats of your inhales and exhales. Inhale for seven beats and exhale for eight.

2. Take a moment to check in with your body. Scan yourself from head to toe. Feel your arms, become aware of your feet, notice your back and placement of hands. If any part of your body is tense or tight (like your jaw or shoulders, especially), spend a few moments trying to relax that part.

3. Check in with your energy, thoughts, and feelings. Are you feeling positive or negative? Tired or energetic? Hungry or full? There are no wrong answers here; it's just time to observe.

4. Take some time to be grateful. Find three things in your life for which you are grateful, and take a moment to focus on each one.

5. Choose one of the following prompts and meditate on it for three to five minutes. As you reflect, try to consciously open your mind so that new ideas can come in. You may find your mind wandering, and that's okay. Just bring yourself back to the prompt and keep meditating.

   – *What has inspired you this week? Why?*

   – *What are some ways having these qualities or characteristics will enhance your life or bring you more joy?*

   – *What are some ways these characteristics will help you create an abundance identity?*

   – *How can these new characteristics or qualities help you in your Meaningful Mission?*

   – *What's one way you can begin adopting these new qualities? How can you practice it?*

— *Meditate on this phrase from your Meaningful Mission Manifesto by repeating it over and over:* When I move through the world aligned with my truest and highest self, I can achieve my Meaningful Mission, help others, attract abundance, and create positive opportunities for myself.

Meditation is calming to our nervous systems and trains our brains to come back to the present moment over and over again. This is a good skill to have on hand as you battle negative thoughts and get rid of your limiting beliefs as soon as you feel triggered or overwhelmed. As you continue to build your new identity, make sure you make time to meditate; you'll find it to be inspiring, peaceful, and beautiful.

YOU ARE THE INSPIRATION

When you have the courage to heal, get rid of toxic thinking, and build a new identity, you will inspire others to do the same. Your inspiration will ripple throughout everyone with whom you come into contact. It's hard work building a new identity, but the quiet persistence with which you set and achieve your goals will inspire others, just as you have been inspired. There are no mistakes in who you are, what you are up to, and where you have been placed in life. You are here to be an inspiration—so keep going.

> **When you have the courage to heal, get rid of toxic thinking, and build a new identity, you will inspire others to do the same.**

Bonus Exercise: Your Mantra Creator

I have a thing I do when I'm running and want to quit. When I want to stop or feel fatigued, I repeat a mantra to myself. *I'm fast. I'm healthy. I'm free.* With each running step, *I'm fast. I'm healthy. I'm free.* And as I run, my fatigue seems to disappear, my pain diminishes, and I start to run a little faster. Our thoughts and output are closely connected. This exercise will help you to create mantras that serve you as you build your abundance identity.

1. Write down the things you most desire. It can be anything—from business success to a loving relationship to becoming the world's foremost lemon expert. Whatever it is, write it down.

2. Next to each one, write a declarative and positive statement.

3. Imagine that you already have what you want most. If you wrote down *I want to find the love of my life*, next to it, write down *I am lovable. I am loved.*

4. Whittle your statement down to a few words to create a mantra that is short and easy to remember and repeat.

Here are a few tips for writing your mantra:

•   Keep your mantra in the first person. Begin with *I* or *My*.

•   Make your mantra specific.

•   Make your mantra positive with no negative words.

Using this formula, create mantras for any part of your life where you need to overcome an obstacle, deal with a difficult situation, or steer your mind away from negative thoughts and into positivity. And, as I do, repeat the mantra anytime you need it, with every step or every breath you take. Nothing is more powerful than changing your negative thinking in the present moment.

Chapter 11

THE MINDSET-IN-MOTION CYCLE

If you were to set this book down, walk to your bathroom mirror, and look at yourself, what would you see? Chances are, you'd see the *you* you've always been. Sure, you'd see yourself as you are today, but you probably would not see the minute changes that have taken place even since you finished the activities for the last chapter. These changes happen every minute, every hour, and every day on this journey of life.

Contrast that to seeing someone else for the first time in a long time. Maybe it's a childhood friend that you haven't seen for 20 years, a past love, or maybe even a relative you haven't seen since you were a child.

In those cases, you'd notice a *drastic* difference. The person you remembered from your past is gone. That person may have been younger, had more or different hair, a different wardrobe, or maybe even a different posture or way of walking and talking.

It's ironic that in others, change seems to happen all at once, while in us, it seems to sneak up on us. Only after a long movement in the same direction do we seem to see the effects of change in ourselves.

But pursuing greatness is all about change.

As we have discussed, greatness comes from both healing our past pain and finding our identity as we *become* someone new, someone different and better. And these kinds of changes take time, effort, and energy. They also take an awareness that change happens when we examine three major components nestled under the one big idea of *mindset*. Mindset consists of three interwoven and overlapping components:

- Your thoughts (how you think)
- Your emotions (how you feel)
- Your behavior (how you act)

We'll unpack these elements more in this chapter, but I wanted to first discuss why these three things mix together to impact mindset. When talking about how powerful negative emotions can be on behavior, Dr. Joe Dispenza, author of *Becoming Supernatural*, said, "If I don't overcome that emotion, then I'm living in the past and that's karma, because that emotion is going to drive my behaviors and my thoughts. My future is going to look a lot like my past."[1]

> ## Pursuing greatness is all about change.

Emotions can cause us to live in the past (where hurt or trauma took place), which affects your present behaviors, which stunts your future growth. Emotions impact behaviors.

As communication pathologist and cognitive neuroscientist Dr. Caroline Leaf told me:

> You cannot control events and circumstances, but you can learn to manage your mind . . . COVID, trauma, death, life happens, but . . . greatness comes from us, managing our

mind. And greatness doesn't necessarily mean that you've got millions in the bank and are this famous superstar. It means that you have mental peace or you are actually growing. You are satisfied as a person.[2]

Events—especially traumatic or negative events—create emotions within us. These emotions lead to thoughts. And these thoughts must be managed or else they can control our behaviors in a negative way.

Marisa Peer, world-renowned Rapid Transformational Therapy trainer, states:

Every thought you think you make real. And if you doubt that, think of this: if you think of something embarrassing, you will blush. If you think of something sad, your eyes will fill up with tears. If you think of food, your stomach rumbles. If you think of something sexy, you can get physically aroused. So the body makes thoughts. Whatever thought you are thinking, your body is very busy making it real. If you think better thoughts, you get better emotional reactions and better responses.[3]

> **Emotions impact behaviors.**

Think. Feel. Act. See how things can get tangled up?

Becoming doesn't happen all at once. It happens gradually, over time, as your thoughts become actions, your feelings become thoughts, your behavior leads to more feelings, and your emotions affect your actions. And so it goes.

Let's unpack that connection further.

THE CIRCLE OF LIFE

The path to anywhere worth going requires taking action. Chances are you've seen this reality played out in your own life. Simply thinking, *I should exercise; I need to eat better; I should listen to different people; I need to take a break from social media; I should really reach out to that person and make amends* doesn't result in greatness.

The same could be said of emotions. Feelings such as *I feel lonely when I'm by myself at night in my apartment, I feel shame because I said those unkind words, I feel angry because that person cut me off in traffic,* or *I feel grateful because of what that person did for me* don't change your behavior.

The path to anywhere worth going requires taking action.

The thoughts require action.

And that requires dealing with both internal and external forces, between who you were (healing your past) and who you are becoming (finding your identity), and between your very real past with all the things you are working to heal there and your ideal future, the new *greatness* identity you are striving to create.

It's a process that takes time. It's direction in motion.

Consider this graphic of what I call the Mindset-in-Motion Cycle:

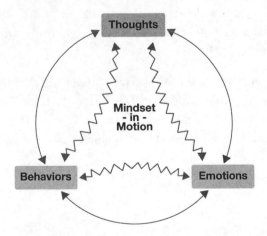

The Greatness Mindset is the sweet spot where how you think, how you feel, and how you act all come together. Mindset by itself is neutral. It can be positive or negative. It can be messy or it can be clean. That's what the two different types of lines in the illustration represent. The jagged lines represent the opposite of a Greatness Mindset. Thoughts, emotions, and behavior are connected, but not in a way that leads to growth and greatness.

When these jagged lines are in play, your thoughts might be largely negative and self-defeating, resulting in a shrinking of your mindset. Thoughts like, *I'll never be enough to reach my goal; I'll never be what someone is looking for in a partner; Every time I try something new I fail;* and *This kind of thing always happens to people like me.* These thoughts obviously have a toxic and negative effect on your emotions. They make you feel defeated, powerless, stuck, anxious, small, and stagnant. And when you feel like that, you aren't inspired to act. Your negative mindset tells you that action is futile.

On the other hand, there is a cycle that leads to expansion and growth—to greatness. The smooth lines on the outside represent a Greatness Mindset where things flow smoothly. Your thoughts are mostly good, positive, and boost your emotions. In other words, they feel like they flow smoothly as you feel *confidence, security, positivity, and excitement.* These emotions affect your behavior. When you see an opportunity, you seize it! You act with purpose. You push through obstacles with grit and

When you see an opportunity, seize it!

determination. When you succeed, you are flooded with new positive thoughts like, *I did it. I overcame the obstacle. I grew through that. I didn't react the way I used to in that kind of situation.*

The right thoughts produce better behavior and lead to better emotions.

The right emotions lead to better behavior and lead to greater thoughts.

The right behavior reinforces better thoughts, which leads to better emotions.

The challenging part is navigating the tension between thoughts, emotions, and behaviors. It's a little like trying to balance on a stand-up paddle board. You may get to your feet and be able to balance when the water is calm, but when the waves pick up, you can get shaky. Try rowing, and you can get shakier still. Bump into something under the water, and you can get pitched off. It takes an internal strength to lock in your core, stay on your feet, and keep moving toward your goal.

That's how the Mindset-in-Motion Cycle works. It's an invisible and constant awareness of the thoughts, emotions, and behaviors that impact you daily as you make micro-adjustments to gain steadiness. But as you learn to navigate these three components, you gradually move from who you were to who you are becoming.

UNLOCKING THE THREE COMPONENTS

Since the three mindset components can get tangled up, it's best if we unpack them one at a time and then tie them all back together. Let's start with thoughts, then move into emotions, and finally wrap up with behaviors.

Optimizing the Thought Cycle

I'm no stranger to battling my thoughts and striving to find the right mindset. For many years, the silent dialogue in my head would run on repeat, telling me I was worthless. That I was stupid. That no one could ever love me again. The worst part was that I thought I was the only one who felt this way. The reality is that most of us have a challenge like this. The lies may be different, the recording may play at different times or be triggered by different catalysts, but the message can still be just as damaging.

What's even more challenging is that it was *my voice* in the recording. And who do we trust more than ourselves? So when my voice was telling me those things, it seemed to have weight and a ring of truth.

Dr. Joe Dispenza told me:

Some people wake up in the morning . . . and the first thing they do is they think about the problems. Those problems are memories that are etched in the brain that are connected to certain people, certain objects, certain things at a certain time and place. Every one of those problems . . . has an emotion associated with it. So then all of a sudden they start feeling unhappy. Now the body is in the past, because thoughts are the language of the brain and feelings are the language of the body.[4]

Did you catch that last part? *Thoughts are the language of the brain and feelings are the language of the body.*

It's the Mindset-in-Motion Cycle at work. Our thoughts talk to our brain, and our feelings talk to our body. When these thoughts lean to the negative or are linked to a painful past, it affects the way we move and act in the present. And this impacts our future and who we are becoming.

> **The right thoughts, emotions, and actions lead to who we want to become.**

"Some people have emotions that influence thoughts," Joe continued. "Some people are more analytical. They have thoughts that influence feelings, but it's a loop. It's that cycle of thinking."[5]

The challenge then becomes, how do you change that cycle of thinking? This is a critical question to answer because it ties directly into our *identity.* The right thoughts, emotions, and actions lead to who we want to become. The wrong thoughts, emotions, and actions keep us stuck.

WHO DO YOUR THOUGHTS SAY YOU ARE?

We all have high-level identity questions that intersect with our thoughts. Who am I? What's my purpose? Why am I here? Why do I act the way I do? Who am I becoming?

At the root of each of these questions is a thought. And, as we've discussed, that thought is tangled up with our emotions and our actions. That's why it's critical to begin to recognize and, as best we can, shape what we are thinking. We need to learn how to reject the thoughts that don't align with our greatness identity and to accept and solidify the ones that do.

I like how Dr. Ethan Kross, author of the book *Chatter*, put it:

> We don't have control over the thoughts that pop up, but what we do have control over is how we engage with those thoughts once they surface. We can choose to immerse ourselves in the thoughts. I can also choose to distance myself from my thoughts or challenge my thoughts. There's a range of things we can do when thoughts pop up—that's where the control comes in.[6]

We need to learn how to reject the thoughts that don't align with our greatness identity and to accept and solidify the ones that do.

Thoughts are going to happen. But you have a not-so-secret superpower, potentially untapped, at your disposal, and ready to push past the you that you used to be and toward the you that you are becoming.

Just as an army of soldiers can quickly fall apart without structure and leadership, the army of thoughts in your mind can do the same thing rather quickly too. Those little ideas that bounce around your brain hundreds of times a day may be big, or they may be small. They may be positive, or they may be negative. They may build you up or tear you down. They may help you achieve your biggest dreams—greatness—or they may hold you back and keep you living life on the sidelines.

Greatness demands that you learn to order your thoughts and make them work for you.

TAKING CHARGE OF YOUR THOUGHTS

At this point, you may be thinking, *That's great, Lewis, but how do I make my thoughts work for me?* Here are a few things I've learned over the years as I've interviewed experts on this topic.

For starters, you've got to establish a sort of "thought bouncer" that stands at the doorway to your mind and lets the good thoughts in while keeping the bad thoughts out. I heard this term from author and motivational speaker Mel Robbins, who said, "I am constantly training my mind to work for me."

How does she do this? By accessing the power of something called the reticular activating system (RAS). Here's how Mel explained it:

> **Greatness demands that you learn to order your thoughts and make them work for you.**

> Imagine a hairnet on your brain, only it's electric, meaning it's alive. The RAS has one job, and the job is to block out 99 percent of what's going on and let in 1 percent of what we need to know at this moment in history. Your RAS has a monster job. It's like a bouncer at a bar that says, "You're not coming in."[7]

The ways this applies to our thoughts is intriguing. Mel says that there are four things that our RAS lets in: the first three are the sound of our name, any threats to our safety, and when someone is interested in us. But it's the fourth one that can drastically alter how we think (emphasis mine):

This is the billion-dollar thing that everybody needs to know. The bouncer in your brain lets in *whatever you think is important to you.* So when you get intentional about telling your brain what's important to you, your brain's literally like, *come on in!* Here's the downside to this. If you have told yourself that you are a bad person for the last 10 years, guess what your brain thinks is important.[8]

Remember that track I had on repeat for years? *I'm worthless, stupid, and unlovable.* I was training my RAS to let more of those thoughts flood in. I was essentially (even if it was unintentional) shaping my identity to become that person.

Mel explains, "When you get intentional about what you want to think about yourself, it changes in real time what your brain lets in and what it doesn't."[9] Thoughts connect to emotions and actions. Debilitating thoughts lead to negative actions.

Here's how to break that cycle. It's something Mel calls having a "high-five attitude." She challenged me this way:

> Starting tomorrow. After you wake up and make your bed and kind of settle your nervous system, high five yourself after setting your intention. Now you're sending yourself into your morning routine in a totally different way, with a calmed down nervous system and clear intention, this boost of feeling supported and loved and celebrated.[10]

To fully push past the negative thoughts that interrupt the Mindset-in-Motion Cycle, you need to reprogram the bouncer in your brain. Look at yourself in the mirror each morning, give yourself a high five, and make sure you are only letting in positive thoughts that will lead to positive emotions that will translate into positive actions.

In her book *Super Attractor,* Gabby Bernstein describes her "Choose Again Method" as a way to take control of your thoughts. "The first step," she says, "is to notice the negative thoughts that you have on repeat and notice how they make you feel."[11] It takes practice to catch yourself at this early stage, but it will become a habit. Step two is to "forgive yourself for having the thought.

When you forgive yourself for having that thought, what happens is that you no longer identify with it."[12] This separates the negative thought from your identity and allows you to dispassionately view it from a greater distance. The third step, she says, "is the fun part. That's when you can *choose again* where you can reach for the next best feeling thought."[13]

Here's an example that may help lock this in. Suppose you are worried about all the things you don't have, and it's causing you to be really selfish and have a scarcity mindset instead of an abundance mindset. The Choose Again Method helps you flip the script to focus on serving other people. You may not have massive amounts of money or time to give everyone, but you can open a door, volunteer your time and energy, or help someone carry a stroller up a set of stairs. By doing that, you feel more valuable. You feel like you have value because you added value to someone else's moment in their life. The more moments you build like this throughout the day, the more you're going to feel like a million dollars. Here's the secret that starts with a simple thought: you don't need a million dollars to feel like a million dollars.

Emotions

We each understand what it means to feel feelings because we feel them all the time. Feelings by themselves are neither good nor bad. Just as a thermometer simply tells us the temperature, feelings tell us what's going on inside our minds at any given moment. But unlike a temperature reading, our feelings and emotions are often tied to things that happened in our past or could happen in our future.

This has huge implications for what's going on in our present.

As Dan Millman put it on my show, "by focusing on the present moment, the here and now, *that's* our moment of power. It's our moment of reality. Our moment of sanity. We can always handle this moment."[14]

He then shared a powerful story of a workshop he once led at a retreat in Costa Rica. On the retreat, one of the events was to race down a zip line. As he took his group up a spiral staircase that wrapped around a giant tree in the middle of the forest, A woman in the group was noticeably and audibly feeling nervous. He asked her if she'd ever walked up a flight of stairs before. Obviously, the answer was yes. "That's all we're doing right now," he said, and she relaxed. Next, they reached the top of the platform, surrounded by guardrails and clipped into the safety cable that surrounded the tree.

Dan could tell the woman's nerves had kicked in again.

Dan told her, "The only way we can get hurt standing here is to take off our helmets and bang our heads against the tree." She smiled and this brought her back to the present, and her emotions were once again back under control. Finally, they clipped into the zip line and stood at the edge of the platform. The nerves were once again evident on her face. Dan said, "Now you can be scared. At least it's appropriate in the moment."

Then Dan brought the story home: "By focusing on the moment, it simplifies our life. This is the moment of power to focus on, not our cosmic purpose or ultimate purpose or twenty-year goal, but focus on what I need to do now. What is my purpose right now?"[15]

Feelings and emotions can often hijack our thoughts, freeze our actions, and keep us from greatness right now in the moment. That's why it's critical to process them in a way that frees us.

STIFF, STUCK, AND STUNTED

Sometimes we get caught up in what happened in the past or we worry about the future and what might happen. This stops us from enjoying the present or moving confidently into our future.

Dr. Susan David, the author of *Emotional Agility*, defines emotional agility this way:

> It's the ability to be healthy human beings. And what I mean by that is that every day we have tens of thousands of thoughts and emotions. The emotions might be emotions about loneliness, anxiety, and those turn into stories

that we tell ourselves about who we are in the world. And we have these every single day. When we are experiencing stress and ambiguity and complexity, often these thoughts, emotions, and stories become more pervasive and they have a greater level of hold on us.[16]

Physical agility allows us to act and react nimbly. It means we can move quickly and effectively, pivoting to face new opportunities or avoid danger. As an athlete, my physical agility is something I worked on constantly to make sure it was an asset. It turns out that emotional agility—working to keep our emotions and feelings healthy—is just as important, maybe even more so.

When we are emotionally stiff and stunted, it keeps us from greatness. It keeps us locked up in the past, and our feelings spiral out of control. We get caught in a vicious cycle, a whirlpool of negativity and doubt.

Susan described three ways we can process these emotions. The first two are by bottling and brooding. Bottling, as you can probably guess, is when we lock our emotions inside or simply try to push them aside. It can manifest itself as forced positivity or simply ignoring something that's bad and replacing it with something that makes you feel better. In Susan's words, "bottling is when you have a difficult emotional experience and you're pushing it aside with really good intentions; you're trying to get on with your day or your life. But bottling over time is actually associated with lower levels of well-being." Since "you haven't been practicing emotional skills, you are completely at a loss with how to deal with a situation that is fundamentally out of control."[17]

Brooding can be just as bad. It's where we get stuck in our emotions and feel like all we can see is the unfairness and injustice. Brooding keeps us from seeing anything else but our pain and how we feel.

All of this bottling and brooding wreaks havoc on our bodies and nervous systems. It keeps our stress hormones off the charts. Personally, when I feel stress and anxiety building up inside of me, I focus on my breathing. Instead of staying in my pain, bottling it up and brooding over it, I try to connect my body with my breath and breathe through my entire body. This helps me calm myself down, and then I can ask myself, *Is this a feeling or a thought that is supporting me, or is it something connected to my past that I haven't worked on yet?*

Gabby Bernstein told me, "At the point when you notice yourself in that freak-out mode, step aside and say an affirmation, like, 'I'm safe, just breathe.' Or you could say, 'I'm loved. I'm supported.' Because under every trigger is a feeling of not being safe."[18]

Until we learn to create that safe space to examine our feelings and emotions, the sad truth is, we will remain stuck where we are and far away from greatness. The same thoughts like *I'll always be bad at money*; *No one will ever love me*; *My future is out of control*; and *I'll never reach my goals* will stimulate feelings like scarcity, loneliness, fear, and futility.

But it can and will change.

FEEL AND MOVE FORWARD

Feelings, like pain, often serve an important purpose. They let us know when something is wrong. I like the way Dan Millman put it:

> There's a saying that fear is a wonderful servant but a terrible master. And it can serve us. If our fear is physical, if we could be injured or killed doing something, fear may be a wise counselor saying, "Wait a minute, step away from this. You're not ready yet," or prepare better or take precautions. But if the fear is subjective, if we're afraid of looking foolish or being embarrassed or ashamed or awkward, just do it anyway. So those are the two kinds of approaches. When do you know when to listen to fear? When do you cut through it?[19]

Great questions. And you must answer them for yourself if you hope to unlock the Greatness Mindset.

Fear (or any emotion, for that matter) is really just a filter to help us clearly see what matters. In the case of fear, if it's because of a physical danger, then you need to evaluate where you are, what your next steps should be, and how to keep yourself safe. But in many cases, our emotions have nothing to do with a physical life-or-death situation. Rather, they are a mental block that keeps us from greatness.

First, our feelings can indicate a problem to address. Like a check engine light on your car's dashboard, when an emotion pops up, it means there is something you need to look into. It's time to pop the hood, so to speak, and look a little deeper. When you are fearful, you need to ask yourself why. *What is it that I'm afraid of?* Is it, as Dan Millman says, "the god of opinion"[20] and worrying about what other people think? Even identifying that can help you push past the emotion and think more rationally.

Author and lecturer Nir Eyal offers this interesting perspective:

> We are sold this unrealistic and unhealthy fixation and obsession with happiness. And most people don't understand that we are not evolved to be constantly happy. You want a species to be perpetually perturbed. You want us to always strive to always want more, to always be discontented so that we fix things.[21]

Feelings of discomfort are important. They push us to find and fix what's broken.

Nir says the way to do that is to start "reimagining the internal trigger. Reimagining the purpose of discomfort. When we feel bored, lonesome, uncertain, anxious, fatigued, fearful, we have to start by understanding that these uncomfortable sensations are a gift. A gift to help us use that discomfort as rocket fuel toward traction, rather than trying to escape it with distraction, what most people do when they feel lonesome, bored, indecisive, fearful, whatever it might be. They look for escape."[22]

Psychologist Dr. Susan David adds, "Our emotions are data, not directives."[23] This means we have to learn how they fit in the Mindset-in-Motion Cycle, making sure the data we receive is properly interpreted and leads to the types of thoughts and actions that drive us toward our greatness goal.

The second thing our feelings can do is indicate an opportunity to explore. When we experience feelings that are more positive, like excitement, wonder, hope, and joy, we are energized and driven onward. It's like there's something just around the corner that we must discover.

The important thing to remember—whether they're good or bad, positive or negative—is that feelings aren't final. And this is critical to remember when we think about building our new greatness identity. You may want to make a quick decision based on your intuition and your gut. But a momentary feeling doesn't paint the whole picture. For example, I feel angry right now, so I'm going to break up with you. Or I fell in love with you within 24 hours, so I'm going to ask you to marry me. Or I feel excited about this business, and I just want to launch it without researching and testing the market.

Feel those feelings, but pause before committing to action. Get curious and start asking questions about the feeling. Feel the butterflies of a new relationship? What does that mean? Feel a sense of excitement about a new business venture? What does that mean? Dive deep into these questions before moving forward.

> **It takes more than good emotions to lead to transformation and greatness.**

Professional dancer and frequent *Dancing with the Stars* champion Derek Hough told me that "emotions are there to give you messages."[24] He said he thinks of it like someone knocking on the door. You can either ignore the knocking and barricade the door, which only makes these emotions pile up until one day they come spilling in, or you can invite them in one by one, examine them, and deal with them one at a time.

Feelings come and go. The bad ones won't last forever, but you have to deal with them. The good ones won't sustain you, but it takes more than good emotions to lead to transformation and greatness.

Dr. Susan David said that once we get past bottling and brooding, there's a necessary third step she calls "gentle acceptance," critical to developing emotional agility. Susan defines gentle acceptance as "being compassionate and kind to ourselves, not invalidating ourselves or telling ourselves that we shouldn't feel what we feel. Having our own back actually allows us literally to explore, to take risks, to be vulnerable, to give love, to put your hand up for a business opportunity, because you know that if something goes wrong, that you will be forgiving and kind to yourself."[25]

And that's a good feeling.

Behavior

Now we consider the final part of the Mindset-in-Motion Cycle—our behaviors. Thoughts and feelings are predominantly in your head, where few people around you fully know what is going on in your mind. But everyone around you can see your behavior.

You can allow feelings to push you to act in a way that is contrary to who you want to be. Or you can act in a way that is aligned with who you are becoming. This is how you shape your identity.

As Nir Eyal explains it, "Behavior change is identity change."

Let's unpack that a bit. He continues, "Our perception of who we are—our identity or self-image—has a dramatic effect on our future actions. Self-image is a cognitive shortcut that helps our brains make otherwise difficult choices in advance, thereby streamlining the decision-making process."[26]

This means that when we decide who we want to become—our definition of greatness, our Meaningful Mission—then that becomes our identity. And when our identity is clear, then our behaviors are easier to establish.

Say you want to run a half marathon. Assuming you have the basic health and physical abilities to start training, what do you need to believe about yourself to get started?

Go back to identity. There is a big difference between *wanting* to someday run a race and actually *being* a runner. The wannabe runner doesn't have a plan for training. Whether they run or not today depends on how they are feeling. But if the runner has already decided, *I am a runner,* they then do what runners do—run. They don't have to think about it. They don't have to feel like it. They *do* it.

It expands outward from there. When it comes to indulging in a pint of pity ice cream when they feel bad, they don't ask if they should. They ask if this gets them closer to their goal of running the race. The answer is no, because that's not what runners do. The ice cream may still be tempting, but because their *identity* has been decided (*I am a runner who is training for a race*) then their actions become easier to decide and manage.

Obviously, this is an oversimplification, and I'm not downplaying your thoughts and emotions, but the principle is solid. I like this example from Nir:

> In the same way, telling yourself that you are indistractable can empower you to overcome distraction. You'll empower yourself yet further by saying this not just to yourself, but to others as well. For example, when they ask why you do "strange" things like meticulously plan your time, refuse to respond to every notification immediately, and so on, you can explain that you are indistractable and that these acts are typical for an indistractable person in the same way that, say, prayer and fasting are to a religious one.[27]

Who do you want to be?

- An entrepreneur? What do entrepreneurs believe about themselves?

- A better friend? How do good friends behave?

- A more involved citizen? How do involved citizens act?

- A better partner? What does that look like?

- Small changes in how you describe yourself can lead to big changes in your actions.

ACTIONS SPEAK

The stories we tell ourselves about who we are and who we are becoming are immensely powerful. What story are you telling yourself? Does that story align with your identity?

Gabby Bernstein told me, "When I'm just being me, I have nothing to prove. I'm just in the truth of who I am. I think that one of the secrets to confidence is to accept that your authentic truth is the coolest part of who you are. That's when we can start to lay down the pretenses of who we think we should be and just be real in the moment."[28]

We touched on this earlier, but it bears revisiting. Who are you becoming? Can you define it? If you haven't already, I challenge you to take a moment to write it out in a sentence and then make it your mantra going forward. Then make sure you align everything you do with that identity.

Seth Godin shared:

What if we could simply say, I am choosing to be passionate about what I do. And my purpose is whatever I am doing. I'm going to be here for it. I'm present for it. I'm merely going to do it. So, you know, I decided a long time ago that my passion and my purpose was a certain kind of teaching to a certain kind of audience in a certain kind of way. But I could have been a totally different thing. And I would have been passionate about that too.[29]

Once you are clear on who you are becoming and lean in to it with passion, then you need to look at the behaviors that *reinforce* that identity and the behaviors that *restrict* that identity. Restrictive behaviors keep you stuck in your past. They circle back to that fear of failure, judgment, or even success. They keep you trapped in a cycle of inaction or wrong actions that don't lead to greatness. They lead to stagnation.

Reinforcing behaviors are aligning behaviors. They are the actions that match up with your identity. Even if you don't *feel* any different or *think* you are different, your actions indicate otherwise.

They are lacing up your shoes and running, even when you are tired, because your identity says *I am a runner*. It's putting in the extra hours at night to start your side business because your identity says *I am an entrepreneur*. It's agreeing to go to couples therapy, even if it's going to uncover some painful feelings, because your identity says *I am committed to building this relationship for the long haul*. It's taking ownership of your past mistakes and moving forward because your identity says *I am in control of my future*.

ENGAGING GREATNESS

The journey to greatness is a lifelong one, but you can put what you just read into motion in your own life right now with these activities designed to help you harness your thoughts, feelings, and behaviors.

Exercise: The Abundance Matrix

One of the best things we can do for ourselves when faced with big feelings is to keep the feeling going and fight the urge to suppress it. You've heard me say this over and over again: Don't suppress! Bring things into the light!

Next time you have a strong feeling (even a good one, like excitement), a negative thought (or an intrusive one), or have a major decision to make, try out this exercise.

STEP 1—STOP AND BREATHE

Before exploring anything, let's get your nervous system in check.

- Sit up straight.
- Place your feet flat on the ground.
- Breathe deeply for at least one full minute. You want to feel as calm and relaxed as possible.
- Take note of any strong, persistent thoughts or feelings. Don't try to stop them. Observe them as

though you are an outsider. Allow these thoughts and feelings to wash over you, much like a wave in the ocean.

- Picture yourself standing just a bit off the shore, inside the ocean. Your feet may shift under their weight, but you are strong enough to withstand their force. The waves come, but these emotions and thoughts won't knock you over.

When you feel calm, move to Step 2.

STEP 2—REFLECT

We don't want to pull the trigger on something based on in-the-moment excitement, even when it's positive. Explore your feelings and thoughts by asking yourself the following questions. Consider yourself a curious outsider.

- I am feeling _____. What do I think it's trying to show me?
- What brought on this feeling?
- What response to this feeling would make me proud?
- Is the action I want to take right now going to support or hurt my Meaningful Mission?
- Is this feeling serving me or is it holding me back?
- Is this feeling coming from a place of healing or from a place of hurt?
- How can I handle this feeling so that I don't feel consumed or crippled by it?
- What are the positive outcomes from this feeling?
- What is this feeling trying to show me? What can I learn from it?
- How would my highest self react to this feeling?
- Does this feeling support my abundance identity?

As you answer these questions, keep your breathing measured. This isn't a time to shut down, react, or become defensive. Remember, you are a curious outsider.

The goal is to evaluate your feelings *without* using them as a definitive call to action or identity marker. You can move away from the place of identifying yourself based on something fleeting. If you want to fully heal, you can't rely on feelings as a foundation for your identity. You can only use the information they provide.

STEP 3—FILL OUT THE ABUNDANCE MATRIX

Now that you have taken time to reflect, take your current thoughts and feelings and plug them into an Abundance Matrix.

Sketch this matrix on your whiteboard, notebook, journal, or wherever you have lots of room to write your observations. This matrix should serve you every time you want to process your innermost activity.

	Abundance Identity	Neutral Identity
Crucial to My Mission		
Not Crucial to My Mission		

FIRST QUADRANT (UPPER LEFT)

If you believe your thoughts and feelings are part of an abundance identity and will lead to actions crucial to your Meaningful Mission, place them here.

Some examples might include excitement over a positive meeting with someone who can help you in your Meaningful Mission or pride over a new skill you're honing. Perhaps you're feeling overwhelmed by positive things happening quickly, and you don't know what to pursue first.

Ask yourself if it is crucial to your mission and the abundance that comes with it. If the answer is yes, place it in this box.

SECOND QUADRANT (UPPER RIGHT)

If your thoughts and feelings are crucial to the mission but are part of a more neutral identity, meaning these particular thoughts and feelings are important but not particularly abundance-building, place them here.

An example of this type of feeling is justified anger. If part of your Meaningful Mission is to help marginalized people, you need to stay angry at the system without internalizing that anger. Another example of a neutral thought that is also crucial to our mission would be "I need to learn Spanish, but I am struggling to find the time."

Prior to the earlier step of Reflection, either one of those examples could have been harmful and led to a scarcity mindset. But because you took the time to explore them, they have been neutralized.

THIRD QUADRANT (LOWER LEFT)

If your thought or feeling is not crucial to your Meaningful Mission, but leads to an abundance mindset, place it here.

Perhaps when you began the earlier reflection portion of this exercise, you were feeling incredibly burned out and wanted to quit. But now, after calming your nervous system, you've recognized that the solution is to lose an activity or two so that you have more room for joy. This realization isn't crucial to your mission, but you are building an abundance identity by creating more space in your life for relaxation and happiness.

FOURTH QUADRANT (LOWER RIGHT)

If your thoughts and feelings are both not crucial to your Meaningful Mission and do not build an abundance identity, place them here. These are likely going to be your negative feelings, time-wasters, and debris from old thought patterns.

With your matrix filled out, you can now make decisions and take action.

Your highest priorities for your Meaningful Mission will be in the upper left, upper right, and lower left quadrants.

The lower right quadrant is very informative. This quadrant reveals the personal work ahead of you to maintain your abundance identity. *These are the things you need to consciously rid yourself of.* In this quadrant are the thoughts and feelings that, if not harnessed, will lead to a neutral and limiting identity. You weren't created for neutrality. You were created for greatness.

No matter who we are, or what we accomplish, negative thoughts and feelings will slip in. We need to quickly bounce them right out of the Abundance Club. Kick out the thoughts that are causing problems so that you can heal from the feelings that lead to negative thinking.

REFLECT ON YOUR JOURNEY

As you strive to become better at processing your thoughts and feelings, consider a nightly reflection practice. Before you end your day, ask yourself a few questions.

- *How did I do with my thoughts today?*
  - *When thoughts came to me that weren't abundant-mindset, abundant-identity, loving-identity, or powerful-identity-minded, did I let them stay inside my mental home? Or did I bounce them out?*
  - *Did I guard my mental home with limitless thinking, or did I limit my thinking and allow scarcity to confine me?*

As you ask and answer these questions, don't judge yourself harshly or be unkind to yourself. You are simply collecting data. Think of yourself as your own coach. A coach collects data on his athlete or client, provides feedback, and helps them improve. The silent conversations we have with ourselves impact everything from our mission to our health to our relationships. Let's make our silent conversations intentionally positive and affirming by coaching ourselves to greatness.

Let's make our silent conversations intentionally positive and affirming by coaching ourselves to greatness.

The Game Plan for Greatness

It may be helpful to contrast The Greatness Mindset with its natural opposite, The Powerless Mindset.

The Powerless Mindset is where we naturally tend to operate unless we intentionally choose a new direction. As you can see in the image, when we are influenced by The Powerless Mindset, we feel trapped and isolated, as if we have few options and little hope for a better life tomorrow.

But there is a path to embracing the liberation of The Greatness Mindset. This requires moving through what I call The Transformation Zone. It begins with gaining Awareness of the problem and realizing the need to do something about it. Then we make the Decision to take action. Finally, we need to make a Commitment to persist in spite of challenges we meet. That is where the Game Plan for Greatness comes into play.

The key to understanding The Transformation Zone is knowing that the process is never easy. As you can see in the image, the way can get narrow when moving from one mindset to the other. But once you make that journey, and continue to live it out, an abundance of options open to you. Then there is no lid on your potential. Soon all the world will see the greatness within you!

I encourage you to power through the challenge of The Transformation Zone and the progression from The Powerless Mindset to The Greatness Mindset.

Greatness Mindset

Driven by a Meaningful Mission
Turns Fears into Confidence
Overcomes Self-Doubt
Heals Past Pains
Creates a Healthy Identity
Takes Action with a Game Plan

COMMITMENT

The Transformation Zone → **DECISION**

AWARENESS

Lacks a Meaningful Mission
Controlled by Fear
Crippled by Self-Doubt
Conceals Past Pains
Defined by Opinions of Others
Drifts Toward Complacency

Powerless Mindset

At this stage of the journey, I hope you're feeling pretty good about having identified your Meaningful Mission and honed your Greatness Mindset. But now what? How do you turn that into activity that moves you toward significance and purpose each and every day?

I'm glad you asked, because it is time to get practical.

The Game Plan for Greatness is the proven process I have used to pursue my own Meaningful Mission, and the steps have been validated by the many experts I have engaged over the years. You can use these steps to guide you as you pursue your Meaningful Mission. I suggest you tackle them in order from 1 to 7 so you don't miss any critical steps, because each step builds on the one before.

Each person will move through these steps at a different pace—and that is totally fine. But the key it to actually move through them.

Starting right now.

**For additional resources to help
you live out the Greatness Mindset,
visit TheGreatnessMindset.com/resources.**

Chapter 12

ASK COURAGEOUS QUESTIONS

"What has been holding you back from starting your Meaningful Mission?"

"The fear of doing it wrong."

Rachel Rodgers, a Black business owner, self-made millionaire, and author of *We Should All Be Millionaires,* founded Hello Seven to help people from marginalized communities learn how to develop seven-figure businesses. Driven by the belief that "when more marginalized people have money, it [the world] will become more equitable," she built a membership community affectionately called "The Club."[1] Hello Seven was a multimillion-dollar success, but she felt her role in the business wasn't completely fulfilling her mission.

At the time, Rachel had been sitting on her idea for a nonprofit for nearly a year. She confessed to me, "I know how to build a business and make money. But building a nonprofit and doing it right and not screwing it up, I'm really nervous about that."[2]

So I did what I have done with a lot of people and began asking her questions.

First, I asked her what she could accomplish with an extra $10 million. As it turned out, she knew exactly what to do with it. She shared with me her dream of starting that nonprofit to serve Black mothers.

The nonprofit would provide three main services: doulas to help new mothers before and after delivery, night nurses to allow mothers time to rest, and subsidized childcare to help give mothers the opportunity to build their careers. We calculated that with an extra $10 million, she could provide these services to more than 1,000 mothers.

Next, I asked Rachel, "How would that make you feel?"

"I'd be on top of the world."

So I pressed her with a follow-up question to help her get practical: "Let's say you're going to help one mom. And this mom is watching and listening right now. What places would she need to contact? Who could she e-mail? What does she need to say?"

I had a reason for pushing Rachel. She had achieved so much. She had already mastered money-making and team building, but her fear of failure ran the risk of holding her stagnant. I wanted to know what would get her excited, what passion fueled her heart, and what first actions she might take to see her next dream come to fruition.

"I think what I imagine doing in this nonprofit is really just having a simple application that people fill out."[3]

"Okay," I said, "Give me the URL to an application page that you can say right now that you'll make available in the next couple of days."

"HelloSeven.org."

But we did not stop there. Since she already had a couple of people in mind to help execute her ideas, I gave her a second challenge: "Call those two people with nonprofit experience right after this interview."

Lastly, there was the business of making that $10 million a reality: "Who are three people you can call today and ask for a $100,000 check?" The amount did not really matter. It was about keeping her momentum. I kept pushing: "Have a form up in a day, call these two friends who have the nonprofit experience, and contact three to five potential donors in the next twenty-four hours. Text me tonight."

Rachel took all of the action I suggested and, as a result, she quickly raised $200,000, enabling her to immediately serve 40 mothers.

And that is how the Hello Seven foundation was born. By asking the courageous questions, defining goals and deadlines, and taking imperfect action, Rachel Rodgers took her mission to the next level.

All too often, people focus on the *how*, when they should be thinking about *what* they really want to do and *why*. When you do that, the how will follow.

FIVE COURAGEOUS QUESTIONS

When you get your Mindset in Motion, things feel good. Really good. The right thoughts, emotions, and behaviors open up possibilities. The future begins to look bright.

For a moment.

And then the questions kick in. *What if . . . What about . . . How will I . . . What will they . . . ?*

The wrong negative questions can quickly derail you on your greatness journey. The right questions, however, are the ones that require real courage to ask and answer.

> **The right questions are the ones that require real courage to ask and answer.**

Questions unlock potential *in* you and *through* you. That's why the Game Plan for Greatness begins by asking courageous questions.

There are five questions that you need to answer to get to the heart of your personal greatness and push yourself to action. I have used variations of these questions time and again to coach people to push past fear and doubt. You can walk through these in any order you like, but each one will help you create a bias for action and inspire you to move forward as quickly as possible.

1. **The Purity Question: If you were to be 100 percent authentic to who you are, what would you do differently?**

    We all tend to present curated versions of ourselves. Maybe it's because we aren't sure if people will like the "real" version of us. But maybe it's also a crutch that keeps us from becoming great. This question empowers you to own who you are and strive for who and what you want to accomplish and become.

2. **The Priority Question: If you absolutely had to double your goal in the next 30 days, what would be your first three moves?**

    I like asking this question because it forces people to not simply think outside the box, but to shatter it. I even dare to ask it this way: If you knew you or someone you love would die if you didn't double your goal and achieve it in 30 days, what would be your first three moves? This may seem like an extreme exercise, but if you lived with a sense of urgency and you absolutely had to accomplish this thing you wanted but have allowed fear to hold you back, what would you focus your attention on to make it happen? You can change the time frame to fit your situation, but

> **Questions unlock potential *in* you and *through* you.**

206

the important thing is that it feels pretty impossible to do at first glance.

Too often we don't live with urgency. We accept the status quo and settle for less than we could achieve just because it feels comfortable, and no one will die if we don't achieve it. But in fact, every day we live is one less day we have to achieve those goals and live out those dreams. If you are not okay with letting those dreams go unfulfilled, then maybe you need to raise the stakes mentally to think and act differently.

3. **The Possibility Question: What would be possible for you if you could** _____ **?**
    (insert your goal/dream/mission here)

    This question allows you to insert the details of your situation into it and try on another potential reality. For example, what would be possible for you if you could leave your current job and devote all your effort to growing your side hustle? What would be possible for you if you could dramatically improve your family relationships? You get the idea. This question lets you explore how your path might feel if you achieved certain goals and positions you to ask the next question.

4. **The Passion Question: What would it feel like if you could** _____ **?**
    (insert your goal/dream/mission here)

    We are all emotional beings at the core, so this question frees you to explore how it might feel to experience success in the areas that are important to you. What would it feel like for you if you could leave your current job and devote all your effort to growing your side hustle? What would it feel like if you could dramatically improve your family relationships?

5. **The Prosperity Question: If you won the lottery today, what would you do next?**

This question allows you to remove the constraint of money and frees you to think about what you really want to do without shutting yourself down because you don't think you have the resources to achieve it. You wouldn't have made it this far in the Greatness journey if you weren't looking to grow, but oftentimes we shortchange our growth goals by making them too small. What if you thought big—really big—where money was not an issue? Go ahead, dare to dream.

These questions aren't exhaustive. In fact, I encourage you to think of others to help you push forward and make courageous decisions. Perhaps the most important thing you can do is to develop the habit of asking yourself courageous questions like these on a regular basis.

FROM STAGNANT TO SPECTACULAR

I have known entrepreneur and real estate mogul Grant Cardone for over 12 years now, and he has been a guest on *The School of Greatness* several times. He has an incredible résumé, including authoring eight books, producing 13 business programs, acting as CEO of seven privately held companies, and appearing as a regular on huge networks like Fox News and CNBC.

> **Develop the habit of asking yourself courageous questions.**

I can say with confidence that he acts with courage and isn't afraid to ask challenging questions. He has shared some incredible stories with me, not the least of which is the story of how he lost everything and built it back tenfold. After a trauma like that, most people would play it conservative and pad their emergency funds. But not Grant.

Grant literally has the bulk of his money invested. Let that sink in. He has no savings. That might sound outrageous, but Grant knows what he can do with his investments and his cash flow. Clearly, he is an *all-in* kind of guy.

Yet, a few years ago, on an episode of my show, I challenged him for thinking too small. At the time, his real estate business was bringing in millions, but I knew that was not representative of Grant's talents. I didn't want him to settle, so I brought on the questions.

"What would it take to get to a billion?" I could see my question surprised him.

"It's just not possible," he replied.

Well, you can probably guess how I feel about the impossible. "What do you mean it's not possible?"

"I just don't have enough contacts anymore."

"Okay," I said, "what would it take? Who do you need to meet? Who has the money that you need to borrow?"

I wouldn't let up because I recognized the limiting thoughts. As I asked him the questions, I saw those limiting thoughts begin to dissipate and his mind open to bigger possibilities right then and there.

Later, he told me that the interview changed everything for him. He kept asking himself, *How can I grow faster?* He realized his business was only reaching a limited, wealthier population. It dawned on him that most of his own family members would not have the money to benefit from his business. So he got started making a fund available to a variety of income levels, where people could invest incrementally in larger real estate deals.

Two years after that interview, Grant returned to my show as the proud CEO of a $900 million business. Can you guess what I did next?

"What would it take to get to $3 billion?" I asked.

"That's just not possible," he said. "We don't have enough time."

"What if it was possible? What would need to happen?"

After some thought, he started listing steps.

"Okay," I challenged him, "what are you waiting for?"

And Grant made the impossible happen—again. When I last saw him, his business had blown past $4 billion. And this time I didn't even need to ask. He told me his team is planning to top $40 billion within the next three years.

From impossible to $40 billion. That's the power of courageous questions. And they work for everyone.

NO LONGER A DOCTOR

When we first spoke on my show, Ali Abdaal was a part-time doctor in the U.K. But his real passion had become that of being an online creator. At the time of our interview, his YouTube channel had over two million subscribers, where he focused on how people can lead happier, healthier, and more productive lives under the five pillars of health, wealth, love, happiness, and impact.

But not long after our conversation, he made the decision to move completely away from being a practicing doctor. His move to becoming an *ex*-doctor happened partly as a result of being asked two questions that are variations of the ones we discussed earlier:

What would it look like if in the next 30 days, you completely stopped being of service, hands-on, one-on-one as a doctor?

How would it make you feel right after you made that decision to stop practicing medicine?

Ali had essentially become a dabbler in the medical field. There were a host of reasons it made sense for him to stay. He had invested more than eight years of his life and many thousands of dollars into medical school. Being a doctor was prestigious. It's how he built his brand on YouTube. Now I was asking him what it would be like to walk away.

His response was fair and honest. "I think it would feel very scary, mostly for selfish reasons. I think even now I can still convince myself that this YouTube channel, the business, everything else, is all just a side gig."[4]

But with this side gig, he was pulling in multiple six figures, much more than he was making as a part-time doctor. And by his own admission, he was helping more people as a YouTuber than as a doctor:

> The fear of not having that old-world prestige of medicine, which is not quite the new-world prestige of being a YouTuber, those fears are all selfish things. I wouldn't be concerned at all about not having an impact on people, because I know that I am. I'm not special as a doctor. Anyone in my position can do the same thing.[5]

I could see that these questions were giving him lots to think about, so I threw a big concept out there: "In a sense, you're doing a disservice by giving ten percent of your time and energy to helping people in an area you're not passionate about as opposed to the people that really want to do it full-time."

"That's an interesting way of looking at it," he replied. "I hadn't quite thought of that."

I was very respectful of Ali, of course. I wasn't pushing him just to push. I just knew that sometimes you need someone to push you to make a courageous bet on yourself.

Being a doctor is a noble calling—*if* it is your calling. What I was hearing Ali say was that it was more about fear and sunk cost. He felt he was having the most impact on the world with the work he was doing as an online creator. Over the course of the rest of the show, we talked about several more questions related to his goals:

- If you had 10 million subscribers, would you continue practicing medicine?

- What if you reallocated those 10 part-time hours a month working as a doctor to develop the next program or focus on things to help your digital business expand?

- What type of impact do you think you would make if you solely focused on your digital platform?

After our conversation, Ali asked himself even more courageous questions. In fact, he shared a YouTube video a few weeks later where he walked through his decision to leave medicine for good.[6]

Before he could make that decision, though, the questions he asked himself helped him get to the core of his mindset. Some of the questions he had to nail down were:

- What if this YouTube thing doesn't work?

- Why not stay a doctor as a safe backup option?

- What if people on the Internet hate me for leaving medicine?

- Will my channel and business die if I don't continue to call myself a doctor?

- Why don't I do everything part-time?

- Is the only reason I'm practicing medicine because I want to continue to hold on to this badge of being a doctor to set myself apart from most of the other YouTubers?

These are all fair and valid questions. But in the end, he realized that he couldn't let fear hold himself back from his greatness goals.

You don't have to be a doctor or YouTuber to use courageous questions to make a change. Questions like these will help you get from where you are to where you want to be. When you discover what you really want to do, and eliminate the things that hold you back, you free up energy to go toward your passion. I've seen it time and again—when people go all in on the things they love, magical things start to happen. Maybe it doesn't happen right away, but greatness will eventually follow.

COURAGE IN A QUESTION

Once you learn to challenge yourself and to silence the easy, lazy questions that pop up when you are trying to do something great, you discover that questions aren't the enemy. Rather, the right kind of questions—courageous questions—can quickly unlock something in you that's been buried deep within.

Courageous questions are focused and direct. They expand possibility thinking while helping you eliminate distractions. They help you zoom out and see things you may have overlooked. They offer you fresh perspective and new horizons to explore.

When people go all in on the things they love, magical things start to happen.

Best of all, they create in you a bias toward action. Dreams of what could be someday suddenly become possible today. And this often leads to an avalanche of momentum.

What questions do you need to ask yourself to get started? Don't wait.

The world needs your greatness.

ENGAGING GREATNESS

Exercise: Ask Yourself Courageous Questions

Let yourself dream of what could be. It's time to dare to ask yourself and answer some courageous questions. Invest some time into thinking about each of the Courageous Questions and jot your answers down in your notebook or in your notes app. As you do, you'll probably stumble across other questions that scare you. Don't ignore them. Jot them down as well and take the time to answer them authentically. Don't let preconceived barriers, fears, or negative thoughts hold you back.

Have the courage to dream about what could be possible for you in pursuit of your Meaningful Mission:

The Purity Question: If you were to be 100 percent authentic to who you are, what would you do differently?

_____

The Priority Question: If you absolutely had to double your goal in the next 30 days, what would be your first three moves?

1.

2.

3.

The Possibility Question: What would be possible for you if you could _____
(insert the next step in your Meaningful Mission here)

_____ **?**

The Passion Question: What would it feel like if you could *(achieve your goal/dream/mission)*?

_____

The Prosperity Question: If you won the lottery today, what would you do next?

_____

List any other questions that surfaced. If you need to, schedule time on your calendar to do nothing but think about each of them and answer them courageously.

_____

_____

_____

_____

_____

_____

_____

_____

_____

_____

Chapter 13

GIVE YOURSELF PERMISSION

My friend Roger is a talented financial advisor who struggled to break through beyond the commission threshold of $80,000 a year. He had a dream of building a robust business, but just always seemed to end up getting stuck. He tried practicing on his own, with a partner, and on his own again—nothing he did seemed to make any difference. He kept asking me, "How can I work with clients who have more money to invest?" I sent him some referrals, but they weren't the big hitters Roger was looking for.

But then an opportunity arose when a friend messaged me about a 19-year-old man who had just won hundreds of millions in the lottery. As it turned out, one of the lottery winner's latest tweets was about an episode of *The School of Greatness*. I reached out to the young man to congratulate him and warn him of the challenges that would be coming his way. After all, about 70 percent of people who win the lottery go broke, become drug addicts, or die by suicide within a few years.[1] I offered support and made myself available if he ever wanted to jump on a call for guidance.

He ended up taking me up on my offer. Over the course of several phone calls, I learned his story. Although he seemed to have a solid support team around him, I offered to connect him with my friend Roger and encouraged him to talk with other advisors as well, to make sure he had a fiduciary in place to guide his financial decisions. He agreed.

I went back to my friend Roger and asked if he would be willing to have some calls with the young man, not selling anything, just being of help and seeing where it might go. He agreed, and before long, we had several calls take place among the three of us. The young man also connected with several other professionals before letting me know he really liked Roger and wanted to work with him.

Imagine my excitement when I called Roger to tell him the great news: "Dude, this is going to change your life right now because this client's going to make you a multimillionaire." And then he said something that totally surprised me.

"I'm not ready for it."

"What?!" I gasped. "What do you mean, not ready for it?"

"I've never had a client that big. I don't know how to manage that much."

I practiced a little tough love. "I'm telling you right now, I don't think I can be your friend if you're unwilling to take this risk and take this on. You've been asking me for years for bigger clients. Now here I am helping you and you're telling me you can't work with him because you don't feel ready?"

Then I let him have it. "I can't send you business if you're not willing to go for it."

Why was I so annoyed with Roger? Because life was offering him an opportunity, one he had dreamed of and desired for so long, but he was unwilling to give himself permission to take it.

He was living in self-doubt and fear, and this was keeping him from fulfilling his Meaningful Mission.

Roger agreed to think about the opportunity. After a few days, he decided he would take on the new client but with the help of another firm—one that would take 50 percent of the commission to partner with him—that had the experience and resources for managing larger clients. This partnership gave Roger the comfort he needed at the start, but it only took a couple of years for him to grow the confidence to manage not only the young man's financial matters but also several other bigger clients on his own. He then made 100 percent commissions instead of only 50 percent.

In a way, by bringing in a partner, Roger gave himself partial permission to succeed. He didn't fully trust his abilities, so he felt he needed someone else's credibility to take on bigger clients. It was a step in the right direction because he was willing to act. When he eventually realized the people he leaned on did not know much more than he did, he had the confidence to give himself full permission to go all in. (And yes, we're still friends.)

A PRISON OF YOUR OWN MAKING

It seems everyone is looking for permission these days. Whether it's from a therapist, coach, friend, client, or family member, we're all looking for someone to give us permission.

As I think about our desire for permission, it seems there are three forms you might need to give yourself on your way to accomplishing your Meaningful Mission: to become your ideal, to eliminate, and to show emotion. If you withhold permission from yourself in any of these areas, you set yourself up for problems.

1. Give yourself permission to become your ideal.

A result of not permitting yourself to become your ideal is jealousy and insecurity. I love how Gabby Bernstein expressed this idea: "Jealousy is a form of witnessing undeveloped parts of ourselves."[2] You might look at someone else and resent the qualities they reflect, but nothing is preventing you from developing those same qualities. You just have to give yourself the affirmation and permit yourself to become your desired self.

As Seth Godin put it, so many of us are waiting to be picked:

> Our cultural instinct is to wait to get picked. To seek out the permission, authority and safety that comes from a publisher or talk show host or even a blogger saying, "I pick you."

Once you reject that impulse and realize that no one is going to select you—that Prince Charming has chosen another house—then you can actually get to work.

Once you understand that there are problems just waiting to be solved, once you realize that you have all the tools and all the permission you need, then the opportunities to contribute abound.

Most of all, when you buckle down, confront the lizard, and ship your best work, you're becoming the artist that you are capable of becoming.

No one is going to pick you. Pick yourself.[3]

Our hesitancy to give ourselves permission to succeed is born out of fear, not from our Greatness Mindset in pursuit of our Meaningful Mission.

2. Give yourself permission to say no.

When it comes to eliminating things from our all-too-cluttered lives, a lot of people struggle with saying no because they feel they need affirmation from others. It goes back to the identity issue. Are you letting other people's expectations define who you are?

If you don't practice giving yourself permission to eliminate tasks, you risk getting distracted with all the tasks others ask of you. Successful people say no to some things so that they can give a fully committed yes to other things.

My friend Rory Vaden is an expert on productivity. As the author of *Procrastinate on Purpose*, Rory has developed an entire system for thinking about using time effectively. As he puts it, "When you have diluted focus, you get diluted results."[4] In other words, the more you try to accomplish to gain others' approval, the less you actually get done as time gets away from you. You have to give yourself permission to eliminate things from your to-do list and from your life so you can focus on what is most important to *you*.

3. Give yourself permission to show emotions.

Can you think of a time when you did not permit yourself to feel the full range of emotions you needed to in order to heal your past? Maybe you didn't give yourself permission to feel that pain because it was uncomfortable or awkward.

Gabby also speaks about this form of permission. She refers to a category of emotions she calls "impermissible feelings."[5] She says everyone has endured some level of trauma, and within that trauma are often shameful feelings of inadequacy, rage, or self-hate.

People may avoid these feelings because it is the only way they know to protect themselves from past wounds, but those coping mechanisms are often unsustainable. They can lead to all sorts of coping behaviors or addictions that only hold you back from greatness. You have to allow for entry into those memories and permit yourself to feel emotions if you want to come out on the other side of them.

> **Successful people say no to some things so that they can give a fully committed yes to other things.**

YOU'RE IN CHARGE OF YOU

Stephen R. Covey is perhaps most famous for his book *The 7 Habits of Highly Effective People*. Habit One is "be proactive."[6] But I like the children's version that his son created even better for its simplicity: *You're in charge of you.*[7] That simple expression, if internalized, can help you avoid the permission pitfalls we talked about earlier. It means you have the power to navigate your way to greatness. You don't need someone else to give you permission to do that.

The guiding principle in Covey's teachings is the difference between reactive and proactive attitudes. Reactive people let their environment shape their story with language like "I can't" or "I have to." They overlook how much influence they have on their circumstances. Meanwhile, proactive people recognize they are powerless over certain aspects of their lives, but they focus on what they can do in response to what comes their way. Proactive people take responsibility for their story, and it all begins with giving yourself permission to take charge of your greatness journey.

Taking charge means living intentionally. For example, Rory Vaden teaches that the key to multiplying time is "giving yourself the emotional permission to spend time on things today that create more time tomorrow."[8] He calls this formula the "significance calculation." It means you take command of your time and use it to do things that will save time in the long run.

> **Successful people know to have internal flexibility and grace for themselves instead of beating themselves up over not being enough.**

Scheduling is not just about calendars and to-do lists. Beneath our objectives are feelings of guilt, fear, anxiety, ambition, and drive. Even if we aren't aware of it, these emotions factor heavily into all our decisions.

I seldom struggle to tackle a new challenge. I'm usually raring to dive in right away. Where I tend to struggle is giving myself permission to slow down or adjust my approach to achieve a goal. For example, I felt a lot of guilt about this book when I didn't get it done as quickly as I had planned. It took me a while to realize it was okay to push the deadline, that the priority was making it great and not necessarily making sure it fit my self-imposed initial timeline.

When I took the pressure off myself, I became more excited about it.

I think when people put pressure on accomplishing their goals the "perfect" way, they often don't achieve those goals. Successful people know to have internal flexibility and grace for themselves instead of beating themselves up over not being enough.

Above all, you need to know to give yourself permission to step up, step back, step aside, or take whatever steps you need to in your journey to greatness.

ENGAGING GREATNESS

Exercise 1: A Matter of Life or Death

It can be difficult to see beyond our own self-doubt. It might even feel like we are being responsible or realistic when we discourage ourselves from big dreams. This exercise will provide a new point of view by helping you to imagine the stakes are higher. Record your responses in your journal, notes app, or other place of your choosing.

STEP 1—CHOOSE A GOAL

Think of a goal you have been wanting to accomplish but have not made progress toward and write it down.

STEP 2—RAISE THE STAKES

Imagine you live in a society where only the most productive people are allowed to live. Each year, a tribunal assesses each person's accomplishments and decides their fate. Now it's your turn to be assessed. They look at your list of achievements but see you have failed to accomplish the main goal you set for yourself (the goal from Step 1 above). Someone steps forward to take you away. You break out in a cold sweat, fall to your knees, and beg them for another chance. After a few tense moments, they agree to give you one final year to make it happen, but you have to submit a convincing plan for how you will do it.

STEP 3—MAKE IT HAPPEN

Take 30 minutes now to write a plan to submit to the tribunal. Take it seriously. Your plan has to be realistic and convincing. Whatever it takes, you must make a plan.

THE REAL PRICE

This scenario is unlikely to ever happen in real life, but the exercise puts your time in perspective. You might not lose your life by failing at your mission, but you may likely lose the *kind* of life you desire. Those are the real stakes, not as pressing, but I would argue as equally high.

Exercise 2: Grant Yourself Permission

STEP 1—CHOOSE A GOAL

Either use the goal from Exercise 1 or write down a new goal.

STEP 2—IDENTIFY CRITICISMS

When you think about chasing after the goal you named in Step 1, what doubts arise? Using the outline below, write the self-criticism preventing you from working toward your goal.

I am not _____ enough.

I am too _____ .

It is too irresponsible/selfish to go after this goal because

_____

_____

In my past, I experienced _____

(identify a trauma)

and that makes me afraid that _____

_____ .

I should not feel _____ .

STEP 3—CRAFT PERMISSION STATEMENTS

Using the outline below, create permission statements to combat the critiques you identified in Step 2.

I give myself permission to control _____

_____ .

I give myself permission to forgive myself for _____

_____ .

I give myself permission to _____

(list action needed to pursue your goal)

imperfectly.

I give myself permission to feel _____

_____ .

FALL FORWARD

We all have self-doubts. We all lack certain skills or traits. I wasn't a professional runner, but I ran a marathon. I wasn't trained to be an interviewer, but I created a podcast. I almost failed out of English class in high school, but I'm now a *New York Times* best-selling author. You have to be able to say, "That's true, I'm not those things, but I give myself permission to do this anyway." Maybe you fall, but you fall forward. And that is still progress in my book.

> **Sometimes we have to give ourselves permission *not* to take action and focus elsewhere.**

OWN YOUR MISSION

Just like we have to give ourselves permission to take imperfect action, sometimes we have to give ourselves permission *not* to take action and focus elsewhere. Remember your mission, and permit nothing to get in the way of that mission. Be your own source of affirmation because no one has the mission's best interest in mind more than you do.

Chapter 14

ACCEPT THE CHALLENGE

When I joined Toastmasters to overcome my fear of public speaking, I received a workbook with 10 types of speeches to deliver. Each speech was to last from five to seven minutes and forced me to practice a different technique.

My first speech style was called "The Ice Breaker." The goal was to tell an interesting story for five straight minutes about myself. I was absolutely terrified. There was no way I could make it through five minutes without blanking or stumbling over my words. Yet I went *all in* and did it.

For other speeches, I practiced using props and presentations and focused on shaping intonation and style. However, the scariest part of the meetings for me was an exercise called Table Topics. In this activity, the leaders assigned us a random topic and we had to stand up and deliver a one-minute speech on that topic—without any preparation. Talk about torture! But I did it because I knew I had to overcome this fear of public speaking and be able to verbally communicate my message in order to become successful in business.

I set a goal to give my first free speech outside of Toastmasters within three months and my first paid speech within nine months.

That felt like an impossible goal, but I was *all in*. Sometimes I even attended five Toastmasters meetings in a single week.

The mentor who advised me to attend Toastmasters also encouraged me to take a baptism-by-fire approach and choose the group that scared me the most. And when I came across a group of professional speakers, I thought, *Crap, this is where I need to be.*

So, there I was, a 24-year-old bum in a room of suited-up professionals in their 40s and 50s. For a year I obsessed over fully participating in this group, fine-tuning my presentation skills. Then it happened. I got my first free speech through LinkedIn. It was a 30-minute local-community gig. Nothing big. But it was the next step toward my goal. Then I got a speaking engagement that paid $500. Before I knew it, I was delivering speeches for over $5,000 per speech!

Even when I started making that kind of money, it never got easy. I had to consistently advocate for myself by messaging people and forming connections. I did this all while giving myself permission to be the professional speaker I had previously thought was impossible and going all in on the challenge, putting myself in a constant state of discomfort.

I believe a lot of our social fears, like the fear of public speaking, come down to community boundaries. We see a community we are not part of and think, *I don't fit. I don't belong. I'm not accepted here yet. This is a community, and they speak a language that I don't know.*

This sense of being an outsider was especially strong when I decided to learn how to salsa dance. I confess, I really struggled with the intricate footwork. And believe me, I was acutely aware that I was a tall white man who just could not dance. A lot of the women I asked to dance turned me down again and again. For three to four times a week for about three and a half months, I faced the fear, though, and it helped me to learn to love myself, even when everyone else was rejecting me. I learned how to stay committed to the goal, and I eventually became fluent in the dance.

A lot of people care so much about being accepted by the people in a community that they don't try new things long enough.

Even at this stage of my life, I still force myself to dwell in the uncomfortable. The only reason I feel able to risk judgment is because I have learned to be okay with myself. I have already given myself all the approval I need, so I can risk meeting rejection and endure friction to learn something new.

For example, I am currently learning Spanish. It is uncomfortable because it is part of a community to which I don't fully belong yet. Yet while I realize my accent might not be correct, I speak Spanish with my girlfriend and her friends and family and stay committed to the challenge.

Meeting new challenges is always going to be uncomfortable. But if you can make the uncomfortable fun, then you are already halfway to overcoming your fear.

When I began practicing public speaking, I found a more experienced speaker who was probably 15 years older than me to coach me one-on-one. He reminded me that the people I spoke in front of at Toastmasters all wanted to see me succeed. He also gave me the support I needed to forgive myself, not just for making mistakes, but also for my procrastination.

If you can make the uncomfortable fun, then you are already halfway to overcoming your fear.

We put a lot of shame and guilt on ourselves when we are not where we think we should be in life. All this does is delay progress more. It does not matter if you wanted to do something years ago. You are doing it now. Rather than beating yourself up over hesitation in the past, it is much more useful to tell yourself, *I haven't had the tools, courage, or confidence to take this on before, but now I am all in.*

Giving myself permission to have fun was also how I learned to deal with the discomfort of networking. I used to always be the youngest person in the room in the business world and didn't have experience. I didn't have a job. I didn't have anything. But

I found a way to get into the rooms, to get to dinner tables, and to meet with the influential people because I was playful. I would joke. I would ask funny questions. I was curious, and I made it a game. I would create fun challenges for myself: There's a speaker on stage. How can I meet him afterward? What can I do to get in the same room with him?

This approach led to a pretty cool door opening for me, simply because I went *all in* and had fun doing it. Back when I was virtually unknown, I saw that Tim Ferriss was doing a conference where he planned to share all his secrets on how he wrote and launched a *New York Times* bestseller. My only problem was that tickets were $10,000.

I thought, *Well, I want to go to this event, but I can't afford to pay for a ticket, so what would it take for me to get in free? Actually, what would it take to be able to give a speech at this event? Actually, what would it take for me to have Tim Ferriss interview me onstage?* It was the ultimate impossibility, but I dared to ask, **In order to be possible, what would need to happen?**

Give yourself permission to tackle the thing you want, then accept the challenge and go *all in*.

I had met Tim Ferriss's assistant Charlie at a conference a couple of times and discovered he was helping launch this event. I learned the event was going to be all about book marketing and book launches. I said to Charlie, "You've got all these big names, all these fancy people. But no one is talking about virtual book tours." I hadn't even written a book yet, but I had some good relationships within that space, and I had a perfect case study for the topic. In a webinar with Gary Vaynerchuk, I promoted his book and sold 800 copies.

I broke down the framework for Charlie, showed him the case study, and laid out how beneficial the topic would be for those in attendance. I ended by asking Charlie to run the idea by Tim and told him I was happy to do it for free.

To my shock, I soon found myself pitching my idea on a three-way call with Charlie and Tim, and they said, "Okay, let's do it." *Holy— Are you kidding me?!*

So I sat on stage in front of an audience that had spent 10 grand to be there, and, yes, Tim Ferriss interviewed *me*, a nobody who dared to ask, *What would it take to be possible?* That is how you pursue greatness. Give yourself permission to tackle the thing you want, then accept the challenge and go *all in*.

THE VALUE OF A CHALLENGE

As anyone who follows me will know, I love challenges. I get energized by tackling a 30-, 60-, or 90-day challenge and overcoming it. If you want to become fearless, you have to check off the items on your Fear List by going all in on your fears until the fear disappears. I start by taking one fear at a time and creating challenges to help face it.

When I was younger, I was afraid to talk to girls. I asked myself, *How can I overcome that through a challenge?* I committed to talking to a girl every day for the entire summer. By the end of the summer, I had all the confidence in the world. At age 17, I was confidently talking with 40-year-old women, simply as a challenge to see if I could.

I discovered that with every fear I overcame, I believed myself more capable going into the next fear challenge. Overcoming my fear of speaking to women gave me the boost I needed to face my fear of rejection in salsa dancing. The details of the fear didn't matter as much as the fact that I was proving to myself that I could overcome my fears. Because I could learn to talk to women and salsa dance, that confidence transferred into believing I could be a public speaker, make successful webinars, and write a best-selling book.

Once you can identify your core fear, you can go all in on that fear. Nothing is more empowering than facing the fear that controls you. The key to overcoming fears is self-assessment and action. Create 30-, 60-, 90-day challenges for one of your fears, take action, and watch your confidence skyrocket.

The enemy of this *all-in* mentality is procrastination. Once again, my friend and author Rory Vaden nails it. He shared with me that psychologists say the cause of procrastination is self-criticism.[1] That inner voice starts saying, *I'm not good enough. I'm not smart enough.* Then you find yourself thinking, *Why bother?* But when you realize that you are enough, right now, you can take the steps to also become more.

> **Nothing is more empowering than facing the fear that controls you.**

I do not believe anyone truly wants to fail at their mission, yet most people say they feel stuck in their lives. Why do so many of us remain in a place we do not want to be? Katy Milkman, economist and professor at the Wharton School of the University of Pennsylvania, sheds an interesting light on this subject. She says people have "internal barriers," the greatest of which is a *status quo* bias. This is the idea that people tend to keep to the path they know. Any change from that path feels risky, so risky that they are willing to endure a lesser path if it is familiar.[2]

That's why, in my experience, living a "good" life is one of the hardest spots to get out of. A person who is 80 percent happy with their good life often feels too comfortable to risk trying for a *great* life.

ACT NOW!

Rory Vaden gave me a helpful way of thinking about challenges. He says everyone wants to avoid pain, even small pain like boredom. We procrastinate to avoid unpleasantness. But the reality is that we do not always get to choose if we will experience discomfort. Sometimes our only choice is whether we go through that discomfort *now* or *later* when the pain has accumulated. With this mentality, the time spent in discomfort does not seem like a sacrifice; it's a short-term down payment on a richer future.

Rory calls this practice "taking the stairs" and states, "The shortest, most guaranteed path to the easy life is to do the hardest parts of things as soon as possible."[3] Notice that this practice is not about working harder. You are actually taking the easier path this way. What it does take is discipline.

This idea rolls right into a concept discussed by Greg McKeown, best-selling author of *Essentialism* and *Effortless*. Greg teaches the disciplined pursuit of less, which is the antidote to priority dilution. Focus on a few important things at the price of all the frivolous things. You will be tempted to lose focus, but that is when you remember that you do the hard thing now to avoid harder things later. Take massive action to create momentum and see change happen.

If you are one of the many people who struggle with one or many forms of procrastination, don't beat yourself up. You are just operating from a place of survival. It is normal to want to conserve energy. But according to Rory, procrastination only conserves physical energy, when most of the energy involved in decision-making is emotional energy. Working out is a perfect example of this. Often the emotional energy spent getting to the gym is greater than the physical energy of the workout. This is because we procrastinate and exaggerate how painful the task will be.

Now, I am going to be completely honest with you here. Going *all in* is going to be painful at times. Sometimes you will have to make some scary leaps with both feet into the unknown.

Katy Milkman and her fellow researchers have discovered a phenomenon called the "fresh start effect"[4] that could help people tackle challenges. Motivation to change tends to fluctuate depending on a number of factors (such as business, energy, optimism). With so many factors, these fluctuations can seem random, but Katy's team found a pattern. As it turned out, people respond to certain moments that mark a fresh start. These moments can be a new year, a birthday, the first day of a new job, or even a Monday.

We tend to step back in these moments and reflect on our lives, goals, or priorities.

Depending on the fresh start, it can even feel like an identity change. For example, when a child turns 18, they might feel a shift because they are legally an adult. This shift means new rules, responsibilities, and privileges, and such a switch can inspire other changes. Knowing and harnessing the power of this "fresh start effect" can empower you to intentionally build fresh starts into your life more often and make the most of them.

Another way to set yourself up for facing challenges is to use *New York Times* best-selling author Shawn Achor's 20 Second Rule. With this rule, you strategically control the amount of energy required for any activity. You base this amount of energy on whether it is something you want to do more or less often.[5] For example, if you want to decrease how often you watch Netflix, you might delete the app from your computer and prevent Netflix logging you in automatically. This way if you want to watch Netflix, you have to search the Web for the website and type in your credentials to access it. Just this little extra effort might deter you from mindlessly gravitating to Netflix.

On the other hand, if you want to cook at home more often, you might invest in prewashed and cut vegetables or other prepped ingredients to decrease the amount of energy required. In other words, you have more control than you might think about tackling a challenge to push past fears or make significant life changes.

I recently challenged myself to run in the L.A. Marathon. Although I spent a long time building up my endurance, I never actually ran a full test run. In fact, the week before the marathon, I ran about 13 miles (half the full marathon distance), and that just about wrecked me. I was so sore that I didn't run at all the entire week before the marathon. It would have been easy to believe I was underqualified and underprepared and just quit. But luckily I had already given myself permission to take imperfect action and committed to tackling the challenge.

The thing that got me through was telling myself, *The marathon is not going to be hard. It's going to be fun*. I made a plan to keep it fun.

I decided I would walk up every hill and past every water station. When the day came, I didn't deviate from that plan. Every time there was a little hill, I walked. Every time there was a place to get water, I walked while I drank and then I started jogging again.

For 26 miles I smiled at people with their signs and exchanged high fives. I laughed and marveled at what my body was doing. I did not try to race at all. I just enjoyed the process. And you know what? I finished the marathon in less time than I thought I would—and I felt great.

When I first took on the challenge of running a marathon, I thought I would never do it again. Then, just a few days after I finished that first local one, I registered for the New York City Marathon.

Challenges help us work toward who we want to become. I box with a guy at the gym whose weight has fluctuated a lot in huge swings over 10 years. When I asked his trainer why this happens, he said it is because if the guy doesn't have another challenge as soon as he finishes the current one, he goes back to his former lifestyle. Right now he's training for a big boxing match, so he's eating right and has lost a lot of weight. But already he's afraid he will gain the weight back after the match unless he takes on something else.

Challenges help us work toward who we want to become.

Challenge yourself. Challenges give you consistency in your life, encourage self-reflection, and build confidence. Always have two challenges, one under your feet and one queued up to tackle next.

To get you started, here are some activities to help you identify and accept your first challenges.

ENGAGING GREATNESS

Exercise 1: Pursue the Impossible

I created an unbelievable opportunity for myself when I secured a public platform in front of Tim Ferriss. Initially, that dream seemed outrageous. I made it happen by asking myself, *What would it take to make it possible*? I gave myself permission to dream really big, and I went after it, not knowing if it would pan out. This exercise will help you make a plan to go *all in* on your impossible dream.

STEP 1—IDENTIFY YOUR CHALLENGE

Reread your Meaningful Mission Manifesto (page 161). Think of the ultimate accomplishment that would launch you on the path to achieving this Mission. Do not hold back. Think of the most impossible thing and write it down.

STEP 2—ASK WHAT IT WOULD TAKE

My dream to be interviewed by Tim Ferriss required developing a relationship with Ferriss's assistant. Therefore my first step was to capitalize on my encounters with his assistant and reach out to him. What would it take for your impossible dream to be possible? What are the steps you can take right now to get closer to that impossible dream? Be as specific as you can.

1. _____

2. _____

3. _____

4. _____

STEP 3—MAKE THE UNCOMFORTABLE FUN

Some, if not all, of the steps you just listed might make you squirm a bit. Joining Toastmasters was just about my worst nightmare, but it was the step I needed to take to meet my seemingly impossible goal of a free speech invitation. To make the process bearable, turn the uncomfortable tasks into games. You can try to beat your personal best or give yourself a time limit to complete a mini task. You can even make a game of looking for humor in uncomfortable or taxing situations. Choose one of the steps you listed in Step 2 and come up with a plan to make it fun.

LEAN INTO THE CURIOSITY

You may have struggled with that last step. Maybe you were thinking, *Lewis, you don't understand. I'm terrified of this challenge.* If that is you, try leaning into what makes you curious about that thing that scares you. I would see people giving these incredible speeches in movies and think, *Man, that looks exciting.* And I would wonder what it felt like to be onstage and influence people in a positive way. Just like I did when those Table Topics got to be too much, remember that curiosity.

Exercise 2: 30-Day Game Plan

Our brains are wired to think in story form. If we think of our lives as stories, each new "chapter" is a fresh start. A birthday is a fresh start. A graduation is a fresh start. Even a new morning can be a fresh start. This exercise capitalizes on Katy Milkman's fresh start concept by building benchmarks into your schedule.

STEP 1—CHOOSE A GOAL

Choose a goal you want to accomplish in the next month and write it down.

STEP 2—DECONSTRUCT YOUR GOAL

Break down your goal into smaller goals. For example, if your big goal is to land a job more in line with your passion, your smaller goals might be to update your résumé, set up job alerts on popular sites, review possible jobs, and fill out applications. List the small goals you need to accomplish to reach your larger goal.

1. _____

2. _____

3. _____

4. _____

5. _____

6. _____

7. _____

8. _____

9. _____

10. _____

STEP 3—ORGANIZE THE SMALL GOALS

Of the small goals you listed, which ones can you complete in three days?

1. _____

2. _____

3. _____

4. _____

5. _____

Of the small goals you listed, which ones can you complete in one week?

1. _____

2. _____

3. _____

4. _____

5. _____

Of the small goals you listed, which ones can you complete in 30 days?

1. _____

2. _____

3. _____

4. _____

5. _____

STEP 4—INDICATE FRESH STARTS

Create a visual on your calendar to indicate the 3-day, 1-week, and 30-day checkpoints. You might use stickers, a symbol, or a meaningful word. Try to choose something celebratory. These are your fresh starts!

Refer back to this exercise and check off the small goals at their various checkpoints as you complete them.

STEP 5—REFLECT

At 3 days, 1 week, and 30 days, come back to this space and reflect on the window of time that just passed and write down your thoughts. Use these prompts to generate thoughts if you get stuck.

- How do you feel about what you accomplished?
- Is there anything you would change about the way you spent your time?
- Did you spend too much time on any one task?
- What did you find challenging about working with this deadline?
- Is there anything you want to do differently for the next deadline?

PROTECT YOUR TIME

It is usually best to give yourself tight deadlines because it forces you to accept imperfection. For example, if you want to write a blog post, you might give yourself three days to complete a rough draft, revise it, and post it. The goal is to take action and see what results you can create. You not only protect your time this way; you also create momentum and build your confidence each time you meet a goal and reach a fresh start.

Chapter 15

DEFINE YOUR GREATNESS GOALS

Ever since I was a kid, the Summer Olympics have always been inspiring to me. A few months after I got my cast off and had taken up residence on my sister's couch, I watched the 2008 Beijing Olympics all day and all night for two weeks. Michael Phelps was the breakout athlete, swimming his way to medal after medal. All across different sports, Olympic records were broken. And there I was on the couch, wondering if I would ever play sports again.

Then late one night, around 3 A.M. actually, I saw highlights for a sport called team handball. I was blown away. I'd never even heard of it before, but now I was intrigued and googled everything I could about team handball.

It's big in Europe, but few people play it in the U.S. It's a mix between basketball and lacrosse/soccer but using hands. Super fast-paced, the games are only 60 minutes long. Players shoot a mini soccer ball into a little soccer goal, trying to score more goals than the opposing team. It's similar to basketball, but players can take three steps before they have to dribble, pass, or shoot.

I became convinced this was the sport I was meant to play. I had just retired from playing football, but didn't feel like I was done as an athlete. So I started googling more and e-mailing and calling people trying to find out about a U.S.A. handball team. I wanted to make the Olympics. I wanted to play with Team U.S.A.

I discovered there were no teams in Ohio where I was. There wasn't even any professional league in the U.S.A. There were only club teams around the country, and the top one was in New York City. I found out no one gets paid to play; it's just for fun. But that didn't matter. I needed to figure out a way to make enough money to move to N.Y.C. to learn handball, play with this team, and make the U.S.A. national team to go to the Olympics.

As I'm sure you can guess by now, I went *all in*. I became obsessed. I repeatedly contacted the U.S.A. organization, but it was nearly impossible to get anyone on the phone or to respond to an e-mail. By early 2010, two years later, I had finally made enough money from my online marketing business to go to N.Y.C. I still couldn't reach anyone, but I found the New York City Handball Club website. They didn't have an e-mail or a phone number, just a physical address where they practiced.

When I went to New York for a month for a couple of speeches, I decided I would show up at this handball thing and see what I could do. When I got there, I discovered I was the only native-born American. There were about 30 players from every country in Europe speaking a wide variety of languages.

I tried the direct approach: "Hey, my name's Lewis from Ohio. I'm here to learn the sport of handball, make the U.S.A. national team, and go to the Olympics."

They laughed at me.

They started talking to each other in every other language but English. Finally someone translated.

"Who are you? You're outrageous," they said. "We just won the national championships last weekend, and this is our last practice of the year. We're just doing it for fun. We're going to play soccer today. We're not even playing handball. Come back in three months when we start to practice again."

I told them I'd be back then, and I started building a relationship with some of the guys. One of them taught me a little bit to prepare for the next time. I ended up staying in New York, and a few months later, started practicing with them.

I just dove in, took on the challenge, and did the uncomfortable thing by moving to a new city to learn a new sport I'd never played before with people who were from different backgrounds and cultural experiences. I spoke a different language than they did, but I was determined.

I started practicing consistently. I had a skill set from football, but I wasn't a skilled handball player. My surgery from a couple of years prior meant I still wasn't at full capacity, but I did have athleticism and was willing to do the hard work.

Nine months after I first showed up in N.Y.C., I made the U.S.A. national team and went to the Pan-American Championships in Buenos Aires, Argentina, for my first international competition. I was one step closer to making this dream come true. And I became even more obsessed.

For nine years, I played with the U.S. national team, representing my country while building my business. I played in Spain for a little while for a professional team. I went *all in* playing the sport and went on to play all over the world—Israel, London, Luxembourg, Brazil, Uruguay, Mexico, Canada, and all over the United States.

The challenge for making the Olympics was that the only way to do so was qualifying at one tournament every four years called the Pan-American Games. It's not like most Olympic sports where most countries get to send a team or representative. Only one team from North and South America advances to the Olympics. All the countries of North and South America come together for a half-world Olympics to determine who will be that team. So you have to win the Pan-American Games to advance to the Olympics in handball.

Brazil, Argentina, and Chile have professional leagues. They've been playing for years and are really talented, but we were all amateurs in the U.S.A. It didn't matter how good I could get personally;

the team would have to win. It wasn't impossible, but it was *so* hard. However, if we were the host country of the Olympics, we would have had an automatic qualification. We tried for 2016 and 2020, but the U.S.A. didn't get it then. But the Summer Games are happening in Los Angeles in 2028, so anything is possible! Either way, one of the proudest moments of my life was playing on the U.S.A. team.

WHEN YOU DON'T SET GOALS

If you don't set goals, you will have a hard time achieving greatness because you won't have a clear picture of where you're going. When you can't see your direction clearly, you can't map out a strategy to get there. In football, for example, the goal is to win the game by getting the ball into the end zone to score enough points needed to win. Without this set goal to strive for and a strategy for getting there, players would just wander aimlessly around the field. It would be no fun to watch and no fun to play.

> **If you don't set goals, you will have a hard time achieving greatness.**

As an athlete, I've always thought that it's super smart to have goals. I've always had goals for every season of life and every season of my sports career. Goals give me the focus and determination to get to where I want to go.

After I stopped playing professional sports and was trying to figure out the rest of my life, I realized I didn't have the same confidence off the field. A lot of my confidence had come from clearly knowing my goal and the strategy. Without a goal to achieve, I lost my focus and wandered aimlessly. Maybe you can relate.

You need to have set goals and the focus and drive to achieve them. If you aren't getting the outcome you want, you probably need to evaluate your goals and focus. Without clear goals, it's easy to get distracted by other people's values and goals. As usual, Rory Vaden gets right to the point:

> You just have to decide what you are willing to do and wanting to go after and realize that until you accomplish those things, everything else is a distraction. But focus is power. When you have diluted focus, you get diluted results. Most people are getting diluted results in their life, not because they're not smart enough or not good enough, but because they're distracted. They are allowing their time, attention, and resources to fragment. What you need is focused energy to create a breakthrough.[1]

Diluted focus equals diluted results. That is especially true as you become more successful and have even more potential distractions and competing priorities. The results you want simply won't happen without being laser-focused on your Meaningful Mission.

That is what leads a lot of people to feel like they're not making progress. Dr. Benjamin Hardy, co-author of *The Gap and the Gain* with Dan Sullivan, described it to me this way:

> One thing that leads people to burn out is spending a lot of energy and not actually feeling like they're making progress. I have a lot of energy when I achieve a goal. Achieving goals gives you energy. It's exciting. If you actually give yourself deadlines, create a result, and watch yourself succeed, you just build confidence because you measured yourself against where you were before you achieved the goal, rather than against your ideal. When you see yourself move forward, that gives you excitement. Success creates confidence and motivation. Watching yourself get some wins, both big and small, gives you energy.[2]

Perhaps nowhere is focused strategy more crucial than in the military. Former Navy SEAL Jason Redman told me when they identify a target, they break it down so they know exactly where they are going and what they are dealing with. They also establish a very defined course for how to get there. Every single action is broken out and every contingency planned for so there is no deviation from the plan. In other words, they set goals and support those goals with a plan of action.

Jason told me the process is a lot like when he decided as a kid that he wanted to become a Navy SEAL. Because he knew his goal, he could create a clear strategy for getting there. He'd need to enlist in the navy, get accepted, get a SEAL contract, pass the SEAL screening test, and pass a specific academic test with a high enough score to be a SEAL.[3]

> **If you aren't getting the outcome you want, you probably need to evaluate your goals and focus.**

When he broke the journey down in this way, it was easier to see the path he needed to take to achieve his goal. It works the same way for you. You can easily take it one step at a time, chipping away at the steps needed to get you where you want to be.

Instead of wandering aimlessly through life, I challenge you to take time to define your goals and map out the strategy to achieve your Meaningful Mission.

MY PERSONAL GOAL-SETTING

I've been a big fan of the technique of scheduling your goals after learning the value of it from my football coach. At the start of the season, he would establish our goals as a team by asking us questions.

"What is our goal, team?" he would ask. "What do we want to accomplish? Do we want to win the championship? Do we want to go to the playoffs? How many games do we want to win? Do we want to become better in each position?"

We would then come up with our shared goals.

I remember the first day of practice, I had a schedule in my locker. So did every person in the locker room. I was 15 years old, and it was the first time I ever saw a calendar like this for every minute with intentional actions to help us reach the goal for that day. There was a five-minute break for water. There was a 10-minute stretching break. There was an offense section and a defense section. It measured the goals and easily showed how far away or how close we were to achieving them. Every single thing had been accounted for and planned out.

That's when I said, "Oh, I need to do this in my life." And I've never gone back.

Even after professional sports ended, I didn't know why anyone would do anything but schedule what they want and actually follow through on it. I've used that system for the last 20 years. Everything I want to do has to be in the calendar. If I want to talk to my mom, it's in the calendar. If I want to work out, it's in the calendar. If I'm writing a book, it's in the calendar. It's not just a matter of writing out a list of things I want to do for the day and then getting distracted. I live each minute by my schedule. It brings clarity to my life and assures I'm taking the steps necessary to achieve my goals.

I've found that one of the most impactful things for my schedule is how I start the day, so I developed a personal morning routine that allows me to be consistently as productive as possible.

To start my day off right, I need to . . .

- **Sleep**—Getting a full seven to eight hours of proper, restful sleep affects the energy and focus for my entire day.

- **Make my bed**—Accomplishing something little first thing when I wake up builds my momentum for success.

- **Move my body**—Exercising helps to cleanse my mind and body.

- **Get a cold shower**—Showering in cold water makes me feel awake and alive and is great for the immune system.

- **Meditate**—Releasing tension and expressing gratitude clears my mind.

A good morning routine sets the tone for the rest of the day. You're able to control and set your schedule better. The more positive the first hour, the more powerful the rest of the day. When you come from a place of creation and not reaction, you *make* your life, as opposed to letting it make you in a negative way.

> **When you come from a place of creation and not reaction, you *make* your life, as opposed to letting it make you in a negative way.**

As I have interviewed so many of the elite performers who are accomplishing their goals and pursuing their dreams, I have found that they invest in their goals and dreams by setting up a schedule and structure, and building accountability and coaching into it all.

Katy Milkman says research shows you'll get more results if you follow through with a schedule rather than merely expecting it to happen. Planning for success is key. What are you going to do and when? Milkman says it's also important to have "if/then" plans. Based on research by Peter Gollwitzer, who studied how people plan their goals, the people with the most follow-through had specific structure and details in place. They were more likely to accomplish their goals by using expressions such as "If X happens, then I will do Y"—*if* it is Monday at 5 P.M., *then* I will go to the gym to train for my marathon. Instead of merely focusing on the outcomes and knowing what needs to be done, you will be more likely to act if you write down specific times and details.

Tracking your goals and seeing the difference your actions make is also key for implementing behavioral change. Milkman explained that if you can't easily see where you are in the journey, it becomes difficult to reward yourself, which is important for your feeling of fulfillment as you move forward.[4]

THE GREATNESS PERFORMANCE SYSTEM

Your goals can change in different seasons of life. When I was playing sports, my goal was to be in the best shape of my life. When I was living on my sister's couch, my goal became to get off the couch and live a productive life.

It begins with your Meaningful Mission statement for this season of life. Remember, not having a clear Meaningful Mission is the Enemy of Greatness. It's important to write it down and keep it visible as you seek to set goals to help you achieve it. Without it, you have no guide, no direction, and nothing to work toward. Who are you? What do you want to create? When you get control of your vision, mission, and goals, you can start living an intentional life throughout the day and ask yourself, *What am I doing today to support my mission?*

In my own life, I've found a lot of power in the simplicity of the number three. So I developed a way of thinking about performance using a focus on three—three players, three goals, and three questions. I used this system to create the **Greatness Performance System (GPS)**, or the game plan for my life.

I like to think of the different domains of life as Three Players I have on the field at any given time: Business, Relationships, and Wellness. It might be tempting to focus on only one or two of these areas, but all three are important for lasting success. If you're not healthy, your relationships and business will eventually suffer. If your relationships aren't vibrant, they'll distract you and cause your business to fall short. But when your wellness and relationships thrive, your business or career dreams are positioned to soar. I prioritize these Three Players in this way to best position myself to achieve greatness.

Each Player has three areas that require attention to be well balanced and healthy:

- **Business:** Income, Influence, Impact
- **Relationships:** Personal, Professional, Community
- **Wellness:** Physical, Mindset, Emotional Health

I go through a process to develop my top goals for each area, so I end up with nine total. But that is still too many to really give them focused attention. I then choose the single most important goal for each Player—Business, Relationships, or Wellness—and focus only on achieving those three goals at any one time.

When it comes to goals, a lot of people feel stuck, and I think it's because they don't set goals correctly, including because they have too many goals. They end up with a to-do list that feels overwhelming. As counterintuitive as it may seem, you need to focus on fewer goals to achieve more. That doesn't mean you ignore certain areas of your life entirely; they simply do not have your most intense focus in terms of the goals you are pursuing.

Once I have chosen my top three goals for each of the Three Players, I ask myself three crucial questions:

- **What do I want?** Answering this question forces me to bring clarity to my vision and the end I have in mind.

- **Why do I want it?** Answering this question helps me reconnect to my Meaningful Mission and tap into my deep motivation to take action. Sometimes when I ask this question, I struggle to answer, which may indicate I need to ask myself another question: *Do I really want it?*

- **What's the next step?** Answering this question causes me to focus on the next practical move I need to take to move forward. I don't have to know what I will do six months from now, only what I need to do next to keep moving forward.

Using this Power of Three approach in the Greatness Performance System (GPS) gives me focus in all areas of my life and specific goals to achieve greatness. I can then schedule the next steps and break down my goals into daily, actionable steps. I love seeing members of our Greatness Coaching community apply this proven GPS process to their own lives and businesses to experience breakthrough success. And I look forward to hearing your stories of what you achieve by applying it to your own Greatness journey.

ENGAGING GREATNESS

People who are part of our Greatness Coaching program get to use an entire Greatness Playbook we created to guide people through the goal-setting and achievement process to get results. Here is a piece of the broader goal-setting activity to help you get started in setting and scheduling goals using the paradigms I just shared:

Exercise: Your GPS Goal-Setting Plan

For each of the Three Players and nine areas, answer each of the following questions:

1. What do I want my life to look like in this area in three years?

    This dream question gets the imagination moving. Answer the question as if there were nothing standing in the way of making it happen. This isn't formal. No need to be neat and grammatically correct—just let your imagination flow.

2. Why do I want it?

    Sometimes we think we want something until we dare to drill down into why we want it. When we do, we may discover we don't really want it at all. Other times, we can tap into deeper motivation to fuel us as we move toward it. You may need to ask this question a couple of times to really get at the core of your motivation.

3. Based on your answers, what is the single most important goal for each of your nine areas?

BUSINESS

Income

Goal: _____

_____

_____

Influence

Goal: _____

_____

_____

Impact

Goal: _____

_____

_____

RELATIONSHIPS

Personal

Goal: _____

_____

_____

Professional

Goal: _____

_____

_____

Community

Goal: _____

_____

_____

WELLNESS

Physical

Goal: _____

_____

_____

Mindset

Goal: _____

_____

_____

Mental Health

Goal: _____

_____

_____

4. Choose only one goal from each Player (Business, Relationships, Wellness). Then answer the following three questions about each goal to position you to take action. Repeat the process as you take the next steps to keep giving yourself the clarity you need to keep moving forward.

1. What do I want?

2. Why do I want it?

3. What is the next step?

Chapter 16

ENLIST SUPPORT

One reason sports were always a big part of my life was that they gave me a sense of community. Having a team to support me equipped me to stand strong in the face of adversity. When challenges came, I had teammates to lift me up even as I lifted them up to achieve our goals.

When I left sports, I missed that support—until I found CrossFit. Then I started going to the gym four or five days a week because I got that feeling of accountability again through being in a group of people going through the same workout together. Not only was a coach guiding and supporting the class, but all my peers encouraged and supported one another to keep moving forward. As a result, CrossFit really helped me stay accountable to my health goals for many years.

No matter if your goal is in the area of Business, Relationships, or Wellness, accountability and support are the magical keys and can make the difference between success and failure.

When I think of accountability, I see, not surprisingly, three levels:

1. Accountability to yourself

2. Accountability to someone else

3. Accountability to a community

Accountability to yourself. The first level is the personal pride and integrity of holding yourself accountable. Most people overlook the value of this level because they undervalue themselves and discount their own voice and personal pride to keep their own commitments. But when you learn to appreciate who you are right now and who you are becoming, you can leverage your personal integrity to value and keep your word. Are you shaping your identity around your individual integrity? In other words, are you a person who says, *I will do this thing*—and then does it? Or are you a person who says one thing and does another, particularly when it's for yourself?

Your word to yourself is everything. When you keep it, you build self-esteem, self-confidence, and self-love. Imagine being able to say to yourself at the end of each day, "I am proud of myself for doing what I said I was going to do." That's the accountability of your personal pride and your integrity at work. That should really be the foundation, but life happens, challenges happen, responsibilities happen. This is where the other two levels come in.

> **When you learn to appreciate who you are right now and who you are becoming, you can leverage your personal integrity to value and keep your word.**

Accountability to someone else. I like to call this person an accountability buddy. It could be a friend, partner, spouse, coach, or another professional of some sort. For example, if you and a friend both want to commit to being more active, maybe you walk together every morning. The point is that you have enlisted their support specifically to hold you accountable for taking the next step to achieving a goal. On those days when you struggle to act based on a sense of personal pride and integrity (and we all have those days), this person can support you and hold you accountable to continue taking action.

While explaining accountability and why it works, Katy Milkman introduced me to the concept called "commitment devices."[1] Commitment devices are consequences or penalties that we place upon ourselves to keep ourselves in line. We're all used to having to comply with limits placed on us by others (think speed limits and the fines that come from exceeding them). But we also seem to respond well to limits and consequences we place upon ourselves. When you give permission to someone to hold you accountable, you have created a commitment device that either implies a penalty of embarrassment or shame by letting someone down or actually delivering some sort of consequence you would prefer to avoid.

When I was at my lowest point—without a job, recovering from an injury, doubting myself completely—both my sister and my brother gave me this incredible gift of accountability. My sister said, "Okay, Lewis, you've been here sleeping on this couch long enough. It's time. You either move out or start paying rent."

Initially, I thought I could just move to my brother's couch, but he told me the same thing. It was only $250 a month, but it forced me to make plans, make money, and make stuff happen in order to pay the rent to them. If I didn't make rent, I would fail, and my siblings would know it. The potential embarrassment and consequences outweighed the discomfort of anything that might come from taking a risk. So I got busy.

Accountability to a community. Community can come from a lot of different places: clubs, memberships, churches, masterminds, support groups—you name it. It can be formal or informal, super structured or more casual, and meeting and interacting frequently or not, depending on the need. The point is acknowledging that we are, at the heart of it, community beings who respond well to positive peer pressure. When we know that others are counting on us, skipping means we're admitting a lack of commitment to the others.

According to productivity expert Thomas Frank, a subgroup within community accountability is accountability to a team, where a group's success *depends* on your performance. It can be your business partners, co-workers, or even family members. Team accountability can be especially intense because you not only have to admit your failure to the group, but your failure is their failure. This is why challenges are so effective when done with a community, especially when tied to team success.[2]

For example, you might engage in a 30-day weight-loss challenge with a team of people who experiences a shared reward for success or suffers some sort of shared consequences for failure. The shared team effect becomes a powerful motivator for everyone to step up and help the team experience a shared win. Harnessing the power of community can give you the edge in achieving your greatness goals.

> **Harnessing the power of community can give you the edge in achieving your greatness goals.**

Here are a few examples of how these levels work. When I played football, I had my own goals, such as scoring a certain number of touchdowns in a season. I would push myself to achieve that goal; that's personal accountability. My coach was also there to hold me accountable every day of practice. If I didn't show up or give 100 percent, there were consequences. I'd have to run a few miles or maybe even ride the bench for a game. I didn't want to let the team down by not delivering my best, so that community support motivated me to keep moving forward.

Another example is my relationship with my girlfriend. My girlfriend is obviously a very important person to give me feedback about whether or not I am staying on course. I first monitor my own feelings and do a self-check to ensure I am being true to who I am and always acting with integrity. Then we have accountability check-ins and share how we are both feeling. I get to see real-time results based on any moment of how I show up with my relationship, with my emotional availability, my intimacy, my connection, and my presence. If that's off for a period of time, there's going to be a disconnect in my relationship.

I also enlist the support of a therapist that I meet with every two weeks to process emotions and reflect and refine where I'm at personally. And finally, I get the advantage of feedback from our friend community as we engage with one another around other people. I try to surround myself with friends who are willing to speak honestly about my life and let me know if they detect any cause for concern.

In every area of life, we can be intentional about setting up and monitoring these three levels of accountability to ensure we take action and do what we say we want to do in pursuit of our Meaningful Mission.

HELP FROM THE PROS

I enlist support from professionals all the time. These professionals can be therapists, coaches, pastors, and mentors. They are experts in the skill for which you want accountability. This type of support can be absolutely critical to your success because they give you an opportunity to learn new skills or just get outside your own head for a valuable perspective. But it may be helpful to think of them more as accountability coaches rather than accountability buddies.

The other thing about professional accountability is that it usually does not come cheap. I hire trainers to help me stay in shape and it works. Because I pay for their services, I know how silly I will look if I skip out on something I have already paid for. But if you cannot afford a professional, I encourage you to seek other options such as community organizations or nonprofits that may be of help.

"Olympic athletes have coaches. Why do we think we can do it without them?" Jen Sincero, best-selling author of *You Are a Bad-Ass* hit me with that great question when I interviewed her.[3] Why would we be surprised that we fail when we try to build a new skill set from nothing? Pride looks obvious when we step back and see it for what it is. Even Tom Brady had an entire team of coaches and experts surrounding him.

So does star tennis player Novak Djokovic, who has been on *The School of Greatness* show twice. I've personally seen his professional team at work as they keep him accountable on things like stretching and recovery and ensuring he gets the ideal sleep after all of his tennis matches. He travels everywhere with a custom trailer that houses a complete recovery system, including a sauna and everything else he needs to stick to his fitness regimen.

> **The more layers of accountability you put in place, the more likely you will stick to your commitment.**

Jen noted that although professionals may not be cheap, they can save you time and money in the long run because they have the expertise to help you progress much more quickly than you would on your own. I have found that I can make progress in some areas on my own, but I just don't know everything, and I especially don't know what I don't know. A professional can help you see what you can't see and learn what you don't even know is available to be learned. That's why I often rely on professional accountability coaches to help me improve my Business, Relationships, and Wellness.

Professional accountability doesn't even have to be with a person. Sometimes when I'm traveling, I'll use an app online that gives me workout routines, meal plans, and advice on mindset, meditation, and sleep. The app helps hold me accountable because it provides a calendar for all the dates that I'm supposed to work out. And at the end of each workout, I have to take a photo to prove to myself that I accomplished the goal. For me, I just want to make sure I get to that photo.

Another example might be using an app like Mint.com or similar tools in place of a professional accountability partner in your finances. The options are endless to enlist support from professionals, and I can guarantee you will need to do so in some way as you progress on this greatness journey.

When she was on my show, cognitive neuroscientist Caroline Leaf advocated for therapy as one of the best support systems. I've talked a lot about the value of therapists, but even then you need to recognize that therapists won't do the work for you. As Caroline put it, "You're still living with yourself twenty-four seven."[4]

That's why you need all the layers of accountability, even when enlisting professional support. Like I said earlier, you are always in charge of you. And that's good news! The more layers of accountability you put in place, the more likely you will stick to your commitment. Experiment and see what combinations work for you.

DANGERS TO AVOID

There are some things to consider as you put support and accountability in place. In general, it's hard to go wrong, but here are a few tips I've learned that can help you avoid speed bumps along the way.

First, avoid choosing accountability partners who are no fun. It sounds simple, but achieving your goals doesn't need to be a chore you dread. I have found that I am much more likely to keep up with something if I can make it fun, and a large part of this depends on the other people involved. For example, I am currently training with the great boxer and former Olympic bronze medalist Tony Jeffries. He really puts me through a strenuous workout every time we meet.

He could make it feel grueling and unenjoyable, but we actually have fun with it. Almost every time while I'm putting on my gloves, I start razzing him: "Hey, what's it feel like to know that you're about to get destroyed by your student? What's it feel like being an Olympic medalist, knowing that a beginner is about to whoop your butt?" Then he starts saying stuff back, and before we know it, we're smiling, having fun, and getting a great workout. He just makes the experience enjoyable, even though he destroys me every time. So, it is worth the effort to find the coach, mentor, or accountability buddy that you're actually excited to be around.

Second, avoid choosing partners who bring negativity, as opposed to positivity, into your life. Being around toxic people will only drain you, not help you. In all that you do, ask yourself whether the people and actions involving them are bringing you more joy and health. If the answer is no and shows no evidence of becoming a yes, rethink that partnership.

How many times have you set goals that you were super excited about only to feel like they were unachievable after sharing them with some friends and getting ridiculed? More than you'd probably like to remember, right? That may mean you need to distance yourself from communities that have become toxic to your growth. And that's okay. As you grow and change, those needs change.

Third, avoid people who are not invested in your success. You have to ask yourself, *How important is it to this person that I succeed?* You do not want to lean on anyone who is rooting for you to fail or is indifferent to your success. Thomas Frank shared a story with me that perfectly contrasted a good partner with a bad one.

Thomas made a goal for himself to read 25 minutes of nonfiction every day. To hold himself accountable, he promised a friend a hundred dollars if he missed a single day. This friend had exactly the right attitude everyone needs from an accountability partner. "I don't want your filthy money if you fail," he told Thomas. "So don't fail." Compare this response to another "friend" who wanted to take Thomas up on his deal so he could actively root for Thomas to fail—and make an easy hundred bucks. The moral of the story is to be careful to choose accountability partners who will not take pleasure in your failure.[5]

Fourth, avoid holding on to irrelevant or unsolicited advice. You do not always get a choice about who is involved in your life. People will hurl unsolicited opinions your way, but it is up to you whether you stick your hand out and catch them or let them whiz by. Former U.S. Secret Service Special Agent Evy Poumpouras shared with me a way she makes this choice intentionally. Anytime someone offers their opinion, Evy asks herself, *Who is this person, and why should I listen to them?* If those questions have no good answer, Evy lets the criticism go by without notice. Evy has discovered that often people base their opinions on their own lives instead of your situation.[6] This is why it is so important to continually align yourself with your values and Meaningful Mission. Because if your values are different from your critics, your decisions should probably be different too.

Another way to avoid being influenced by others' irrelevant advice is to think through your mission carefully. Jordan Peterson has found that people's comments usually only influence us if we already have doubts. If you have thoroughly planned and prepared, you will be able to respond to criticism and securely know that you are enough, you are ready, and it is possible. When you believe that, no one can stop you.[7]

Fifth, avoid going too extreme with your goals. Trying to do all areas of your life in the most extreme way all at once simply will not work. For example, if you are trying to accomplish financial goals and physical health goals all at the same time with the same energy, you might say something like this:

> I'm not going to spend any money for the next three months. That means I'm not going to buy any more coffees on the way to work. I'm going to cook everything at home and personally prepare all my meals every week. I'll go grocery shopping every few days to make sure all my ingredients are fresh and healthy. I'm going to do everything perfectly and save and eat as healthy as possible. And I'll work out every day, twice a day!

That's an extreme mentality. And it will probably fail miserably, leaving you more discouraged than ever. Going super extreme on things is the opposite of the natural flow of life, which consists of working in phases and allowing things to progress.

For example, if you really need to make a drastic change in your health, you might decide to go *all in* and tackle a 90-day challenge. However, you need to recognize that it will take an emotional toll and impact the rest of your life. So you may need to dial back your commitments in other areas to support that change for a season. Otherwise, you will run yourself ragged and end up slipping in your other commitments. That will hurt you more in the long run because you might be tempted to take a slip-up as permission to give up completely.

ENGAGING GREATNESS

Exercise 1: Handling Irrelevant or Unsolicited Advice

Before you act on anyone's advice, you should ask yourself some important questions about that person. In fact, I advise you to think carefully before you even share your goals with someone. Before you bring your Meaningful Mission to someone, you want to know that person will treat it and you with respect. With this exercise, you will practice assessing and responding to potential accountability buddies.

> You have a right to be choosy about who you let influence your life.

STEP 1—IDENTIFY

What is a decision you are currently making about your Meaningful Mission? This might be an investment decision, a choice about the next appropriate step, or the choice to start on that mission. Who has the potential to influence this decision? Is it a spouse? A parent? A friend? Keep in mind the people who influence you might not be the same people you go to for advice. People often share their thoughts whether you ask or not. You might even be influenced by their actions. Have you ever tried something because it seemed to work out well for someone else? Note this decision and the involved person(s).

STEP 2—ASSESS

You have a right to be choosy about who you let influence your life. You probably have some professional accountability partners such as a trainer, therapist, or financial planner. Did you research these people before trusting them? Why should your accountability buddies be any different? Answer the questions below about the person(s) you answered in Step 1.

- Is this person qualified to give advice in this area?
- Is their advice specific to my situation or is it based on their experiences (good or bad)?
- Is this person invested in my success?
- Does this person have anything to gain from my failing or not trying?
- Will this person be a coach or a critic?

STEP 3—RESPOND

What did you learn from your research? Is this person(s) worthy of being an accountability buddy?

If the answer is yes, how do you want them to hold you accountable? Be sure to build in a commitment device. This could be financial, a blow to your pride if you attach honor to your word, or maybe some other creative form of embarrassment. Write your plan below.

If the answer is no, what is your plan to remove this person from this process? You might not want to cut the person out of your life, but you might need to avoid the topic of your mission.

Plan now what you can say if this person asks a question related to your mission. One strategy is to remain vague and quickly get off the topic.

ONLY THE BEST

> **Make sure the partners in your life bring out your best.**

On your greatness journey, you deserve great partners to hold you accountable and share advice. Make sure the partners in your life bring out *your* best. Not their best, or what they think should be your best. *Your* truest and best self.

Exercise 2: Be Your Own Worst Critic

It has been said that the only reason criticism hurts is because we already have doubts. As with a lot of things, the best way to avoid problems later is to front-load the work. This exercise will help you lay a strong foundation so you can confidently face any criticism.

STEP 1—CRITIQUE

You probably believe strongly in your mission. I hope you do. But set aside that confidence for a moment and imagine you are a critic. Write down every opposing argument you can think of. A good place to start is with whatever you feel most insecure about, whether that is something about yourself or about your idea.

STEP 2—RESOLVE THE ISSUES

If you gave that step your all, it was probably uncomfortable. That's good! Discomfort now means confidence later when it counts.

Now what do you need to do to overcome those insecurities and counter those arguments? Do you need to do more research? Do you need data or other forms of evidence? You might need to bring a new member to your team if you do not have the expertise to overcome an objection.

For example, if your mission involves designing a new product, you might need to consult with an engineer. Write out your game plan for addressing the weak spots in your ideas. This is a perfect time to enlist the help of your accountability support to help make sure you see your plans through.

CONSTRUCTIVE CRITICISM

We all want great missions. The whole reason you take on a mission is because you care about something strongly enough to devote yourself to it. This passion makes it painful to see our plans as anything but great, but if you don't critique it, someone else will. If you are so close to your mission that you cannot fault it at all, go to someone you trust and ask them to give an honest critique.

Exercise 3: Gamify

Hard work and dedication will only take you so far. The best way to ensure success at something is to enjoy the process. That means bringing intentionality into the way you structure your goals so that it appeals to your fun side. First, you need to identify what fun means to you. Then you can plan that type of fun into your tasks. Those are the objectives for this exercise.

STEP 1—DEFINE FUN

Fun usually involves a reward of some sort. If you are a parent, you may have awarded prizes or stickers to your kids to make chores fun. Some competitive athletes are driven by the reward of a win.

Others might feel that beating their personal best is the greatest reward. What kind of reward motivates you? Circle all that apply to you.

Material rewards

Physical evidence of progress

Words of affirmation from others

Money

Cheats (like a cheat day)

Beating your personal best

Beating someone else

STEP 2—STRUCTURE FUN INTO CHALLENGES

For each of the rewards you circled, consider the ways you can build that type of reward into your tasks. Here are a few suggestions to help you out.

Material rewards: Unfortunately, as adults, we don't have anyone rewarding us with trinkets or stickers, but you can do something similar for yourself. There is nothing wrong with allowing yourself little indulgences now and then, as long as they do not harm yourself or others. This is not permission to spend beyond your means or indulge in harmful coping mechanisms, but if flowers make you happy, buy yourself a bouquet. If renting a movie helps you unwind after a week of hard work, go for it.

Physical evidence of progress: The options are nearly unlimited for you. Track your progress using graphs, checklists, photos, or "completed" piles or folders. Calendars can be a great place to visually reward yourself for tasks that repeat daily.

Words of affirmation from others: This is where your accountability support really helps. Your accountability partners should be people you can count on to bring positivity and praise into your life. Remember, though, that *you* need to be your own main source of affirmation. Something you can do is write yourself affirming notes or letters to yourself to refer back to whenever things get tough.

Money: One option is to arrange a financial penalty for yourself. It is possible that your successes could make or save you money, though. Consider if you are reaping any financial benefits not immediately obvious. For example, your goal might be to eat healthy, but you might reap the side benefit of saving money when you skip eating out.

Cheats (like a cheat day): Build in limited compromises for yourself. If you need to, revisit Marissa Sharif's "emergency reserve" strategy (page 73).

Beating your personal best: See if your task can be quantified in any way. You might track time, production, speed, profit, etc. Track these numbers and see how far you can push yourself. Another option is to create challenges for yourself and see if you can figure out a way to make the "impossible" happen.

> **Whether it be time, money, or relationships, an investment in your happiness is an investment in your long-term success.**

Beating someone else: Try involving your accountability buddy in some friendly competition. Just be careful not to let this reward turn toxic by comparing yourself to unrealistic counterparts.

INVEST WISELY

Remember, whether it be time, money, or relationships, an investment in your happiness is an investment in your long-term success.

Chapter 17

GET STUFF DONE

Have you ever seen Steph Curry shoot a basketball? It's a work of art.

If you aren't familiar with basketball, the three-point line is an arc-shaped line that surrounds the basket on each end of the court. At its most distant point, it's 23 feet, 9 inches away from the rim. Players who shoot successfully from beyond that line get rewarded with a satisfying swoosh as the ball drops in—nothing but net.

Curry has gotten so good at shooting threes that there's even a five-minute YouTube video of him making *105 three-pointers* in a row before finally missing a shot.[1] What's his secret? A practice routine that would make your head spin. Consistently.

With a combination of shooting drills, footwork, endurance training, working backward from his mistakes to correct them, dribbling two basketballs at once,[2] dribbling a basketball in one hand while bouncing a tennis ball in the other and even neuro-cognitive training using special goggles[3]—what happens *before* his games is impressive.

But while practice is so important, even Steph Curry has to eventually suit up and play.

You are now well on your way on your journey from wherever you are now to where you want to be. It's been a journey toward *greatness for you*. It's been a discovery of your Meaningful Mission and why the world needs you to bring it to life. And what all the greats know is that there is a time to prepare and then there's a time to get stuff done.

That's what this chapter is all about. It's a highly practical way to get you ready to jump in the game and feel the way Steph Curry describes his flow state: "Every shot I take from the ground up, my rhythm is locked in. And honestly, you are not thinking about anything, you are just hooping."[4]

So, now that you're ready to start living out greatness, let's go!

THE 1% RULE

As you pursue greatness, there is one battle that you'll constantly have to fight—the battle against perfectionism.

Although perfect seems like a worthy target, it actually can be a devious enemy. Brené Brown says, "Perfectionism is something we don't understand very well. We think it's being our best selves. Perfectionism is actually a defense mechanism that says to us, 'Hey, if you look perfect, do perfect, and accomplish perfect, you can avoid or minimize shame and judgment and blame.' So, perfectionism is not about striving for excellence or being our best selves. It's how we self-protect."[5]

> **Greatness is found when you take massive imperfect action.**

Ouch. So true. The problem with trying to be perfect is that chasing greatness means you've got to be willing to put yourself out there *before you feel ready*. It's easy to get stuck in learning mode or practice mode. That feels safe. It feels comfortable. It's the safety net that says, *It's okay to mess up, something is there to catch me.* But that's not where greatness is found. Greatness is found when you take massive imperfect action.

I like how productivity expert Thomas Frank put it to me: "My favorite thing for overcoming perfectionism is what I call the 1 Percent Rule."[6] Here's how I would paraphrase the 1 Percent Rule and how to use it to overcome perfectionism—set a schedule to create or learn, grow, or move, etc., and then each time you act, determine to get just 1 percent better. Pretty simple, right?

The 1 Percent Rule acknowledges that you won't be perfect right out of the gate. But you can become 1 percent better. We all can do that. Here's how that might look in your life:

- Exercise—strive for 1 percent better form during a push-up

- Music—aim for 1 percent better control of the note

- Business—write a 1 percent better customer service e-mail

- Writing—draft a 1 percent stronger sentence in a paragraph

- Relationship—get 1 percent better at making eye contact in a conversation

This is a really simple way to give yourself some grace while continuing to move the needle toward getting better. It's the antidote to fear and failing to launch. Brené Brown finished that talk about our focus on perfectionism by saying, "I think the question to ask is, 'What am I afraid of?'"[7] Right back to those fears that support the Enemy of Greatness.

Don't let the tension between where you are now and what you

> **Don't let the tension between where you are now and what you don't know hold you back from where you want to go or who you are becoming.**

don't know hold you back from where you want to go or who you are becoming. At some point you've got to push back fear, strive to get better, and move forward—even if you don't feel ready.

The truth is, none of us ever are.

DO WHAT YOU CAN DO

When it comes to getting stuff done, there are five words that have become my mantra: *Done is better than perfect.*

Perfect is a nice thought, but an impossible target. Even though Steph Curry shot three-point shots for five minutes and racked up 105 beautiful shots in a row, on the 106th shot, he missed.

> **Done is better than perfect.**

That's the futility of waiting to act until you're perfect. Imagine if Curry refused to play a game until he never missed a shot. Not happening.

I've created a lot of things in my lifetime—a podcast and several books, coaching programs, live events, businesses—and there's not one product I've put out that is perfect. However, I feel like a lot of things I've put out are great. It doesn't have to be perfect in order to be great, and impactful, and helpful, and of service, and meaningful, and fulfilling, and expressive, and artistic, and powerful, and get big results. You can always make things better, but you can't let that stop you from starting.

Done is better than perfect.

But there's a catch—you must stay connected to your Meaningful Mission that lets you see past your fears. If your goals are tied to self—how you think you look or sound or will be viewed—it will never feel enough to move you past perfection. You'll remain just this side of the action, convincing yourself you are "practicing" or "getting prepared." You'll stay stuck.

I like the way author Jon Acuff put it:

Perfectionism offers us two distinct distractions: hiding places and noble obstacles. A hiding place is an activity you focus on instead of your goal. A noble obstacle is a virtuous-sounding reason for not working toward a finish. Both are toxic to your ability to finish.[8]

So where are you hiding? What seems noble but is really an excuse? What can you do with excellence *now* that will be helpful, meaningful, fulfilling, expressive, artistic, and get big results? As Brené Brown says, "No one can contribute what you can contribute."[9] That means there's a big void out there in the world that is *waiting on you* to fill it.

When I launched my first book, it was a huge deal for me. In school, I was consistently at the bottom of my English class. So, when *The School of Greatness* came out and then became a *New York Times* bestseller, I was understandably proud. But it also planted some high expectations in my mind about what my next book "should" do. When that book, *The Mask of Masculinity,* was released, I had an even larger audience. I had past success, so of course, in my mind, my new book would become a *New York Times* bestseller too.

It didn't.

To be honest, for a couple of days I was crushed. I was upset, hurt, and angry, even though I was hearing from all sorts of people who were being helped by the book. Honestly, I wasn't much fun to be around. I wanted this thing that didn't happen. I had this expectation, and the expectation let me down. Basically, I had an "expectation" hangover. I soon realized the core reason I had written the book was not to make the list, but to help other people live better lives.

> **What can you do with excellence *now* that will be helpful, meaningful, fulfilling, expressive, artistic, and get big results?**

And the fact is, I had very little control over the bestseller status of my book. Sure, I could—and did—try to do all the things I could to position the book to make that list, but there were plenty of factors outside of my control, including the editorial review board at the *New York Times*. The reality was that my book did make bestseller status on many other respected lists.

The first thing you have to remember when it comes to getting stuff done is that there are things you *can* control and things you *can't* control. You have to know which is which and where to place your focus.

If you tie your confidence to your accomplishments, you're focusing on things you can't necessarily control. A better way to do it is to move toward giving it your greatest effort, impact, creative expression, and consistency. These are things you can control *and* be proud of yourself in the process.

To get the right things done, you must recognize the difference between those things that are under your control and those things that are not under your control.

Take my podcast, for example. At the time of this writing, I've been doing the weekly show *The School of Greatness* for 10 years. That's a long time to do one thing. I certainly don't have the biggest podcast (although it is frequently in the top 100 globally of all podcasts). I've never received an award. Other people have launched after me and grown more. If I placed my confidence solely on accomplishments, that might get me down.

But I have a choice. I can dwell on everything I'm not, or I can remember everything I am and rest in the fact that I am enough and I am becoming more.

What I am is a hard worker whose Meaningful Mission is to *serve 100 million lives every single week*. You know how I do that? I consistently interview the best and the brightest people on the planet and share that wisdom with my listeners. I can't control downloads or rankings or social media shares, but I can be extremely proud of the consistency and the effort and impact I have had on a weekly basis, never missing a week for 10 years. No one can take that away from me. Maybe I didn't win some big awards or get acknowledged by an industry or peers, but I know what I'm creating for people.

I know the direct impact it has.

I know the impact it has on my life and community.

I see how it's impacting our own team's lives.

To get the right things done, you must recognize the difference between those things that are under your control and those things that are not under your control. And then celebrate your consistency, effort, and movement toward your Meaningful Mission.

Do that, and you will be a success.

KEYS TO GETTING STUFF DONE

Let's take a look at some very practical ways to move toward your Meaningful Mission.

First, you need to think about where to begin. Greatness, by definition, is not small. This means that your Meaningful Mission is probably going to have a lot of moving parts.

There are a lot of places you *could* start.

Your first step is to figure out where you *should* start.

As I emphasized when crafting your Greatness Goals, start by thinking about the next right thing you should do. Sometimes when things feel overwhelming (which is often perfectionism raising its ugly head again), it helps to simply do the next

> **Sometimes when things feel overwhelming, it helps to simply do the next right thing.**

right thing. It doesn't have to be huge; it does have to move you forward. There is a four-step process that I use to ensure I'm moving forward: Schedule, Automate, Eliminate, and Celebrate.

Schedule

You may have heard the saying that "what gets scheduled gets done." It's true. Two things tell us what we value—our wallets and what we give our time to. To make sure you are moving toward your greatness goal, you've got to schedule what's important in advance. For example, I have appointments with my therapist scheduled for the next four or five months. Why? Because I perform at my best when I optimize my inner world for emotional agility. Scheduling takes the decision-making stress out of the equation. Just put it on the calendar and keep moving forward.

> **Scheduling helps you create a routine that manages your energy.**

I do the same thing with my health. I know that if I don't exercise first thing in the morning, there's only a 50 percent chance I get it done later in the day. I know myself well enough to understand that I like to work hard. I show up at work fully engaged. And it takes a lot of energy for me to do all my interviews and writing and everything else that's a part of my business. The work I do in the gym is important because it helps me function at my best. I feel the most confident, the most proud, the most self-love, the most joy, and the most healthy when I work out and do physical activity daily. So I schedule that first thing in the morning. I don't have to think about it. It just happens.

Scheduling helps you create a routine that manages your energy. When describing his daily routine, Thomas Frank put it this way: "I have a limited amount of energy during the day. If I have something I need to do that requires me to pull out all my self-discipline, I should put that first. I can then use external self-discipline and accountability to power through the rest of the day."[10]

What fuels you? What restores you? What positions you for greatness? Is it routine?

Why not make your schedule your best friend? Block out time for what matters most. Fill in all the other small stuff around the important things. It's the only way to ensure you are moving toward the things that matter.

Automate

The second step in the process is to automate. Automating repetitive tasks is like walking on one of those moving walkways at the airport. You cover twice as much ground with the same effort! Look for repetitive tasks you can automate. This can be things like meal-planning, bill payments, e-mail responses, subscriptions, or exercise routines. I try to automate as much as possible. If it's around finances, I automate or prepay my bills to maximize my investment goals. I try to automate things with my team to save myself time. I automate training to help my team do things efficiently and effectively to help the business grow.

Take a look at the things you do daily, weekly, monthly, and yearly. What is repetitive? Where are you wasting your time acting on something that could be automated? Who can you equip and empower to take over some of the things you don't need to do?

Make automation a key strategy in your routine, and you'll get more done!

Eliminate

This is a big one. We spend way too much time doing things we either shouldn't be doing because they are unimportant or should be handing off to someone else because they can do them just as well as (or better than) we can.

If you're an entrepreneur, you'll appreciate this—you don't need to be in every meeting, on every e-mail, or part of every discussion and decision. Don't try to manage everything yourself. Empower your team to work in their area of strength so you can do the same. I work to carefully eliminate the things I shouldn't be doing from my schedule, so I can focus on the things that can help everything and everyone else grow.

Elimination can lead to acceleration. Look for things to cut back, strip away, streamline, and dump. Chances are you won't miss them when they are gone and they'll allow you to move forward faster.

Celebrate

Finally, it's good to celebrate your wins! When you've scheduled what's important, automated the things that zap your energy, and eliminated the things that you shouldn't be doing, you'll feel pretty amazing! That's why at the end of the day, I'll say something like, "I'm really grateful that I did these things that I was supposed to do today."

I acknowledge the things I was able to get done and then mentally prepare myself for tomorrow. I bake gratitude into the end of my day, and it helps me create an environment and a process that I enjoy. This gives me energy. It gives me confidence. It makes me feel proud of the effort I made that day to get me closer to my goals.

Each of these things can become habits over time that form a cornerstone of your identity. I like how Jen Sincero phrased it, "Getting into the habit of the habit is really important."[11] Sometimes you build the best habits by doing it tired or not as consistently as you'd like, or with not as many results as you'd like to see. This is getting into the habit of the habit. Over time, it will become easier.

Keep moving forward. Do the next right thing. Get stuff done.

A ROUTINE FOR SIGNIFICANCE

There's a reason high performers often wear the same thing every day, listen to the same soundtrack on repeat, eat the same things consistently every morning, or speak a mantra each evening. Routines keep us focused and help us minimize the overwhelm and distractions that come from making small decisions.

The best of the best have routines that work.

Austin Kleon, author of *Steal Like an Artist*, told me about his "notebook habit."

"I write in a notebook every day," he said. "I do about three pages in the morning, no matter what. That's a constant in my creative life. No matter what's going on, I'm reading and writing."[12]

When I asked Anthony ONeal, author of *Debt Free Degree*, about the habits of wealthy people, he said, "When I think of all the wealthy people in my circle, they have a Monday-through-Friday daily routine."[13]

Rob Dyrdek, former professional skateboarder, entrepreneur, and television personality, agreed. "The only way to get there is through discipline. And discipline and consistency are the hardest things to do. How do you get more disciplined and consistent? You have clarity on where you're headed."[14]

> **The best of the best have routines that work.**

If you don't have a clear idea of where you are heading, you may stay busy, but you won't move toward greatness. You'll get caught up in what everyone else is doing. Greatness requires sacrifice. As former Olympic skier Lindsey Vonn told me, "If you want to succeed at anything you're doing in life, you have to make sacrifices. I honestly feel that the most successful people aren't the most talented; they're not the smartest. They are the people who are willing to go the extra mile that other people are not."[15]

Where are you willing to go the extra mile?

Greatness also requires thinking more about how and where you spend your time. *Take the Stairs* author Rory Vaden shared this gem with me: "The next level of results always requires the next level of thinking."[16] In particular, Rory says we need to change our thinking about *significance*. He teaches something he calls the "significance calculation":

> Urgency is *how soon* does this matter? Most of us live in a world of urgency. It's all about what needs to be done right

now. Importance is different. Importance is *how much* does this matter? But significance is even different still. Significance is *how long* is this going to matter? Instead of thinking about tomorrow and the next day, the significance calculation changes everything, because this is how it's possible to multiply time. . . . The way you multiply time is by giving yourself the emotional permission to spend time on things today that create more time tomorrow.[17]

If you are on a journey to greatness, you'll find there's a lot to do. You need to make sure you have a routine and a process that separates what feels urgent and important from what is actually significant and moving you forward.

> **If you don't have a clear idea of where you are heading, you may stay busy, but you won't move toward greatness.**

The movement toward greatness is ultimately a state of mind. It has no finish line. It doesn't matter if the world is against you or says you can't do something. It doesn't matter if you don't have the resources or if you're not genetically gifted or whatever the obstacle might be.

Getting stuff done is up to one person—*you.*

So, take a deep breath, square up your shoulders, and move forward.

Evaluate your habits. What works? What doesn't? What should change?

Look at your routines. Are they optimized? Do they work for you or against you?

Fight against perfectionism. Where can you start? What is good enough? When can you launch?

Strive for significance. What truly matters? What will last? What multiplies your time?

Celebrate your wins. What are you proud of? What are you grateful for? Where did you excel?

If you believe in yourself and you follow through on the habits that confirm that belief and the actions daily, you can do pretty much anything—including being great.

ENGAGING GREATNESS

Exercise 1: The Significance Strategy

STEP 1—EVALUATE YOUR PERFECTIONISM QUOTIENT

To begin to get stuff done, you've got to measure how much perfectionism is holding you back. You can do that by evaluating your perfectionism quotient. Evaluate the following statements on a scale of 1 to 10.

I tend to put things off until I'm sure they will succeed.

I often set big goals that seem out of reach.

I put a lot of pressure on myself to "get it right the first time."

I beat myself up when I try something and fail or make a mistake.

I'm critical of my skills and abilities.

I worry about how I look to others when I'm trying something new.

I sometimes get lost in the details and fail to zoom out to see the big picture.

Once you've worked through these statements, you should have a baseline for how much perfectionism is holding you back. The aim is to get your number for each of those statements as close to 1 (or even zero!) as possible.

STEP 2—DEFINE YOUR 1 PERCENT

One of the best things to keep in mind as you move forward is that greatness is a marathon, not a sprint. That means that you should be striving for small and continuous improvement. To do that, you must break down the areas in which you need to improve.

Physically. This is movement, exercise, and health. Think about your current level of fitness and identify your 1 percent improvement. It doesn't matter where you are starting; write down how you might get 1 percent better each day.

Relationally. This is the way you relate to others. It may be a significant other, a co-worker, a friend, or a stranger on the street. With each interaction, spend some time thinking about ways you might become 1 percent better in improving that relationship, and write them down.

Mentally. This includes your thoughts and mental resilience. For this one, you'll need to identify the thoughts that guide your day and determine whether they are positive or negative. For the negative thoughts, your 1 percent will move you out of that pattern of thinking and into positive territory. For positive thoughts, you'll need to look for ways to enhance them and make them better.

Intellectually. This refers to the way you work on self-improvement. Take a look at the information you consume and how it affects your output. Strive to make a 1 percent improvement in both what you take in and what it causes you to produce.

STEP 3—MAKE A ROUTINE

High performers have routines that help them multiply their outcomes. There are four ways you can get started. Schedule. Automate. Eliminate. Celebrate.

Schedule. Your schedule is your first tool for getting stuff done. It helps you prioritize what's significant and fit in what's important. Work through the following blocks to build out your schedule.

Things I want to do each day. These may be things like spending quality time with my partner, exercise, reading, or spending time outside. Put these key items on your calendar first. They will help you perform at a high level.

Things I need to do each day. These are things that revolve around your work or life activities. Make a list of what these things are and block out time to do them around the things you want to do.

Everything else you could do. This is a catchall for all the other things you could do—doctor appointments, things that are on other people's to-do list, meetings, etc. The reality is there will always be more of these potential tasks then could possibly be done. Put them on the schedule where they best fit, but work to protect the time where you are most creative or productive.

Automate. Look for ways to streamline tasks by automating. The goal here is to make sure you aren't wasting time on things that don't require your effort. Enlist someone on your team or in your life to help you identify time-wasters. You'll often have a hard time finding these on your own, so a fresh set of eyes is critical.

Eliminate. The goal here is to make sure you aren't wasting time on things that don't require your attention. Use the following questions to identify what to eliminate.

- What is the best and highest use of your time?
- What can you do that *only* you can do?

- What are you working on that someone else could do just as well?

- What are you working on that is a distraction from your real purpose?

- What meetings or e-mails can you remove yourself from?

- Where are you working out of an area of weakness rather than strength?

- Where might someone else on your team be a better fit for a task you don't enjoy doing?

Celebrate. Finally, build in time to celebrate. When you accomplish things, it's a reason to reward yourself. Write a list of the things that make you happy below and give yourself a pat on the back when you push past perfectionism and actually get stuff done!

STEP 4—DEFINE SIGNIFICANCE

This may be the most personal and yet most important thing you do in this exercise. Spend some time thinking about your life so far and what you are doing in pursuit of significance. How does where you spend your time stack up on the significance scale?

Fast-forward 10 years and write a statement defining what you accomplished, why it was important, and how it led to significance. Then assess the way you are spending your time *today* and look for what needs to be adjusted.

Chapter 18

CELEBRATE: YOU ARE ENOUGH!

When I was younger, I never celebrated my accomplishments because I never felt like I was worthy of celebration. No success was big enough for me to feel worthy to celebrate. Even when I accomplished my goals of becoming an All-American athlete twice, of becoming a professional athlete, or of breaking a world record in sports, I never allowed myself to celebrate because I didn't feel like I was enough.

I thought I needed to go bigger and be better—to be more.

It wasn't until I started my healing journey about nine years ago that I allowed myself to really celebrate wins. I don't mean celebrating that I had arrived at my destination and was done. It was more a celebration of what I had achieved and realizing there was still more to my mission to be fulfilled.

I don't ever want to be done. I want to keep growing and learning and developing and creating. Celebrating just allows me to enjoy those powerful moments instead of feeling pressure to keep going because I'm not yet *good enough*.

I have learned to pause and appreciate wins, whatever size they may be, instead of pressuring myself to always do better and never feel as if I were enough. For example, for the last 10 years, I've wanted to have Dwayne "The Rock" Johnson (remember his story from earlier?) on my show. But so far it hasn't happened . . . yet. Then recently, The Rock followed me on Instagram. Now, he only follows about 500 or so people and has more than 300 million followers as of this writing. In the past, I might have seen that and thought, *I still haven't achieved my goal of having him on the show. I need to try harder!* But instead, I paused to enjoy the moment and celebrate a cool step on my journey to the goal.

> **Every day should be a celebration of your consistent effort toward accomplishing your Meaningful Mission.**

The day after he followed me, The Rock posted a video of my show on his Instagram where I was interviewing a friend of his, Jay Glazer. He mentioned what a powerful message it was and tagged me. Again, another win to celebrate as I keep moving forward and, hopefully, as I'm one step closer to interviewing him. It's all a matter of how we reframe the journey.

A great way to do this is to ask yourself every evening, *What's something to be grateful for today? What can we celebrate today?* Appreciate those moments of success and growth, even while acknowledging that there's more to be done tomorrow.

I used to think if I celebrated the little successes that it might make me complacent, but now I know better. Because I have a Meaningful Mission, there is a foundation I can stand on, something more solid than my needing to feel worthy, lovable, and enough. Celebrating doesn't make me complacent. It makes me excited and hungry for more, yet from a place of peace and fulfillment and joy. I know there is always going to be more to create, so it's a different type of energy.

Some days, I just acknowledge the effort I made to follow through on the things I said I was going to do today—*I'm grateful that I showed up for my Wellness today; I'm grateful I showed up for my Relationship and for my Business goals.* I recognize the three things I did that day to move me closer to my goals.

That's why every night I reflect on the three things I'm grateful for. It's a moment of celebration of my effort, consistency, and follow-through. When there's a moment of bigger success or a milestone achieved, you can celebrate that too, but every day should be a celebration of your consistent effort toward accomplishing your Meaningful Mission.

> **What are the actions you want to do tomorrow that you want to be grateful for and celebrate again?**

I challenge you to take the time each evening to celebrate three things that happened that day. Sometimes it might all be related to one of your life players. It might be all Wellness or all Relationship related. Maybe you got to spend extra time with your family. Whatever it is, just take time to acknowledge the good. Get in a routine of asking, *What are the three things that stand out today that I can be grateful for and celebrate?*

Then figure out what you are going to do tomorrow to continue on the path of the Meaningful Mission. What are the actions you want to do tomorrow that you want to be grateful for and celebrate again? What do you plan to celebrate the next night?

YOU ARE ENOUGH *AND* BECOMING MORE

"If you were in a field by yourself with no clothes, no possessions, no trophies, absolutely nothing—just you, by yourself, you are enough. You always have been, and you always will be, no matter what." Celebrity dancer Derek Hough said he finally realized that he truly was enough when someone told him that.[1]

Before that, he always felt like he had to do or have something in order to be enough. Only when he accepted that he was enough already did he really start doing things because he enjoyed them, which, in turn, accelerated his career. The ability to be confident in himself and be a part of something because of the joy it brought him enhanced his work. No longer did he strive to be enough. He already knew he was enough.

> **Instead of measuring our accomplishments to see if we are really enough, we need to flip it and just say the effort itself reveals our worth.**

Author and therapist Lori Gottlieb agrees. "You can be messy," she told me, "and fallible and imperfect and all of those things, but you are enough."[2]

It is true, my friend. You are enough, just as you are. You don't need to do or be anything extra in order to matter.

Instead of measuring our accomplishments to see if we are really enough, we need to flip it and just say the effort itself reveals our worth. Who you are is revealed in the act of doing and the act of being and in who you become in the expression of your gift, your art, and your talent, no matter what someone says about it. As Sarah Jakes Roberts says, "Success is in the process, not the outcome."[3] The process is the prize.

LOVE YOURSELF

To really embrace the reality that you are enough, you need to accept yourself. You have to release the negativity and live your life knowing that you don't need to put any effort into being enough.

I didn't grow up in a commune where everyone loved each other. Growing up in the Midwest, I learned to toughen up and live up to the standards of society. This was ingrained in me for about 22 years. It built me into an athletic, competitive business machine, but it left me feeling unfulfilled, hurt, lonely, sad, jealous, insecure, and afraid because I was often making decisions based on fear.

It wasn't until so many pieces were breaking down in my life that I realized things were off. I was making money and had what looked to be a good life on the outside, but everything inside felt like it was suffering. That's when I started my healing journey.

If people understood the art of falling in love with yourself, the world would be a much better place.

I've gone back to my childhood and allowed myself to reflect and feel the emotions so I can let them go and integrate the meaning behind some of the most painful memories. It's been incredible. I've experienced a lightness about things that used to feel so heavy.

I've had to build up the courage to let myself be vulnerable and express that vulnerability. It's become easier every time to speak what needs to be said and authentically express myself. It doesn't mean there haven't been problems or challenges, but it does feel incredible to be on the other side of that journey. It is all a part of the process of knowing I deserve it and knowing I am enough in every aspect.

If people understood the art of falling in love with yourself, the world would be a much better place. It's a lifelong process but one we all need to learn to engage with.

CELEBRATE EVERY SUCCESS

As you follow through the Greatness Game Plan, setting goals and crushing them, take time to celebrate your successes. Your happiness is found in the journey. Take time to acknowledge how far you've come and celebrate your wins.

Nicole Lynn became the first female agent to represent a top NFL athlete and one of the youngest top sports agents in history. Despite her success at representing top athletes and making the most money she'd ever made, Nicole found she was the most unhappy she'd ever been. She told me she realized that "success does not equal happiness." It wasn't the achievements that made her most happy. It was the journey to achieve them that did: "What I'm trying to do now is learn how to be present in the moment. When I hit the goal, celebrate it. Instead of thinking, *Well, what's next?* I take a moment to really take it in."[4]

> **Take time to celebrate your successes. Your happiness is found in the journey.**

And so should you. Pause to celebrate your success and accomplishments of hard work so you can find happiness along the journey as well. Don't be so concerned about the end goal that you don't enjoy all the little wonderful achievements on your way to the ultimate win.

THE POWER OF CELEBRATION

A number of research studies show the importance of celebrating your wins. On *The School of Greatness* podcast, Dr. Ivan Joseph said he creates a brag list when he's going into a new situation or trying for a new job—a list to remind himself of how powerful he truly is.

I love using this technique and actually created an acronym for it—BRAG, standing for Big Results, Accomplishments, and Goals. To create a BRAG list, write down everything from junior high to high school, college and beyond, reminding yourself of what you've already done. Maybe you feel like you haven't done anything big in a while, but even just finishing high school or college is an accomplishment. Getting promoted recently at work. Finally taking that trip you always dream about. Starting a side-hustle business. Don't take any success for granted. This list will boost your confidence, and you'll remember just how capable you are.

CELEBRATION ACTIVITIES AND FUTURE COMMITMENTS

Exercise: Create a BRAG list

Take a few quiet moments to reflect on your wins through the years, personal and professional, big and small. Think about those times you hit the mark, got the results you wanted, or crossed the finish line—or just felt proud! Every single one of those has been a stepping-stone to reaching where you are today!

Don't take any success for granted.

Write them down, divided into the following categories:

- Early school years (junior high and high school)
- Post high school (college, trade school, etc.)
- Early career (first job, early to mid-20s)
- Late 20s to present day

COMMIT TO A LIFE OF GREATNESS!

Congratulations! It has been a privilege to walk with you on this greatness journey—but it is not over yet. In fact, I suspect it is only just beginning. As you embrace the Greatness Mindset, I look forward to hearing more about your story pursuing your Meaningful Mission.

Your Meaningful Mission:

_____

_____

_____

What next step will you take to implement your Game Plan for Greatness?

_____

_____

_____

_____

**For additional resources to help
you live out the Greatness Mindset,
visit TheGreatnessMindset.com/resources.**

ACKNOWLEDGMENTS

I talked about my younger self in my dedication. I think it's important we all acknowledge our younger selves, the ones who showed up to this world and faced so much uncertainty. So I thank him for having the courage to face all the pain and learn how to heal, even when it felt like there was no hope. You carried me to this season of my life, and I'm so grateful for the courage you had on all those dark days to keep showing up and seek peace and truth.

To my mother, who continues to show up in service to her health, to myself, and the world—you are a light, and your love lifts me up. To my father, who passed the year I wrote this book— thanks for planting seeds in me my entire life that have helped me so much today. Thanks for all the lessons, love, and belief in me and always inspiring me to DREAM BIG!

Thank you to Chris, Heidi, and Katherine. I'm so grateful to have siblings that hold me accountable, accept me for my uniqueness, and love me no matter what happens in my life.

To Team Greatness, all the passionate and dedicated people who have made this journey possible—you inspire me every day to pursue my Meaningful Mission, and I appreciate each and every one of you. I consider it a privilege to be on this journey with you.

To Matt Cesaratto and Sarah Livingstone for showing up side by side on this incredible journey. You both know that none of this would be possible without you!

To Martha Higareda for showing me what conscious love and partnership looks like. Thank you for your full acceptance of my mission, my vision, and who I am. I love you.

Special thanks to my writing partner Bill Blankschaen and his StoryBuilders team for capturing my thoughts and bringing this book to life in such an enjoyable and engaging way.

To Lisa Cheng, Monica O'Connor, Patty Gift, Reid Tracy, and all the team at Hay House—thank you for all your dedicated efforts to deliver this book and your commitment to make a real difference in the world. You all are world class!

To all my coaches, teachers, mentors, and guides, who have given me so much my entire life—thanks for believing in a kid who didn't always believe in himself.

To all the inspiring guests who have appeared on *The School of Greatness* podcast with me and to future guests (I'm looking at you, Dwayne "The Rock" Johnson!)—thanks for the stories and wisdom you have shared and will share to heal, energize, and inspire so many people to greatness.

And, of course, to all my friends and supporters—thank you for being you and having the courage to take the next step on your Meaningful Mission. You inspire me!

ABOUT THE AUTHOR

Lewis Howes is a *New York Times* best-selling author, keynote speaker, and industry-leading show host. Howes is a two-sport All-American athlete, former professional football player, and member of the U.S.A. Men's National Handball Team. His show *The School of Greatness* is one of the top podcasts in the world with over 500 million downloads. He was recognized by the White House and President Obama as one of the top 100 entrepreneurs in the country under 30. Lewis has been featured on *Ellen*, the *Today* show, *The New York Times*, *People*, *Forbes*, *Fast Company*, *ESPN*, *Entrepreneur*, *Sports Illustrated*, and *Men's Health*, among other major media outlets. Learn more by visiting **LewisHowes.com**.

ENDNOTES

CHAPTER 1

1. Viktor E. Frankl, *Man's Search for Meaning* (Boston: Beacon Press, 2006).

2. Paul Conti, *Trauma: The Invisible Epidemic: How Trauma Works and How We Can Heal From It* (S.L.: Vermilion, 2022).

3. John Maxwell, "One Is Too Small a Number," John Maxwell, May 31, 2011, https://www.johnmaxwell.com/blog/one-is-too-small-a-number/.

CHAPTER 2

1. "Anxiety Disorders—Facts & Statistics," Anxiety & Depression Association of America, June 27, 2022, https://adaa.org/about-adaa/press-room/facts-statistics.

2. "Panic Disorder," Cleveland Clinic, August 12, 2020, https://my.clevelandclinic.org/health/diseases/4451-panic-disorder.

3. "Any Anxiety Disorder," National Institute of Mental Health, accessed January 25, 2022, https://www.nimh.nih.gov/health/statistics/any-anxiety-disorder.

4.   Wendy Suzuki, "The Most Effective Ways to Manage Stress & Anxiety w/Dr. Wendy Suzuki EP 1160," September 8, 2021, in *The School of Greatness*, podcast, MP3 audio, 01:42:00, https://lewishowes.com/podcast/the-most-effective-ways-to-manage-stress-anxiety-with-dr-wendy-suzuki/.

5.   Jean M. Twenge, "The Sad State of Happiness in the United States and the Role of Digital Media," World Happiness Report, March 20, 2019, https://worldhappiness.report/ed/2019/the-sad-state-of-happiness-in-the-united-states-and-the-role-of-digital-media/.

6.   "Overweight & Obesity Statistics," National Institute of Diabetes and Digestive and Kidney Diseases, September 2021, https://www.niddk.nih.gov/health-information/health-statistics/overweight-obesity.

7.   Bill Fay, "Demographics of Debt," Debt.org, February 23, 2022, https://www.debt.org/faqs/americans-in-debt/demographics/#:~:text=The%20average%20American%20has%20%2490%2C460.

8.   "The State of Mental Health in America," Mental Health America, January 25, 2022, https://mhanational.org/issues/state-mental-health-america.

9.   Jason Redman, "Navy Seal's 3 Rules for Leadership, Overcoming Near Death Experiences & Breaking The Victim Mentality w/Jason Redman EP 1175," October 13, 2021, in *The School of Greatness*, podcast, MP3 audio, 01:37:00, https://lewishowes.com/podcast/navy-seals-3-rules-for-leadership-overcoming-near-death-experiences-breaking-the-victim-mentality-w-jason-redman/.

10. Jason Redman, "Navy Seal's 3 Rules."

11. Valuetainment, "Consequences of Over Protected Children—Jordan Peterson," YouTube, August 8, 2019, video, 03:26, https://www.youtube.com/watch?v=Ll0opgJ9_Ck.

12. Brian Dunbar, ed., "Tribute to John Glenn from the Glenn Family and the John Glenn School of Public Affairs," NASA, December 8, 2016, https://www.nasa.gov/feature/tribute -to-john-glenn-from-the-glenn-family-and-the-john-glenn -school-of-public-affairs/.

CHAPTER 3

1. The Rock, "Seven Bucks Moment: Dwayne 'The Rock' Johnson," YouTube, February 17, 2022, video, 05:57, https:// www.youtube.com/watch?v=RjATMi9yNd0&t=336s.

2. The Rock, "Seven Bucks Moment."

3. Nicole Lynn, "Nicole Lynn On Breaking Down Industry Barriers & Accomplishing Your Goals EP 1142," July 28, 2021, in *The School of Greatness*, podcast, MP3 audio, 01:06:00, https://lewishowes.com/podcast/nicole-lynn-on-breaking -down-industry-barriers-accomplishing-your-goals/.

4. Gurudev Sri Sri Ravi Shankar, "A Spiritual Approach To Death, Abundance & Purpose w/Gurudev Sri Sri Ravi Shankar EP 1216," January 17, 2022, in *The School of Greatness*, podcast, MP3 audio, 01:23:00, https://lewishowes.com/ podcast/a-spiritual-approach-to-death-abundance-purpose -with-gurudev-sri-sri-ravi-shankar/.

5. Tony Robbins, "Tony Robbins: Key to Success, Wealth and Fulfillment," April 4, 2016, in *The School of Greatness*, podcast, MP3 audio, 00:52:00, https://lewishowes.com/podcast/ tony-robbins2/.

6. Katy Milkman, "The Science of Identity, Believing in Yourself & Setting Goals w/Katy Milkman Part 1 EP 1151," August 18, 2021, in *The School of Greatness*, podcast, MP3 audio, 00:59:00, https://lewishowes.com/podcast/the-science -of-identity-believing-in-yourself-setting-goals-with-katy -milkman-part-1/.

7. Zig Ziglar, "Quotable Quote," Goodreads, February 8, 2022, https://www.goodreads.com/quotes/309132-money-isn-t-the-most-important-thing-in-life-but-it-s.

8. Donald Miller, "Donald Miller: The Power of Storytelling," May 16, 2016, in *The School of Greatness*, podcast, MP3 audio, 00:55:00, https://lewishowes.com/podcast/donald-miller/.

9. Laurie Santos, "961 The 5 Keys to Long-Term Happiness and Prosperity with Dr. Laurie Santos," June 1, 2020, in *The School of Greatness*, podcast, MP3 audio, 01:02:00, https://lewishowes.com/podcast/the-5-keys-to-long-term-happiness-and-prosperity-with-dr-laurie-santos/.

10. Gurudev Sri Sri Ravi Shankar, "A Spiritual Approach To Death."

11. John Brennan, "1051 CIA Director REVEALS All: Making Mistakes, Being a Leader & Inside the Bin Laden Mission w/John Brennan," December 28, 2020, in *The School of Greatness*, podcast, MP3 audio, 01:41:00, https://lewishowes.com/podcast/cia-director-reveals-all-making-mistakes-being-a-leader-inside-the-bin-laden-mission-with-john-brennan/.

12. Robert Greene, "1024 Robert Greene: The Positive Side of Human MANIPULATION (The #1 Skill for SUCCESS)," October 26, 2020, in *The School of Greatness*, podcast, MP3 audio,01:50:00, https://lewishowes.com/podcast/overcome-tragedy-create-abundance-embrace-failure-with-robert-greene/.

13. Donald Miller, "Donald Miller: The Power."

CHAPTER 4

1. Sara Blakely, "397 Sara Blakely: SPANX CEO on Writing Your Billion Dollar Story," October 24, 2016, in *The School of Greatness*, podcast, MP3 audio, 01:05:00, https://lewishowes.com/podcast/sara-blakely/.

2. Emma Fierberg and Alana Kakoyiannis, "Learning to Celebrate Failure at a Young Age Led to This Billionaire's Success," Insider, February 16, 2022, https://www .businessinsider.com/sara-blakely-spanx-ceo-offers-advice -redefine-failure-retail-2016-7.

3. Lauren Thomas, "Spanx Founder Sara Blakely Says Business Will Expand into Denim and More after Blackstone Deal." CNBC, October 22, 2021, https://www.cnbc.com/2021/10/22/ spanx-founder-sara-blakely-says-business-will-to-expand-to -denim-and-more.html.

4. Sara Blakely (@sarablakely), 2020, "Here's a glimpse of the moment i joined Instagram . . ." Instagram video, October 1, 2020, https://www.instagram.com/p/CFzRXzmA1Rs/.

5. Sara Blakely, "397 Sara Blakely: SPANX CEO on Writing Your Billion Dollar Story," October 24, 2016, in *The School of Greatness*, podcast, MP3 audio, 01:05:00, https://lewishowes .com/podcast/sara-blakely/.

6. Robert Greene, "1024 Robert Greene: The Positive Side of Human MANIPULATION (The #1 Skill for SUCCESS)," October 26, 2020, in *The School of Greatness*, podcast, MP3 audio,01:50:00, https://lewishowes.com/podcast/overcome -tragedy-create-abundance-embrace-failure-with-robert -greene/.

7. Wendy Suzuki and Billie Fitzpatrick, *Good Anxiety: Harnessing the Power of the Most Misunderstood Emotion* (New York: Atria Books, 2021).

8. Sarah Jakes Roberts, *Woman Evolve: Break Up with Your Fears and Revolutionize Your Life* (Nashville, Tennessee: Thomas Nelson, 2021).

9. Dan Millman, "How to Develop a Peaceful Heart & Warrior Spirit w/Dan Millman EP 1217," January 19, 2022, in *The School of Greatness*, podcast, MP3 audio, 01:20:00, https:// lewishowes.com/podcast/how-to-develop-a-peaceful-heart -warrior-spirit-with-dan-millman/.

10. Ben Shapiro, "Jordan Peterson's Thoughts on Transgenderism," YouTube, February 8, 2022, video, 12:44, https://youtu.be/3enLBUJ5Od0.

11. Sukhinder Cassidy, "Building Wealth, Overcoming Failure & Rethinking Risk Taking w/Sukhinder Singh Cassidy EP 1150," August 16, 2021, in *The School of Greatness*, podcast, MP3 audio, 01:29:00, https://lewishowes.com/podcast/building -wealth-overcoming-failure-rethinking-risk-taking-with -sukhinder-singh-cassidy/.

12. Robert Greene, "1024 Robert Greene."

13. Sarah Jakes Roberts, "How To Heal Your Past, Build Strong Relationships & Deepen Your Faith w/Sarah Jakes Roberts EP 1105," May 3, 2021, in *The School of Greatness*, podcast, MP3 audio, 01:30:00, https://lewishowes.com/podcast/how-to -heal-your-past-build-strong-relationships-deepen-your-faith -with-sarah-jakes-roberts/.

14. Dan Millman, "How to Develop a Peaceful Heart."

15. Sarah Jakes Roberts, "How To Heal."

16. Sarah Jakes Roberts, "How To Heal."

17. Sarah Jakes Roberts, "How To Heal."

18. Priyanka Chopra Jonas, "1067 Priyanka Chopra Jonas: Create Self Worth, Find Happiness & Choose Yourself," February 3, 2021, in *The School of Greatness*, podcast, MP3 audio, 01:32:00, https://lewishowes.com/podcast/priyanka-chopra -jonas-create-self-worth-find-happiness-choose-yourself/.

19. Ethan Suplee, "Processing Pain, Losing 250+ Pounds, & Dissecting Trauma EP 1025," October 28, 2020, in *The School of Greatness*, podcast, MP3 audio, 01:26:00, https:// lewishowes.com/podcast/processing-pain-losing-250 -pounds-dissecting-trauma-with-actor-ethan-suplee/.

20. Sukhinder Cassidy, "Building Wealth, Overcoming Failure."

21. Ray Dalio, "Create Financial Success, Develop Principles & Understand Your Purpose," December 7, 2020, in *The School of Greatness*, podcast, MP3 audio, https://lewishowes.com/podcast/create-financial-success-develop-principles -understand-your-purpose-with-ray-dalio/.

22. Katy Milkman, "Behavioral Scientist's Take on Accountability, Temptation Bundling & Creating Lasting Habits w/Katy Milkman Part 2 EP 1152," August 20, 2021, in *The School of Greatness*, podcast, MP3 audio, 00:56:00, https://lewishowes .com/podcast/behavioral-scientists-take-on-accountability -temptation-bundling-creating-lasting-habits-with-katy -milkman-part-2/.

23. Katy Milkman, "Behavioral Scientist's Take on Accountability."

CHAPTER 5

1. Jamie Kern Lima, "1074 How to Overcome Self-Doubt & Rejection to Build a Billion Dollar Brand w/Jamie Kern Lima," February 19, 2021, in *The School of Greatness*, podcast, MP3 audio, 01:40:00, https://lewishowes.com/podcast/how-to -overcome-self-doubt-rejection-to-build-a-billion-dollar -brand-with-jamie-kern-lima/.

2. Jade Scipioni, "IT Cosmetics Jamie Kern Lima: 'I Lived Completely Burnt Out for Almost a Decade,'" CNBC, March 9, 2021, https://www.cnbc.com/2021/03/09/it-cosmetics -jamie-kern-lima-on-building-a-billion-dollar-company.html.

3. Phil McGraw, "Dr. Phil's Keys For Creating Success In Your Life EP 1172," October 6, 2021, in *The School of Greatness*, podcast, MP3 audio, 01:11:00, https://lewishowes.com/podcast/dr-phils-keys-to-owning-your-life-future-today/.

4. Phil McGraw, "Dr. Phil's Keys For Creating Success in Your Life EP 1172."

5. Tim Grover, "The Mindset of World Champions w/Tim Grover EP 1111," May 17, 2021, in *The School of Greatness*, podcast, MP3 audio, 01:03:00, https://lewishowes.com/podcast the-mindset-of-world-champions-with-tim-grover-part-one/.

6. Amy Cuddy, "The Science of Building Confidence & Self Esteem w/Harvard Psychologist Amy Cuddy EP 1198," December 6, 2021, in *The School of Greatness*, podcast, MP3 audio, 01:46:00, https://lewishowes.com/podcast/the-science -of-building-confidence-self-esteem-with-harvard -psychologist-amy-cuddy/.

7. Evans, Jonny. 2015. "The Untold Story behind Apple's 'Think Different' Campaign." Computerworld. June 17, 2015. https:// www.computerworld.com/article/2936344/the-untold-story -behind-apple-s-think-different-campaign.html#:~:text=Think %20Different%20became%20TV%2C%20posters%2C%20 advertising.

8. Jamie Kern Lima, "1074 How to Overcome."

9. Tim Grover, "The Mindset of World Champions."

CHAPTER 6

1. Robin Sharma, "988 The Morning Routine of Millionaires, Superstars & History's Greatest Geniuses w/Robin Sharma," August 3, 2020, in *The School of Greatness*, podcast, MP3 audio, 01:24:00, https://lewishowes.com/podcast/the -morning-routine-of-millionaires-superstars-and-historys -greatest-geniuses-with-robin-sharma/.

2. Dan Millman, "How to Develop a Peaceful Heart & Warrior Spirit w/Dan Millman EP 1217," January 19, 2022, in *The School of Greatness*, podcast, MP3 audio, 01:20:00, https:// lewishowes.com/podcast/how-to-develop-a-peaceful-heart -warrior-spirit-with-dan-millman/.

3. Daniel Gilbert (@DanTGilbert), 2018, "He loved bumblers and despised pointers. Not even a question," Twitter post, May 23, 2018, https://twitter.com/DanTGilbert/status/999154208128622592.

4. Erin McCarthy, "Roosevelt's 'The Man in the Arena,'" Mental Floss, April 23, 2015, https://www.mentalfloss.com/article/63389/roosevelts-man-arena.

5. Ellen Vora, "How To Turn Your Anxiety Into Your Superpower w/Ellen Vora EP 1240," March 14, 2022, in *The School of Greatness*, podcast, MP3 audio, 01:28:00, https://lewishowes.com/podcast/how-to-turn-your-anxiety-into-your-superpower-with-ellen-vora/.

6. Rich Diviney, "1058 How to Attract Success, Destroy Laziness & Achieve Optimal Performance w/Former Navy SEAL Officer Rich Diviney," January 13, 2021, in *The School of Greatness*, podcast, MP3 audio, 01:46:00, https://lewishowes.com/podcast/how-to-attract-success-destroy-laziness-achieve-optimal-performance-with-former-navy-seal-officer-rich-diviney/.

7. Joel Osteen, "Joel Osteen: Create Confidence & Abundance In All Areas Of Your Life! EP 1180," October 25, 2021, in *The School of Greatness*, podcast, MP3 audio, 01:13:00, https://lewishowes.com/podcast/joel-osteen-how-to-create-confidence-abundance-in-all-areas-of-your-life/.

8. Priyanka Chopra Jonas, "1067 Priyanka Chopra Jonas: Create Self Worth, Find Happiness & Choose Yourself," February 3, 2021, in *The School of Greatness*, podcast, MP3 audio, 01:32:00, https://lewishowes.com/podcast/priyanka-chopra-jonas-create-self-worth-find-happiness-choose-yourself/.

9. Priyanka Chopra Jonas, "1067 Priyanka Chopra Jonas."

10. Rich Diviney, "1058 How to Attract Success."

11. Wendy Suzuki, "The Most Effective Ways to Manage Stress & Anxiety w/Dr. Wendy Suzuki EP 1160," September 8, 2021, in *The School of Greatness*, podcast, MP3 audio, 01:42:00, https://lewishowes.com/podcast/the-most-effective-ways-to-manage-stress-anxiety-with-dr-wendy-suzuki/.

12. Wendy Suzuki, "The Most Effective Ways."

CHAPTER 7

1. Tim Grover, "Why You NEED to be Selfish to WIN w/Tim Grover EP 1112," May 19, 2021, in *The School of Greatness*, podcast, MP3 audio, 01:05:00, https://lewishowes.com/podcast/why-you-need-to-be-selfish-to-win-with-tim-grover-part-two/.

2. Joel Osteen, "Joel Osteen: Create Confidence & Abundance In All Areas Of Your Life! EP 1180," October 25, 2021, in *The School of Greatness*, podcast, MP3 audio, 01:13:00, https://lewishowes.com/podcast/joel-osteen-how-to-create-confidence-abundance-in-all-areas-of-your-life/.

3. Dan Millman, "How to Develop a Peaceful Heart & Warrior Spirit w/Dan Millman EP 1217," January 19, 2022, in *The School of Greatness*, podcast, MP3 audio, 01:20:00, https://lewishowes.com/podcast/how-to-develop-a-peaceful-heart-warrior-spirit-with-dan-millman/.

4. J'na Jefferson, "Snoop Dogg Explains Why He Thanked Himself during 'Walk of Fame' Speech," *Vibe*, May 24, 2014, https://www.vibe.com/news/entertainment/snoop-dogg-walk-of-fame-speech-explanation-651073/.

5. Dan Millman, *Everyday Enlightenment: The Twelve Gateways to Personal Growth* (Sydney: Hodder, 2000).

6. Joel Osteen, "Joel Osteen: Create Confidence."

7. Seth Godin, "1027 Habits of Success for Creatives, Artists & Entrepreneurs w/Seth Godin," November 2, 2020, in *The School of Greatness*, podcast, MP3 audio, 01:13:00, https://lewishowes.com/podcast/habits-of-success-for-creatives-artists-entrepreneurs-with-seth-godin/.

CHAPTER 8

1. Dale Carnegie, *How to Stop Worrying and Start Living* (S.L.: Jaico Publishing House, 2019).

2. Dale Carnegie, *How to Stop Worrying and Start Living* (S.L.: Jaico Publishing House, 2019).

3. Dale Carnegie, *How to Stop Worrying and Start Living* (S.L.: Jaico Publishing House, 2019).

4. Ethan Kross and Gretchen Rubin, *Chatter: The Voice in Our Head, Why It Matters, and How to Harness It* (New York: Crown, 2022).

5. C. G. Jung, "Quotable Quote," Goodreads, February 15, 2022, https://www.goodreads.com/quotes/44379-until-you-make-the-unconscious-conscious-it-will-direct-your.

6. Todd Herman, *The Alter Ego Effect: The Power of Secret Identities to Transform Your Life* (New York: HarperCollins Publishers, 2019).

7. Wendy Suzuki and Billie Fitzpatrick, *Good Anxiety: Harnessing the Power of the Most Misunderstood Emotion* (New York: Atria Books, 2021).

8. "An Ocean of Bliss May Rain Down from the Heavens, But If You Hold Up Only a Thimble, That Is All You Receive," Statustown, February 16, 2022, https://statustown.com/quote/9693/#:~:text=An%20ocean%20of%20bliss%20may.

CHAPTER 9

1. Ramani Durvasula, "Signs You're Dating a Narcissist & How to Know If You Are One w/Dr. Ramani Durvasula (PART 1) EP 1195," November 29, 2021, in *The School of Greatness*, podcast, MP3 audio, 00:53:00, https://lewishowes.com/ podcast/narcissists-vs-psychopaths-how-to-avoid -dating-one-with-dr-ramani-durvasula-part-1/.

2. RecoveryRevival (@recoveryrevival), "'Stresses Have an Impact on Your Physiology'—Dr. Gabor Mate," TikTok video, February 27, 2022, https://www.tiktok.com/@recoveryrevival/ video/7069601379811216642?_t=8RnnBW7SuAI&_r=1.

3. Dr. Shefali Tsabary, "How to Understand Your Trauma & Relationships w/Dr. Shefali EP 1110," May 14, 2021, in *The School of Greatness*, podcast, MP3 audio, 01:41:00, https:// lewishowes.com/podcast/how-to-understand-your-trauma -relationships-with-dr-shefali/.

4. Nicole LePera, "The Power to Heal Yourself," The Holistic Psychologist, February 16, 2022, https:// theholisticpsychologist.com/.

5. David Perlmutter, "How Your Diet Affects Your Behavior, Risk Of Disease & What You Should Do About It w/Dr. David Perlmutter EP 1211," January 5, 2022, in *The School of Greatness*, podcast, MP3 audio, 01:32:00, https://lewishowes .com/podcast/how-your-diet-affects-your-behavior-risk -of-disease-what-you-should-do-about-it-with-dr-david -perlmutter/.

6. Tim Ferriss, "Paul Conti, MD—How Trauma Works and How to Heal from It (#533)," The Tim Ferriss Show, September 22, 2021, https://tim.blog/2021/09/22/paul-conti-trauma/.

7. Donald Miller, "Your Life Is A Story: Why You Should Write Your Own Eulogy TODAY w/Donald Miller EP 1215," January 14, 2022, in *The School of Greatness*, podcast, MP3 audio, 01:40:00, https://lewishowes.com/podcast/your-life-is-a-story-why-you-should-write-your-own-eulogy-today-with-donald-miller/.

CHAPTER 10

1. Payal Kadakia, "Why You Shouldn't Have A 'Plan B' & The Ultimate Goal Setting Method w/Payal Kadakia EP 1224," February 4, 2022, in *The School of Greatness*, podcast, MP3 audio, 01:25:00, https://lewishowes.com/podcast/why-you-shouldnt-have-a-plan-b-the-ultimate-goal-setting-method-with-payal-kadakia/.

2. Payal Kadakia, "Why You Shouldn't Have A 'Plan B.'"

3. Adam Grant, "1066 Positively Influence Others, Increase Mental Flexibility & Diversify Your Identity w/Adam Grant," February 1, 2021, in *The School of Greatness*, podcast, MP3 audio, 01:37:00, https://lewishowes.com/podcast/positively-influence-others-increase-mental-flexibility-diversify-your-identity-with-adam-grant/.

4. Amy Cuddy, "The Science of Building Confidence & Self Esteem w/Harvard Psychologist Amy Cuddy EP 1198," December 6, 2021, in *The School of Greatness*, podcast, MP3 audio, 01:46:00, https://lewishowes.com/podcast/the-science-of-building-confidence-self-esteem-with-harvard-psychologist-amy-cuddy/.

5. Leon Howard, "From Prison To Financial Freedom: The Journey of Reshaping Your Identity w/Wallstreet Trapper EP 1209," December 31, 2021, in *The School of Greatness*, podcast, MP3 audio, 01:47:00, https://lewishowes.com/podcast/the-simple-keys-to-building-financial-freedom-eliminating-poor-money-habits-with-wallstreet-trapper/.

6. Adam Grant, "1066 Positively Influence Others, Increase Mental Flexibility & Diversify Your Identity w/Adam Grant," February 1, 2021, in *The School of Greatness*, podcast, MP3 audio, 01:37:00, https://lewishowes.com/podcast/positively-influence-others-increase-mental-flexibility-diversify-your-identity-with-adam-grant/.

7. Benjamin Hardy, "The Secret to Avoiding Burnout & Reshaping Your Identity w/Dr. Benjamin Hardy EP 1181," October 27, 2021, in *The School of Greatness*, podcast, MP3 audio, 01:07:00, https://lewishowes.com/podcast/the-secret-to-avoiding-burnout-reshaping-your-identity-with-dr-benjamin-hardy/.

8. Tim Storey, "1078 Finding Spiritual Truth, Understanding Identity & Managing Your Inner Mess w/Tim Storey," March 1, 2021, in *The School of Greatness*, podcast, MP3 audio, 01:19:00, https://lewishowes.com/podcast/finding-spiritual-truth-understanding-identity-managing-your-inner-mess-with-tim-storey/.

9. Donald Miller, "Your Life Is A Story: Why You Should Write Your Own Eulogy TODAY w/Donald Miller EP 1215," January 14, 2022, in *The School of Greatness*, podcast, MP3 audio, 01:40:00, https://lewishowes.com/podcast/your-life-is-a-story-why-you-should-write-your-own-eulogy-today-with-donald-miller/.

10. Donald Miller, "Your Life Is A Story."

11. Donald Miller, "Your Life Is A Story."

CHAPTER 11

1. Joe Dispenza, "1054 Dr. Joe Dispenza: Transform Your Mind for Lasting Love & Magnetic Relationships (PART 1)," January 4, 2021, in *The School of Greatness*, podcast, MP3 audio, 01:08:00, https://lewishowes.com/podcast/dr-joe-dispenza-transform-your-mind-for-lasting-love-and-magnetic-relationships/.

2. Caroline Leaf, "1079 How to Heal Your Mind & Improve Mental Health (Based on NEUROSCIENCE!) w/Dr. Caroline Leaf," March 3, 2021, in *The School of Greatness*, podcast, MP3 audio, 01:49:00, https://lewishowes.com/podcast/how-to -heal-your-mind-and-improve-mental-health-based-on -neuroscience-with-dr-caroline-leaf/.

3. Marisa Peer, "Get Rid Of Your Negative Beliefs, Manifest Abundance & Start Loving Yourself w/Marisa Peer EP 1213," January 10, 2022, in *The School of Greatness*, podcast, MP3 audio, 01:10:00, https://lewishowes.com/podcast/get-rid -of-your-negative-beliefs-manifest-abundance-start-loving -yourself-with-marisa-peer/.

4. Joe Dispenza, "679 Heal Your Body with Your Mind: Dr. Joe Dispenza," August 12, 2018, in *The School of Greatness*, podcast, MP3 audio, 01:20:00, https://lewishowes.com/ podcast/heal-your-body-with-your-mind-dr-joe-dispenza/.

5. Joe Dispenza, "1055 How To Overcome Negative Emotions, Let Go of Your Identity & Truly Love Yourself w/Dr. Joe Dispenza (PART 2)," January 6, 2021, in *The School of Greatness*, podcast, MP3 audio, 01:03:00, https://lewishowes .com/podcast/how-to-overcome-negative-emotions-let-go-of -your-identity-and-truly-love-yourself-with-dr-joe-dispenza -part-2/.

6. Ethan Kross, "Turn Your Inner Dialogue Into Productivity and Confidence w/Dr. Ethan Kross EP 1118," June 2, 2021, in *The School of Greatness*, podcast, MP3 audio, 01:38:00, https:// lewishowes.com/podcast/turn-your-inner-dialogue-into -productivity-and-confidence-%EF%BB%BFwith-dr-ethan -kross/.

7. Mel Robbins, "The High 5 Habit & The Secret To Motivation w/ Mel Robbins EP 1170," October 1, 2021, in *The School of Greatness*, podcast, MP3 audio, 01:38:00, https://lewishowes .com/podcast/the-5-second-rule-the-secret-to-motivation -with-mel-robbins/.

8. Mel Robbins, "The High 5 Habit."

9. Mel Robbins, "The High 5 Habit."

10. Mel Robbins, "The High 5 Habit."

11. Gabrielle Bernstein, *Super Attractor: Methods for Manifesting a Life beyond Your Wildest Dreams* (Carlsbad, California: Hay House, 2021).

12. Gabrielle Bernstein, *Super Attractor*.

13. Gabrielle Bernstein, *Super Attractor*.

14. Dan Millman, "How to Develop a Peaceful Heart & Warrior Spirit w/Dan Millman EP 1217," January 19, 2022, in *The School of Greatness*, podcast, MP3 audio, 01:20:00, https://lewishowes.com/podcast/how-to-develop-a-peaceful-heart-warrior-spirit-with-dan-millman/.

15. Dan Millman, "How to Develop a Peaceful Heart."

16. Susan David, "Why Emotional Agility Is The Most Important Skill You Need To Know EP 1297," February 18, 2018, in *The School of Greatness*, podcast, MP3 audio, 01:28:00, https://lewishowes.com/podcast/susan-david-the-art-of-emotional-agility/.

17. Susan David, "Why Emotional Agility."

18. Gabrielle Bernstein, *Super Attractor*.

19. Dan Millman, "How to Develop a Peaceful Heart."

20. Dan Millman, "How to Develop a Peaceful Heart."

21. Nir Eyal, "Build Life Changing Habits & Become A Productivity Master w/Nir Eyal EP 1097," April 14, 2021, in *The School of Greatness*, podcast, MP3 audio, 01:31:00, https://lewishowes.com/podcast/build-life-changing-habits-become-a-productivity-master-with-nir-eyal/.

22. Nir Eyal, "Build Life Changing Habits."

23. Susan David, "Susan David: The Art of Emotional Agility," February 18, 2018, in *The School of Greatness*, podcast, MP3 audio, 01:15:37, https://lewishowes.com/podcast/susan-david-the-art-of-emotional-agility/.

24. Derek Hough, "How To Pursue Your Dream & Make A Living As An Artist w/ Derek Hough EP 1167," September 24, 2021, in *The School of Greatness*, MP3 audio, 01:33:00, https://lewishowes.com/podcast/how-to-pursue-your-dream-make-a-living-as-an-artist-with-derek-hough/.

25. Susan David, "Susan David: The Art."

26. Nir Eyal, "Build Life Changing Habits."

27. Nir Eyal, "Build Life Changing Habits."

28. Gabrielle Bernstein, *Super Attractor*.

29. Seth Godin, "1027 Habits of Success for Creatives, Artists & Entrepreneurs w/Seth Godin," November 2, 2020, in *The School of Greatness*, podcast, MP3 audio, 01:13:00, https://lewishowes.com/podcast/habits-of-success-for-creatives-artists-entrepreneurs-with-seth-godin/.

CHAPTER 12

1. Rachel Rodgers, "How To Develop A Rich Mindset, Double Your Income & Accomplish Your Dreams w/Rachel Rodgers EP 1184," November 3, 2021, in *The School of Greatness*, podcast, MP3 audio, https://lewishowes.com/podcast/how-to-develop-a-rich-mindset-double-your-income-accomplish-your-dreams-with-rachel-rodgers/.

2. Rachel Rodgers, "How To Develop."

3. Rachel Rodgers, "How To Develop."

4. Ali Abdaal, "Build Multiple Income Streams, Habits To Become A Millionaire, and How To Gamify Your Productivity w/Ali Abdaal EP 1158," September 3, 2021, in *The School of Greatness*, podcast, MP3 audio, 01:59:00, https://lewishowes .com/podcast/build-multiple-income-streams-habits-to -become-a-millionaire-and-how-to-gamify-your-productivity -with-ali-abdaal/.

5. Ali Abdaal, "Build Multiple Income Streams."

6. Ali Abdaal, "Why I Left Medicine . . . Forever," YouTube, April 29, 2022, video, 43:16, https://www.youtube.com/ watch?v=mZOVLrLXKCE.

CHAPTER 13

1. Brandon Gaille, "23 Lottery Winners Bankrupt Statistics," Brandon Gaille, May 26, 2017, https://brandongaille .com/22-lottery-winners-bankrupt-statistics/.

2. Gabrielle Bernstein, "How to Manifest Your Dreams, Replace Negative Beliefs & Attract Abundance w/Gabby Bernstein EP 1103," April 28, 2021, in *The School of Greatness*, podcast, MP3 audio, 01:44:00, https://lewishowes.com/podcast/how -to-manifest-your-dreams-replace-negative-beliefs-attract -abundance-with-gabby-bernstein/.

3. Seth Godin, "Reject the Tyranny of Being Picked: Pick Yourself," Seth's Blog, April 27, 2022, https://seths.blog/2011/03/reject -the-tyranny-of-being-picked-pick-yourself/.

4. Rory Vaden, "How To Beat Procrastination & Rewire Your Brain For Success w/Rory Vaden EP 1144," August 2, 2021, in *The School of Greatness*, podcast, MP3 audio, 00:58:00, https:// lewishowes.com/podcast/how-to-beat-procrastination-rewire -your-brain-for-success-with-rory-vaden/.

5. Gabrielle Bernstein, "How to Manifest."

6. Stephen R. Covey, *The 7 Habits of Highly Effective People* (New York: Simon & Schuster, 2013).

7. Sean Covey and Stacy Curtis, *The 7 Habits of Happy Kids* (New York: Simon & Schuster, 2018).

8. Rory Vaden, "How To Multiply Your Time & Income w/Rory Vaden EP 1133," July 7, 2021, in *The School of Greatness*, podcast, MP3 audio, https://lewishowes.com/podcast/how-to-multiply-your-time-income-with-rory-vaden/.

CHAPTER 14

1. Rory Vaden, "How To Beat Procrastination & Rewire Your Brain For Success w/Rory Vaden EP 1144," August 2, 2021, in *The School of Greatness*, podcast, MP3 audio, 00:58:00, https://lewishowes.com/podcast/how-to-beat-procrastination-rewire-your-brain-for-success-with-rory-vaden/.

2. Katy Milkman, "The Science of Identity, Believing in Yourself & Setting Goals w/Katy Milkman Part 1 EP 1151," August 18, 2021, in *The School of Greatness*, podcast, MP3 audio, 00:59:00, https://lewishowes.com/podcast/the-science-of-identity-believing-in-yourself-setting-goals-with-katy-milkman-part-1/.

3. Rory Vaden, "How To Beat Procrastination."

4. Katy Milkman, "The Science of Identity."

5. Shawn Achor, *The Happiness Advantage* (New York: Random House, 2011).

CHAPTER 15

1. Rory Vaden, "How To Beat Procrastination & Rewire Your Brain For Success w/Rory Vaden EP 1144," August 2, 2021, in *The School of Greatness*, podcast, MP3 audio, 00:58:00, https://lewishowes.com/podcast/how-to-beat-procrastination-rewire-your-brain-for-success-with-rory-vaden/.

2. Benjamin Hardy, "The Secret to Avoiding Burnout & Reshaping Your Identity w/Dr. Benjamin Hardy EP 1181," October 27, 2021, in *The School of Greatness*, podcast, MP3 audio, 01:07:00, https://lewishowes.com/podcast/the-secret -to-avoiding-burnout-reshaping-your-identity-with-dr -benjamin-hardy/.

3. Jason Redman, "Navy Seal's 3 Rules for Leadership, Overcoming Near Death Experiences & Breaking The Victim Mentality w/Jason Redman EP 1175," October 13, 2021, in *The School of Greatness*, podcast, MP3 audio, 01:37:00, https:// lewishowes.com/podcast/navy-seals-3-rules-for-leadership -overcoming-near-death-experiences-breaking-the-victim -mentality-w-jason-redman/.

4. Katy Milkman, "The Science of Identity, Believing in Yourself & Setting Goals w/Katy Milkman Part 1 EP 1151," August 18, 2021, in *The School of Greatness*, podcast, MP3 audio, 00:59:00, https://lewishowes.com/podcast/the-science -of-identity-believing-in-yourself-setting-goals-with-katy -milkman-part-1/.

CHAPTER 16

1. Katy Milkman, "The Science of Identity, Believing in Yourself & Setting Goals w/Katy Milkman Part 1 EP 1151," August 18, 2021, in *The School of Greatness*, podcast, MP3 audio, 00:59:00, https://lewishowes.com/podcast/the-science -of-identity-believing-in-yourself-setting-goals-with-katy -milkman-part-1/.

2. Thomas Frank, "Avoid Burnout, Learn Faster, Improve Your Memory & Overcome Procrastination w/Thomas Frank EP 1205," December 22, 2021, in *The School of Greatness*, podcast, MP3 audio, https://lewishowes.com/podcast/avoid -burnout-learn-faster-improve-your-memory-overcome -procrastination-with-thomas-frank/.

3. Jen Sincero, "How to Build Habits to Create Financial Abundance & Success w/Jen Sincero EP 1101," April 23, 2021, in *The School of Greatness*, podcast, MP3 audio, https://lewishowes.com/podcast/how-to-build-habits-to-create-financial-abundance-success-with-jen-sincero/.

4. Caroline Leaf, "1079 How to Heal Your Mind & Improve Mental Health (Based on NEUROSCIENCE!) w/Dr. Caroline Leaf," March 3, 2021, in *The School of Greatness*, podcast, MP3 audio, 01:49:00, https://lewishowes.com/podcast/how-to-heal-your-mind-and-improve-mental-health-based-on-neuroscience-with-dr-caroline-leaf/.

5. Thomas Frank, "Avoid Burnout, Learn Faster."

6. Evy Poumpouras, "How to Build Command, Authority & Credibility w/Evy Poumpouras 1092," April 2, 2021, in *The School of Greatness*, podcast, MP3 audio, 01:55:00, https://lewishowes.com/podcast/how-to-build-command-authority-credibility-with-evy-poumpouras/.

7. Jordan Peterson, "Jordan Peterson on Marriage, Resentment & Healing the Past (Part 1) EP 1093," April 5, 2021, in *The School of Greatness*, podcast, MP3 audio, 01:23:00, https://lewishowes.com/podcast/jordan-peterson-on-marriage-resentment-healing-the-past-part-1/.

CHAPTER 17

1. PHP, "Steph Curry 105 THREES in a ROW, 5 Minutes Straight without Missing," YouTube, April 30, 2022, video, 05:13, https://www.youtube.com/watch?v=1mi-lCTCvrE.

2. MasterClass, "Stephen Curry's 9 Tips for a Basketball Practice Routine," MasterClass, March 2, 2022, https://www.masterclass.com/articles/stephen-currys-practice-tips#a-brief-introduction-to-steph-curry.

3. Sourabh Singh, "Steph Curry Workout Routine: What Makes Him the Best Shooter in the League?" Essentially Sports, May 19, 2021, https://www.essentiallysports.com/nba-basketball -news-golden-state-warriors-steph-curry-workout-routine -what-makes-him-the-best-shooter-in-the-league/.

4. Bharat Aggarwal, "Steph Curry Details 'How It Feels Like' When He Hits Prime Shooting Form & Achieves a Flow State," Essentially Sports, March 10, 2021, https://www .essentiallysports.com/nba-basketball-news-steph-curry -details-how-it-feels-like-when-he-hits-prime-shooting-form -achieves-a-flow-state/.

5. Motivation Stop (@motivationstop), "Perfectionism Is a Defence Mechanism," TikTok video, April 30, 2021, https:// www.tiktok.com/@motivationstop/video/7082462324438748421.

6. Thomas Frank, "Avoid Burnout, Learn Faster, Improve Your Memory & Overcome Procrastination w/Thomas Frank EP 1205," December 22, 2021, in *The School of Greatness*, podcast, MP3 audio, https://lewishowes.com/podcast/avoid -burnout-learn-faster-improve-your-memory-overcome -procrastination-with-thomas-frank/.

7. Motivation Stop (@motivationstop), "Perfectionism Is a Defence Mechanism."

8. Jonathan Acuff, *Finish: Give Yourself the Gift of Done* (New York: Portfolio/Penguin, 2018).

9. Motivation Stop (@motivationstop), "Perfectionism Is a Defence Mechanism."

10. Thomas Frank, "Avoid Burnout, Learn Faster."

11. Jen Sincero, "How to Build Habits to Create Financial Abundance & Success w/Jen Sincero EP 1101," April 23, 2021, in *The School of Greatness*, podcast, MP3 audio, https:// lewishowes.com/podcast/how-to-build-habits-to-create -financial-abundance-success-with-jen-sincero/.

12. Austin Kleon, "The Habits & Routines Behind Great Artists w/Austin Kleon EP 1123," June 14, 2021, in *The School of Greatness*, podcast, MP3 audio, 01:25:00, https://lewishowes .com/podcast/the-habits-routines-behind-great-artists -with-austin-kleon/.

13. Anthony ONeal, "How To Reshape Your Beliefs Around Money, Love & Your Future w/Anthony ONeal EP 1222," January 31, 2022 in *The School of Greatness*, podcast, MP3 audio, 01:28:12, https://lewishowes.com/podcast/how-to -reshape-your-beliefs-around-money-love-your-future-with -anthony-oneal/.

14. Rob Dyrdek, "How To Reshape Your Beliefs Around Money, Love & Your Future w/Anthony O'Neal EP 1222," September 6, 2021, in *The School of Greatness*, podcast, MP3 audio, https://lewishowes.com/podcast/how-to-reshape-your-beliefs -around-money-love-your-future-with-anthony-oneal/.

15. Lindsey Vonn, "Lindsey Vonn: DISCOVER Your Potential, Destroy Self-Doubt & Develop Habits for SUCCESS EP 1132," July 5, 2021, in *The School of Greatness*, podcast, MP3 audio, 00:58:00, https://lewishowes.com/podcast/lindsey-vonn -discover-your-potential-destroy-self-doubt-develop-habits -for-success/.

16. Rory Vaden, "How To Multiply Your Time & Income w/ Rory Vaden EP 1133," July 7, 2021, in *The School of Greatness*, podcast, MP3 audio, https://lewishowes.com/podcast how-to-multiply-your-time-income-with-rory-vaden/.

17. Rory Vaden, "How To Multiply."

CHAPTER 18

1. Derek Hough, "How To Pursue Your Dream & Make A Living As An Artist w/ Derek Hough EP 1167," September 24, 2021, in *The School of Greatness*, MP3 audio, 01:33:00, https:// lewishowes.com/podcast/how-to-pursue-your-dream-make-a -living-as-an-artist-with-derek-hough/.

2. Lori Gottlieb, "Red Flags To Watch Out For & The Keys To A Healthy Relationship w/Lori Gottlieb EP 1191," November 19, 2021, in *The School of Greatness*, podcast, MP3 audio, 01:04:00, https://lewishowes.com/podcast/red-flags-to-watch-out-for-the-key-to-a-healthy-relationship-with-lori-gottlieb/.

3. Sarah Jakes Roberts, "How To Heal Your Past, Build Strong Relationships & Deepen Your Faith w/Sarah Jakes Roberts EP 1105," May 3, 2021, in *The School of Greatness*, podcast, MP3 audio, 01:30:00, https://lewishowes.com/podcast/how-to-heal-your-past-build-strong-relationships-deepen-your-faith-with-sarah-jakes-roberts/.

4. Nicole Lynn, "Nicole Lynn On Breaking Down Industry Barriers & Accomplishing Your Goals EP 1142," July 28, 2021, in *The School of Greatness*, podcast, MP3 audio, 01:06:00, https://lewishowes.com/podcast/nicole-lynn-on-breaking-down-industry-barriers-accomplishing-your-goals/.